QUAKER CAMPAIGNS.

QUAKER CAMPAIGNS

IN PEACE AND WAR.

BY

WILLIAM JONES,

HON. COMMISSIONER OF THE SOCIETY OF FRIENDS' "WAR VICTIMS' FUND
IN FRANCE IN 1870-71, AND IN BULGARIA IN 1876-77.

WITH ELEVEN ILLUSTRATIONS.

LONDON:
HEADLEY BROTHERS,
14, BISHOPSGATE STREET WITHOUT, E.C.

1899.

HEADLEY BROTHERS,
PRINTERS,
LONDON AND ASHFORD, KENT.

PREFACE.

In offering this book of reminiscences to the public, it should be understood that it does not purport to be a complete autobiography. The main object attempted has been to gather up, at the pressing invitation of many personal friends, some fragments of my experiences at home and abroad, in connection with certain leading events in European history during the last half-century.

Imperfect as these records are, it is hoped that they may be of interest, as a small contribution to the thoughtful consideration of some important questions, especially the subject of the modern ruinous armaments, which have of late obtained so generous a share of national and international attention and effort.

If, in the narratives of travel, the allusions to the Society of Friends may appear to some readers to be rather too frequent, it must be remembered that it was mainly in connection with, and at the request of, that religious body that my journeys in America, and among our English-speaking kindred at the Antipodes, as well as on behalf of suffering humanity in Europe, were undertaken.

These gratuitous services, though often arduous, and at times perilous, were truly a labour of love, as well as of duty.

The many months which I spent in France, in the administration of relief to the impoverished victims of the war of 1870-71, affected my heart with a warm regard for the interesting and intelligent French people, and with a profound desire that they and our own nation may be increasingly and permanently united in bonds of mutual friendship, and in collateral services to civilization and humanity.

In the preparation of this book for the press, I have gladly availed myself of the experience of my friend William Tallack, Secretary of the Howard Association, to whom my grateful acknowledgments for valuable assistance are due. To the eminent historian, Dr. Thomas Hodgkin, of Newcastle-on-Tyne, I am also indebted for highly valued counsel and suggestions.

WILLIAM JONES.

Sunderland,
May, 1899.

CONTENTS.

CHAPTER I.

CHAPTER II.

CHAPTER III.

CHAPTER IV.

CHAPTER V.

CHAPTER VI.

CHAPTER VII.

CHAPTER VIII.

CHAPTER IX.

CHAPTER X.

CHAPTER XI.

CHAPTER XII.

CHAPTER XIII.

CHAPTER XIV.

CHAPTER XV.

CHAPTER XVI.

CHAPTER XVII.

CHAPTER XVIII.

CHAPTER XIX.

CHAPTER XX.

CHAPTER XXI.

CHAPTER XXII.

CHAPTER XXIII.

CHAPTER XXIV.

LIST OF ILLUSTRATIONS.

CHAPTER I.

EARLY LIFE — TOWN OF RUTHIN — ITS ANTIQUARIAN INTEREST — GRANDFATHER JONES — SERVICE IN THE MARINES—MY FATHER ENLISTS—HIS LOVE OF MUSIC—BECOMES A "FRIEND"—CURIOUS WELSH CUSTOMS—GEORGE BORROW AND JONATHAN HUGHES.

RARELY does it fall to the lot of a civilian engaged in the every-day pursuits of commerce, to be placed in the very peculiar circumstances which led the author to become an eye-witness of some of the most stirring events of the latter half of the nineteenth century.

Already a generation has grown up since the close of the Franco-German war in 1871, which can but faintly realise the impressive lessons of that terribly disastrous campaign. These and other considerations would seem to justify some attempt at a simple autobiographical narrative connected with the history of that period.

To ordinary readers any details of the writer's early life and Welsh extraction may appear superfluous, but for the sake of many personal friends a few particulars of those early days are briefly recorded.

RUTHIN.

I am a Welshman. The place in which I first saw the light, May 10th, 1826, is the quaint old town of Ruthin, picturesquely situated near the head of the beautiful Vale of Clwyd, in Denbighshire. It commands a view of the whole range of Clwydian hills, of which the highest, called Moel Fammau, is about 1,850 feet above the sea. This hill is crowned by a tower, erected in 1810, to commemorate the fiftieth anniversary of George the Third's reign. My father, in his boyhood, witnessed the laying of the foundation stone of the tower, of which the upper portion collapsed about thirty-five years ago, and has not been rebuilt.

The only historical event worth recording in connection with old Ruthin is, that Owen Glendower, having headed a formidable insurrection, and having had disputes with the De Greys, lords of the Manor and Castle, concerning some land, surprised and plundered the town on the 20th September, 1400, and also set fire to it. De Grey, in returning the attack, was worsted and taken prisoner. His ransom from Glendower's hands cost him 10,000 marks, and he was moreover compelled to marry Owen's daughter, Jane.

The old house in which I was born, situated in the Market-place, still bears on the first floor the owner's initials, and the date of 1622. Side by side with this is another board, with my father's initials

From a Photo by] [Valentine and Sons, Ltd.

ST. PETER'S SQUARE, RUTHIN.

Part of the stone, Maen Huail, is shown in the left hand corner of above picture, adjoining wall of Exmewe Hall.

and date, "J. J., 5th mo. 1st, 1825." Other houses near by are much older, having been built, it is said, after the fire, in 1401. Among these may be mentioned the present post office, where, in making alterations a few years ago, oaken beams were encountered, black and hard as ebony, in cutting through which many of the workmen's steel tools were spoiled. The "Myddelton Arms," lately renovated, ornaments the Market-place with its three tiers of dormer windows, reminding one of the picturesque old houses of Strasburg. "Exmewe Hall" is another historical ancient house, built by one Thomas Exmewe, a wealthy merchant of London, in the year 1500. His son became Lord Mayor of London, with the title of Sir Thomas Exmewe. The house afterwards became the residence of Edward Goodman, a burgess and mercer of Ruthin, and it was here that his son Gabriel was born, who was distinguished as an eminent scholar and divine, and was Dean of Westminster in Queen Elizabeth's reign. Among other benefactions to his native town, Dean Goodman founded and endowed the Ruthin Grammar School. After an existence of about three hundred years the old school premises have been abandoned, and a handsome new building has been erected in the outskirts of the town, and is now a flourishing Collegiate School for North Wales.

Below the black and white gable of Exmewe Hall stands a rough block of limestone, known as Maen Huail, the greatest piece of antiquity in the town. Huail, who lived in the early part of the sixth century, tradition says, was beheaded on this stone by King Arthur.

Other ancient buildings in the town and neighbourhood possess much of antiquarian interest.

This is notably the case with some old parish churches of venerable antiquity. For example, in the old church of Llanrhaiadr, three miles from Ruthin, there may be seen, among other curiosities, a huge uncouth pair of old wooden dog-tongs (*gefaill cwn*). These are so constructed as to enable the sexton to grip firmly round the body, and carry out of the church with safety to his own person, any savage or fighting dogs during divine service. On such occasions the deafening yells of the terrified dog were far from contributing to the harmony of the proceedings. I have heard my father tell of a scene in a country church, to which sheep-dogs often followed their masters, when two big dogs engaged on one occasion in a noisy stand-up fight, whilst an old cripple seated near was vigorously plying his crutch upon the infuriated beasts. So great was the excitement that even the parson, carried away by the hubbub, leaned over the pulpit and called encouragingly to the cripple in vigorous Welsh, "*Yna Luke, whangiwch nhw allan!*" (That's right, Luke, bang them out of doors!)

Parents and Relatives.

My parents were both of Welsh extraction. My mother was the grand-daughter of Jonathan Hughes, "the old bard of Llangollen," as he was termed, a small farmer at Pengwern Farm, on the slope of the Berwyn mountains. He was interred in Llangollen churchyard, where a beautiful "englyn," or verse, by a brother bard might formerly be read on his tombstone; but of late years, during some alterations to the church, the stone has been carelessly broken up and thrown away, and no copy kept of the verse.

In her early days, my mother attended the Sunday class of the "two Ladies of Llangollen," the Lady Eleanor Butler and the Honourable Miss Ponsonby, at their well-known residence, Plas Newydd. My father, John Jones, had, at the early age of sixteen, followed the example of his father, and enlisted into the Royal Marines, in accordance with the prevailing idea of that day that every man was called to take part in defence of his country against any invasion by Napoleon Bonaparte. My grandfather Jones was a very active, hardy man, who never experienced a day's illness until quite the end of his life. He had seen a great deal of foreign service, and fought in battles both on sea and land. To the close of his life he was fond of talking of the "glorious victory" of Trafalgar, in which he had been an active participator, and had seen his revered commander, Lord Nelson, shot down and carried below. Among my very early recollections are his narrations of some of the scenes of death and carnage on board the ship *Victory*, with which the old man delighted to thrill my young blood, his graphic stories often ending with his favourite Nelsonian maxim, "England expects every man to do his duty." From my remembrance of him, he was a sharp, clever tradesman, of soldierly habits of order and neatness, and was much respected in his native town of Ruthin as an upright man. Being naturally quick, he had little patience with people about him who were slow, untidy, or careless in their habits. To such he was literally a daily terror.

On each recurring anniversary of the victory of Trafalgar he dressed up in his full regimentals and girded on his sword. These he had been allowed to retain as a mark of honour for long service, and for bravery, when he left the King's service.

Another reminiscence of my grandfather is, that after his death there was produced, from its place of concealment, a deep wash-leather bag, full of glittering spade guineas. These were his accumulated prize moneys, earned in many a sea-fight, and which he never would suffer to be touched in his lifetime. They vanished like smoke, however, in the eager hands of his heirs, not one of whom had the grace to present me with even a single coin as a keepsake or souvenir of the old hero, for whom, though always rather in awe of his temper, I felt a sincere regard.

My father had, some time before this, become a member of the most peaceable sect in the community, the Society of Friends. His own account of this complete change from his youthful military career interested me much. He served about ten years in the Royal Marines, chiefly on convoy and garrison duties in the East Indies, China, etc. On their voyage homeward from the East the vessel touched at the island of St. Helena, which gave him an opportunity of going ashore, and seeing the old war eagle, Napoleon Bonaparte, who had so long tormented Europe with wars and bloodshed, chained, as it were, to his ocean-girt rock.

My father sometimes expressed his thankfulness in later life, that although war, by sea and land, was often raging, he had never during his whole ten years of service been called upon to take human life. His mother had furnished him with a small Welsh Bible, and this, with a copy of his grandfather Jonathan Hughes's poems, constituted his entire library. Many of these Welsh poems were of a religious and spiritual character, and being set to well-known Welsh airs which my father could sing admirably, his memory became stored with these hymns, and in later life he would hum them to himself with much enjoyment. When he landed in England he was visited by his youngest brother, the late Joseph Jones of Hereford, who, being a printer by trade, was then in the employ of the well-known firm of Harvey and Darton of London, who were members of the Society of Friends. Here he had become acquainted with the eminent philanthropist, Peter Bedford of Spitalfields, through whose Christian influence Joseph Jones had become a decided Friend. When the two brothers met, my father found to his surprise that his brother had joined a people of whom he had hardly ever heard, and who, he now learned, were carrying out in actual practice the identical Christian principles with which he had become imbued from the spiritual Welsh hymns of his grandfather. He needed no further convincing that all war was incompatible with the teaching of Christ. Conscience would no longer suffer him to bear arms, or to remain in the army. With him, loyalty to Christ, the Prince of Peace, had now become paramount to his loyalty to his earthly King. There were, however, great difficulties in getting out of the army in those warlike days. Ultimately, by paying a fine of one hundred pounds, and finding two substitutes, he was set at liberty. He now applied for, and was received into membership in the Society of Friends, and he remained a consistent member of that body to the end of his life. My mother never having passed through the same spiritual experiences, was not specially drawn to the Society of Friends, but remained attached to the religious body with which she had been connected from her childhood. She died in 1837, at the early age of thirty-two.

With the zeal of a convert, my father soon opened a Sunday School, for teaching his neighbours to read the Bible in Welsh. This school was kept on for a few years in a hired room, in which we afterwards held a meeting for worship, after the manner of "Friends." As long as memory lasts, I shall ever be grateful for the power there acquired of reading my Welsh Bible. To this day, a chapter well read aloud, in this graphic and forcible language, is to me as impressive as the best of sermons. One would naturally have expected that his brethren in the faith would have given him every encouragement in this work, but such was not the case. The Society had in its early years flourished in Wales, and there was a large body of convinced "Friends" in the Principality, but being for the most part engaged in agriculture, they were so continually harried and persecuted for non-payment of tithes and other ecclesiastical demands, that they emigrated in a body with William Penn to the welcome freedom of Pennsylvania, thus taking the very seed of Quakerism out of the ground in their native land of Wales. Seventy years ago English Friends had not warmed as they have so nobly done of late years, to the work of Sunday or "First-day" Schools, and it was not long before intimations were given to John Jones, from some of the leading "Friends" of his "Monthly Meeting," that his Sunday School labours were not regarded as "Friendly," but only as "creaturely activity." His loyalty to the Society caused him to close the school, and thus a well-meant attempt to re-establish the principles of "Friends" in Wales was extinguished, the hired room was given up, and henceforward, for some forty years or more, the small meeting of "Friends" in Ruthin was confined almost exclusively to members of our family, and was held in our own house. One old man, however, named William Williams, a nailmaker by trade, for many years walked from Denbigh, a distance of eight miles, every Sunday, wet or dry, to join in our little silent meetings, and returned home in the evening, at all seasons of the year. We were always glad to welcome this pious, simple-minded old Christian, and in dry weather, generally "set him home" a few miles on his way. He also was received into membership by the Society of Friends.

In his youth my father had spent about ten years of his life in mastering that difficult instrument the triple Welsh harp, on which he became a fairly skilful player. He had a fine ear and a considerable talent for music, so that he became a leader in the church choir of his native village. All this, however, he believed it right to give up when he joined the Society of Friends, whose views with regard to the dangers of music were, in that day, of the Puritanic order. So far did he carry out what he believed to be his Christian duty in this matter, that when his costly instrument, the triple Welsh harp, was broken, he refused to have it repaired, so that it should not become a temptation to his children. The love of music was, however, irrepressible in most of them, and those who cultivated their talent in later years became excellent singers. It is perhaps hardly necessary to say that the modern Friends have come to regard their predecessors' conscientious objection to music as being based upon mistaken, or too narrow, views of the subject, and that music now forms part of the curriculum of their own public schools.

Towards the close of my father's life, he was greatly cheered and consoled by a message coming from Australia from his youngest son, Jonathan Hughes Jones, then within a few hours of his death. He had emigrated to a warmer climate, in the hope of recovering from the effects of severe rheumatic fever, with which he had been seized in England. Assisting his eldest brother, Joseph, in his business at Ballarat, he struggled manfully for some time against the malady, which had, alas, taken so deep a hold of his constitution that, in spite of his earnest efforts to be useful and to overcome his physical weakness, he was compelled at last to succumb. Amid the uncomfortable surroundings of his little room at the store, in physical weakness and utter loneliness, but with a mind perfectly clear and calm, as though filled, day by day, with a renewed sense of peace with God, his young life was rapidly ebbing away. Summoning all his fast-waning strength, he dictated impressively to his brother the dying message which he wished to be conveyed to his beloved father. "Tell father," so ran this message of filial affection, "that before I died I often used to think of him, and have done so for many years. I always thought with great satisfaction of the beneficial influence his life, example, and words had on the minds of his children. Tell him that I was very thankful that I was brought up as a member of the Society of Friends, and that I considered his yielding to God in his youth had been greatly blessed both to him and his family, and although we shall not meet again on earth, I believe we shall meet in heaven. This is the last message from his affectionate son, who died in the full assurance of forgiveness, through the atonement made for him by Jesus Christ our Saviour."

The day before my father's death, his daughter read again to him this touching message. The dying father could not speak, but his eyes followed the reader through every word. Soon afterwards an attack of apoplexy came on, and after a brief struggle, life was extinct. He died at Ruthin on the 27th of June, 1874, aged about 75 years, and was interred beside his first wife in the small burial ground attached to a chapel of the Countess of Huntingdon's connection, situated in Rhos Street, Ruthin, but now belonging to the Established Church.

True and sincere were these words so aptly spoken by my dear youngest brother on his death-bed. Everyone of the six children who grew up to maturity, has similarly been glad of the example of their father's consistent and conscientious life. Four more of the family have since that time passed away, the latest survivor beside myself being my younger brother Henry, who for more than thirty years was Principal of the Government Model School in Melbourne, and after leading for a few years a retired life in the suburbs of that busy city, he peacefully expired on the 31st of May, 1897.

Curious Welsh Customs.

In my boyhood, gas was unknown in Wales as an illuminant; a dim flickering oil lamp, here and there, barely sufficed to make darkness visible in the streets of our little town. On dark nights visits were made by the light of hand-lanterns only. Friction matches had not, up to 1835, found their way to Ruthin. For striking a light we relied solely on the tinder box and sulphur match (a long splinter of wood tipped with sulphur), and many were the weary struggles on cold winter mornings to get a spark, struck from flint and steel, to catch the tinder in the box. How little do we now think of the enormous gain, in time and comfort, through the cheap and ubiquitous lucifer match!

As in most other country towns, there was no water supply laid on in pipes. All the water consumed in the upper part of the town was carried in tins or buckets from a spring situated in a field nearly half a mile from the Market-place. In summertime, on Saturday evenings, when double supplies were required—for our town was intensely Sabbatarian, and would have been shocked to see water carried on Sundays—I have often seen the well exhausted, and people patiently waiting for the spring to gather, before they could fill their vessels.

Another scene occurring in harvest time, in our market-place, to which my mind has often reverted, when reading the Scripture parable of the labourers and the vineyard, was the group of harvesters, with sickles or scythes in hand, waiting from an early hour to be hired for the day. Farmers would come in from the country round, and after some bargaining as to the rate of wages, would hire as many men as they wanted. Others came in after breakfast-time, and others again at the "eleventh hour" to engage labourers for half a day. It was eminently pastoral and simple, and as a boy, standing by to learn the rate of wages paid, I often marked the disappointment on the faces of the poor men, who "stood all the day idle, because no man had hired them."

In country cottages, and even in the kitchens of good farm-houses, rush-lights were generally used in order to save candles. Of rushes there was no scarcity in those days of undrained meadows. The largest were gathered and peeled, leaving a thin strip of peel to keep the pith together. After being drawn through melted grease several times, they were dried ready for use. The rush-stand which had a peculiar sort of pliers for holding the rush light, was to be found in every farmhouse. The light given was dim and feeble, and its only recommendation was its cheapness.

The bread commonly eaten by country folks was made from barley meal, wheat flour being too dear for general use. Bread in the country was usually made with leaven, and the barley loaf, which was very heavy, had a sourish taste, which we town boys rather relished as a change, though in reality we never hankered much after it. The labourers, however, who were accustomed to its taste, preferred it, because they considered it had more "last" in it than wheaten bread.

The sound of the flail had not then departed from the land. As a boy I loved its rhythmic music, and spent many an hour in the farmhouse barn, watching the clever strokes of the two threshers, as, standing face to face, they brought the flails down alternately, with unerring strokes, on the heads of the corn. Sometimes I ventured to wield the flail myself, but, like most inexperienced hands, generally managed to deal on my own head a resounding thump which abruptly ended the experiment. The garden rhubarb was unknown in Wales as an edible up to the date of my going to school, and even at Ackworth, in Yorkshire, in 1835, its hard woody texture bore but a distant resemblance to the modern juicy, well-flavoured esculent. Nevertheless, when mixed with apples, it served to flavour our pies, and schoolboy appetites are by no means fastidious. At eight o'clock every evening in Ruthin, that survival of the Norman Conquest, the curfew, "tolled the knell of parting day." We children called it the "sexton's cow," as it rang from the church tower "*Dyna buwch y clochydd yn brefu*," (the sexton's cow is bellowing), and we were packed off to bed at once. Reminiscences of early life, like these, might be indefinitely multiplied, but more important matters forbid any further enlargement in this direction.

As already mentioned, my mother was granddaughter to the old bard of Llangollen, Jonathan Hughes. His grandson Jonathan, the third of the name, was tenant of the Pengwern Farm in my boyhood, and my venerable grandmother lived there with her son for many years after the death of her husband.

George Borrow, author of the "Bible in Spain," in his book on "Wild Wales," gives an account, in his own racy style, of a conversation with Jonathan Hughes the Third, whom he incidentally met at his farm gate as he (Borrow) was proceeding to cross the Berwyn Mountains on foot, by ascending a steep narrow lane, down which a little mountain torrent flowed past the Pengwern Farm.

Being invited into the house, "I went," he says, "with him and his wife into a neat kind of kitchen, flagged with stone, where were several young people, their children. I spoke some Welsh to them, which appeared to give them great satisfaction. . . . I entered into discourse with the man about Welsh poetry, and repeated the famous prophecy of Taliesin about the Coiling Serpent. I asked him if the Welsh had any poets at the present day.—'Plenty,' said he, 'and good ones; Wales can never be without a poet.' Then, after a pause, he said that he was the grandson of a great poet.

"'Do you bear his name?' said I.

"'I do,' he replied.

"'What may it be?'

"'Hughes,' he answered.

"'Two of the name of Hughes have been poets,' said I, 'one was Huw Hughes, generally termed the Bardd Coch or Red Bard. He was an Anglesea man . . . the other was Jonathan Hughes; where he lived, I know not.'

"'He lived here, in this very house,' said the man. 'Jonathan Hughes was my grandfather'; and as he spoke his eyes flashed fire . . . I then repeated a quartette of his poetry, which I chanced to remember.

"'Ah'! said the man, 'I see you know his poetry; come into the next room, and I will show you his chair.' He led me into a sleeping room on the right hand, where in a corner, he showed me an antique three-cornered armchair. 'That chair,' said he, 'my grandfather won at Llangollen, at an Eisteddfod of Bards. Various bards recited their poetry, but my grandfather won the prize. Ah! he was a good poet; he also won a prize of fifteen guineas at a meeting of bards in London.'

* * * *

"As I went away, he said that both he and his family should be always happy to see me at 'Ty-yn-y-Pistyll,' which words interpreted are the house by the spout of water."

In later years that grandfather's old arm-chair,—an oaken relic of his poetic skill, that would have been specially prized by his grandchildren—was thoughtlessly disposed of at a sale of farm-effects, after my uncle's decease, and thus lost forever to the bard's descendants.

CHAPTER II.

MY SCHOOL-DAYS—STRANGE RAT INCIDENT—MY MOTHER'S LAST FAREWELL—COACH JOURNEY TO ACKWORTH SCHOOL—SKIPPING AS A FINE ART.

THE facilities for education in my boyhood were very different from what they are in the present era of Board and High Schools. The only real educational establishment which then existed in Ruthin, was Dean Goodman's Grammar School, but this school, being entirely under the management of the clergy, and the pupils being expected to learn the catechism, and to attend the services of the Church of England, was not available for Dissenters like ourselves, unless we were willing to comply with these requirements. The only alternative was a private day school in the town kept by a person named Davies, a tall strong man and a thorough adept with cane and birch, which were in frequent requisition in school hours. Here also our father would not allow his sons to learn the Church catechism, a distinction we did not altogether enjoy, as it sometimes led to our being teased as "Quakers," which did not always tend to peaceful relations with our school-fellows, and sometimes even led to pugilistic encounters, causing further disgrace and trouble at home. The education given at this school was elementary enough, little in fact beyond the "three R's," and it was, of course, entirely in English, although the moment we stepped outside the school doors we relapsed into our familiar Welsh. In the home also, Welsh was the language of the household, so that we did not really acquire the power of speaking English properly until we went to school in Yorkshire. In our boyhood we were allowed considerable liberty, and often spent our half-holidays in fishing or bathing in the river Clwyd. My elder brother, Joseph, thus became a good swimmer and found very few rivals in the art when he went to the Friends' School at Ackworth, near Pontefract.

A rather uncommon "rat" incident of this epoch, when I was about eight years old, may be worth recording. It occurred at our cart-shed attached to the stables, when I was helping our outdoor man, Edward, to sweep out the place. Suddenly a large brown rat popped out of a hole, over which Edward promptly pushed a piece of wood, and confronted the rat, broomstick in hand. The rat thus driven to bay, gave a spring and suddenly disappeared from view. Edward gave a startling shriek, as he found that the rat was running up the inside of his trousers. Up and up, under his shirt it climbed, digging its claws into the skin of his back; then crossing over his shoulder, began to descend his arm. There, however, the rat stuck fast, just below the elbow, where the coat sleeve was too tight to allow him to proceed any further. Poor Edward, although a strong and sturdily built fellow, turned ghastly white with the shock, and trembled like an aspen leaf. Begging me to take hold of his coat sleeve, he gently drew out his hand. The rat, probably as terrified as the man, sprang out and made for the open door. Just at that moment, a youth was passing, who, though a cripple from his birth, having only one leg, yet was one of the most nimble in all sorts of games. "Eben Un Goes" (One Legged Ebenezer), as he was called by his playfellows, quickly seized the situation; whipped off his bowler hat, adroitly scooped up the rat in it and clapped it down firmly on his head, coolly saying, "There, I shall take him home for my ferrets." Off he skipped nimbly on his crutch, but whether he succeeded in safely delivering the prey to his ferrets I never heard. A more fearless and dexterous turn I never saw done. Possibly he was ignorant of the fact that a large rat at bay is a most formidable beast.

My pleasantest reminiscences of early life are in connection with the holidays we spent among our country relatives, especially at Grandmother Hughes at Pengwern near Llangollen. Here we roamed at our own sweet will over the Berwyn range, and feasted as often as we liked upon black cherries, which grew in abundance in her orchard. The kind, hospitable, old lady spoiled and petted us, and almost ruined our digestions, with the piles of "indigestibilities" which she heaped upon our plates. We loved the dear old granny; she was always kind to us, and never scolded, no matter what mischief we were guilty of.

In the month of August 1835, when nine years and three months old, my father took me to Ackworth School in Yorkshire, the national boarding school of the Society of Friends, where my eldest brother, Joseph, had preceded me by twelve months. The long journey was, in anticipation, a joyous treat to me, especially the unknown delight of travelling by railway over the recently opened line from Liverpool to Manchester. I well remember the early morning start from home with our horse and car; when my mother, after giving me her parting kiss, stood on the doorstep to see us off. Distinctly can I recall, over a vista of more than sixty years, her tall slender form and delicate peach-blossom complexion, as she bravely kept up a smiling face towards me, at the same time chiding our two maids, who stood by, weeping aloud because their sister was going with us to a situation in Liverpool. "Don't be silly," I heard mother say, "your sister is going no further than Liverpool. My boy is going more than 150 miles away, and I may never see him again." Sadly prophetic words! She never did! She died after the birth of her youngest son, when I had been about two years at school.

This doorstep scene is my last and most touching reminiscence of that dear loving mother. When the then Principal of Ackworth School, Thomas Pumphrey, broke, in the kindest manner, the sad intelligence to my brother and self, I felt heart-broken at the thought that I should see my mother no more, and bedewed my pillow at night with many tears, while trying hard to keep up a brave face towards my school-fellows in the daytime. It was impossible for us to go home to the funeral, there being no one to fetch us, and coach travelling being too expensive. Cowper's pensive lines on the receipt of his mother's picture, served to embalm the memory of our own beloved mother to us two poor forlorn boys, exiled from home, without vacations, or a single visit from any-one from the old home, during the whole of our school-days. Those exquisite lines would often touch me to tears, as I recalled in vivid fancy—as I do even yet—the sweet face of that beloved mother, saying her last farewell to her boy, from the doorstep—

"My mother, when I learn'd that thou wast dead,
Say, wast thou conscious of the tears I shed?
Hovered thy spirit o'er thy sorrowing son,
Wretch, even then, life's journey just begun?
Perhaps thou gav'st me, though unfelt, a kiss:
Perhaps a tear, if souls can weep in bliss."

Our route towards Ackworth, after slowly ascending the three-mile hill out of the Vale of Clwyd, lay through Mold to Queensferry, where we crossed the Dee, and thence to Eastham on the Mersey. Leaving there the horse and car, we took steamer for Liverpool, and the same evening booked to Manchester from Lime Street Station, which, in 1835, was a very sorry affair, compared with the present magnificent terminus.

In 1835, the third class carriages upon the Liverpool and Manchester Railway were open at the sides; all the passengers' luggage was piled upon the roofs, then covered with tarpaulins and carefully strapped down, causing considerable delay in starting. The guards wore brilliant scarlet coats, as was then the practice in the stage coaches, and the trains were started to the strains of a trumpet played by an old trumpeter, who had probably been a mail-coach guard.

My first experience of railway travelling was not an unmixed pleasure. After proceeding a few miles, we came to a stand for some hours, owing to something in front being off the line—a not infrequent occurrence in those early railway days. Our arrival in Manchester was in consequence too late to book by the coaches taking the most direct route for Ackworth. Early next morning we proceeded, by another line of coaches, over Blackstone Edge, up which our coach slowly crawled, drawn by six horses. Travellers in these days, unconscious of the mighty hill above them, are whirled through it in a few minutes, by the Lancashire and Yorkshire Railway, in a tunnel over three miles in length. Passing through several Yorkshire towns, of which no special impressions remain in my memory, we at length reached Pontefract, late in the evening. Leaving our baggage to follow next day (probably in the cart drawn by the noted old bull belonging to the School, which had a collar large enough for a young elephant), my father and I set off on our three miles walk to Ackworth.

Next morning I was glad to see my brother Joseph, but strange to say we were dumb in each other's presence; in a year he had wholly forgotten his native tongue, and I knew too little of English to have any talk with him. That it is possible, in so short a time, to lose one's mother tongue, at nine or ten years of age, I was soon to experience myself, for within six months after coming to school, when my uncle, Joseph Jones, brought his second daughter Sarah from Hereford to Ackworth, he tried in vain, as we walked round "the great garden," to make me talk in Welsh. Even a big thing like a haystack had literally gone from my memory. Do what I would, I could not recall the words, "*y das wair*" (the haystack).

My forgetfulness of Welsh was probably much facilitated by the petty teasing of some of my school-fellows, who lost no opportunity of reminding me that "Taffy was a Welshman," and a somewhat objectionable character all round. The delight taken by some boys in this incessant habit of teasing proved, at times, too much for my hot Welsh blood, and regardless of their age or size, some of my tormentors had to carry into school visible traces on eyes and nose, of my not altogether unpractised fists. Little satisfaction, however, came from outbursts of temper like this; I, of course, was regarded as the aggressor, no matter how sore the provocation undergone, and it was I who received punishment, being left for many an hour to cool down and ponder over my sins, in solitary confinement in the dingy cells, which were waggishly dignified by the title of "the light and airy."

I soon outlived these early difficulties, however, and began to enjoy my school-life. Active and rough games were so much to my taste that the worthy Superintendent added, as a postscript to one of my early letters home, that "William is as wild as a goat from the Welsh mountains." This proof of ignorance of natural history on the part of the good man, in ignoring the fact that no such quadruped as a *wild* goat exists in Wales, afforded me some amusement in later years.

Even the early morning plunge into the old bath, which, for appearance sake among my companions, I made a pretence of enjoying, was in fact a hard test of Spartan endurance, such as would now be condemned as utterly unfit even for the hardiest constitutions. Roused out of sleep at five o'clock on a cold morning, regardless of weather, and trotted over the mile or so of road to the bath, where we had to deposit our clothes on the dewy grass, it then became a point of honour who should be first to plunge through the yellow chalybeate scum on the surface, and take a header across the bath. Often our teeth chattered, and we were blue with cold, and in spite of the small hunch of bread served out to the bathers, we were ready to faint before having our eight o'clock breakfast.

One such fainting occurrence led to a ludicrous circumstance, that has remained in my memory. In the Latin class, as we were standing to recite our lessons before breakfast, after having been to the bath, my neighbour, W. S.——, whose face had been gradually growing whiter and whiter, suddenly collapsed, and fell in a dead faint on the floor. The Master, in alarm, dispatched a boy at full speed downstairs for some cold water to dash on his face. The lad quickly returned with an odd looking bottle, whose contents he emptied over the poor boy's white face. In his haste he had seized the first thing to hand, which happened to be an old *blacking* bottle, containing enough of its original contents to blacken the whole. This was too ridiculous! Much as we felt for our schoolfellow, the sharp contrast of the blacking and the pallid face was too much for our decorum, and the whole class relieved their feelings with a loud burst of laughter. The douche was effective, however, and the boy, after a good wash, bravely turned up at the breakfast table. I never saw him again, after he left school, until we met in the Australian colonies, more than fifty years afterwards, when he was much amused with the recital of the incident.

The art of skipping was much practised among the boys in my school-days at Ackworth, and was brought to a great pitch of perfection.

The Ackworth skipping-rope was really a scientific instrument, and the feats that were achieved by its means could not have been done by a rope of the ordinary form. It was made out of the finest whip-cord, weighted at the sides with two pieces of stout cord, well tarred, these being connected at the bottom with fine whip-cord. The handles were turned out of the smoothest box, or other hard wood, thus allowing the rope to revolve with an ease and speed which caused it to whistle as it cut through the air. With an instrument like this, it was possible to do "treble" and even "four-ble" (in schoolboy's lingo), that is, to make the rope revolve three, or even four times, for each bound in the air of the skipper. More than this, some of the best skippers could cross their arms once, in each of the three revolutions of the cord during one jump. This difficult feat, only to be attained by long practice, was called "cat-tail treble." I remember counting on one occasion the performance of no less than 75 "cat-tail treble" by the then best skipper in the school, the late Thomas Burtt. These skipping feats formed one of the attractions of the Annual General Meeting, when the best skippers used to perform in a ring, surrounded by admiring Friends and visitors.

Notwithstanding various incidents, more or less

unpleasant, I really enjoyed my school-days. I got on well with my school-fellows, and took part in all sorts of active games. The masters, too, were fairly impartial and just in their dealings with us, though we had our strong likes and dislikes among them. For our Latin lessons I acquired a taste, but my favourite study was geography. Until I went to Ackworth, I had never seen a map. When once I understood that the large school-maps represented so many condensed plans of the geographical features of every country on the globe, they fascinated me so much, that I spent many hours of play-time in studying them, and thus at an early age acquired a grasp, often useful in later life, of the main physical features of the globe we inhabit.

VACATIONS.

Vacations were not allowed during my school-days, and indeed they would hardly have been practicable, considering the great distances many of us had to travel to our homes, and the expense of stage-coach journeys. It was a great concession, after the coming of the new Principal (Thomas Pumphrey), that a boy whose conduct was good, was allowed, after *three* years at school, one month's holiday, at the request of his parents. I obtained this privilege in 1838, but instead of the intense enjoyment of my holiday which I had pictured to myself, on reaching my native town, a sense of disappointment came over me, as I found all so changed and different to the old days at home before I went to school.

My father had in the meantime married again, his bride being an English "Friend." Somehow, the Welsh people and the Welsh language she never acquired a liking for, and in accordance with her own strict ideas of management and discipline, she insisted on our using "the plain language," *i.e.*, "thee" and thou" to everyone; and no doubt thought she was doing the best service possible for my little sisters by dressing them up in small quaint "Quaker" bonnets, in which the poor children were ashamed to be seen in the streets.

My visits also to my Welsh relatives, which used to be so great an enjoyment to me, were no longer so, as I, having forgotten my Welsh, could not talk to them, nor they to me. I remember a very countrified aunt on the Llangollen hills exclaiming, "*Pa sut yr ydych chwi yu disgwyl rhiw pagan pen mynydd vel nyni i siarad saesoneg*" (How can you expect a mountain-top heathen like me to speak English).

Everything in fact seemed to conspire against the enjoyment of my holiday at home. I found few, if any, of my old school companions in the town, and in our home everything was so very different from the ways of our own dear mother, that, at last, I fairly broke down, and begged to go back to school.

To Ackworth at the end of the month I returned, and made so good a use of my last year there, that after completing a four years' course, at the age of thirteen years and three months, I was considered fit to enter upon commercial life.

Apprenticed at Liverpool.

To Liverpool I was accordingly sent in 1839, to be apprenticed to a grocer, and after a few months trial, was duly bound, according to the mistaken custom of that day, for seven years. I was far from sorry that after about two and a half years of hard, uncongenial business life, ill-health caused my indentures to be cancelled, and I proceeded home, under medical orders, to recruit in my native air. At the same time, the practical knowledge of colonial and other foreign produce thus acquired behind a grocer's counter has often proved beneficial and useful in after life.

My health was more seriously impaired than at first appeared, and for some months it seemed doubtful whether tubercular consumption might not be the final result.

CHAPTER III.

BURGLAR CAPTURE — ILLNESS — RETURN TO WALES — RECKLESS COACH DRIVING — OLD PENSIONERS' STORIES — EARTHQUAKE IN WALES — TEACHING AT RAWDON—LIFE AT DARLINGTON—HOW I LEARNT TO SPEAK FRENCH.

A CURIOUS burglary incident occurred on the premises, during my apprenticeship in Liverpool. It was then customary to keep grocers' shops open till midnight on Saturdays. As I was getting supper in the house late one Saturday night, I heard a strange noise in the room over my head, and ran upstairs to ascertain the cause. As I entered the bedroom a man was disappearing out of the window. He dropped into the yard below, from the first storey, and then, after a hard scramble, got over a wall into a long narrow passage communicating with the street. By this time, our principal, a wiry little man, had rushed out at the front door, and pluckily grappled with the burglar in the narrow passage, calling at the same time loudly for the police. As the burglar was a powerful fellow, he would very soon have got away, had not one or two policemen come promptly to the rescue. He was seized and brought into the house by them, and afterwards taken to the police station. On Monday, we had to appear to give evidence before the Magistrate, and as the man was not absolutely caught on our own premises, there appeared to be a risk of his being discharged, for want of evidence. At this moment, I asked that his clothing might be examined, to see whether a brace button was wanting, for on Sunday morning, when looking in the back yard, at the way the man had escaped, I had picked up the outer rim of a bone button, which without telling anyone, I quietly put in my pocket. In court, the policeman reported that he found a piece of broken button on the man's clothing. I then handed up the bone rim in my possession, which was found exactly to fit the piece of the broken button on his clothing. This settled the question of his having been a trespasser upon our own premises, and he was committed to the coming Assizes. At the Assizes the judge complimented us, saying that as every Englishman's house was his castle, we had done bravely in capturing the thief. He was sentenced to seven years penal servitude. Soon afterwards the gang of which he was the chief were all captured by the police, and about two thousand pounds worth of plate and jewellery were found in their possession.

I was reduced, after my return home to Wales, to great physical weakness, and scarcely had strength enough left to walk even a short distance. Many hours of the night were spent in wakefulness, and in nervous tremor. These feelings were not improved by the howlings of a big dog in the neighbourhood, making night hideous, which the force of old associations (in spite of better feelings), would, in my then weak state, convert into presentiments of death. An accident also, about this time, helped to bring matters to a crisis, for I was thrown from a lofty seat on a coach, upon my right shoulder, on the hard road. suffered long from this injury, the arm having to be carried in a sling, until the shoulder-joint gradually stiffened, and its free action became impeded for the rest of life.

In this connection may be mentioned an instance of recklessness in driving, arising from the competition amongst stage coaches, which occurred whilst I was obliged to carry my right arm in a sling, owing to the accident previously referred to. My brother Henry and I were going from Ruthin to Rhyl. At a steep hill on the journey, the passengers got down to walk, and before we could all resume our seats at the top of the hill, the coachman, seeing that the opposition coach was overtaking us, was very impatient to start his horses. Whilst waiting for my brother to get into the seat before me, I was standing on the fore wheel, when the coachman whipped up his horses and started the coach. I made a spring with one hand at the rail above my head, but instead of getting hold of it, I only got hold of a loose coat, and fell down in a dangerous position between the front and hind wheels. How I raised my head in time to avoid being run over by the hind wheel, I never knew, but I suffered no worse consequences than a blow on the back of the head as it passed me. By this time the passengers had made the coachman aware of my dangerous position, and I was enabled to get up and take my place again on the coach as though nothing had happened. But the careless driver had reason to congratulate himself that the accident had not proved fatal.

Reading was my chief resource during this time of enforced idleness, but my father's scanty library was soon exhausted. It contained, however, one or two books which influenced me for life. One of these was "Barclay's Apology," regarded then as the chief text-book of Quaker theology, which I read carefully through twice, and portions of it three times. Another book which attracted me strongly, at that time, was a treatise on "The Indwelling of the Holy Spirit," by a mystic, one Michael De Molinos, a Spanish monk, who was immured for twenty-eight years in the prisons of the Inquisition, for his so-called heretical writings. Molinos' book, though intensely mystical, served to enlighten my mind in regard to the doctrine of the indwelling and guidance of the Holy Spirit, far beyond anything I had previously learned on this subject, either at Ackworth School, or from any "Friends'" books.

From later experiences, and from wider acquaintance with the Gospel of Christ, as the "power of God unto salvation, to every one that believeth," I have, however, been led to see that the tendency of writings like those of Molinos and of Madame Guyon, on the whole, did not contribute to real healthfulness of soul. The constant atmosphere of self-introspection induces a morbid, unpractical state of mind, which tends to a life of seclusion, wrapped up in self-musings, rather than to the wholesome teaching of the gospel to "look on the things of others" also.

Nevertheless I feel that, instrumentally, I owe much to the pious Spanish Monk, for the light which shone into my soul from the study of his book, in regard to the practical operations of the Spirit of God on the human heart.

Old Pensioners' Stories.

My father's shop, being in the centre of the town of Ruthin, was frequently the *rendezvous* for old comrades and other men who had served in the wars, to look in, and enjoy "a chat with John Jones." On these occasions I was often a listener, and heard many interesting stories of campaigning under the "Great Duke," in the Peninsular wars.

I well remember a tall, slender old man, who used to travel about the country as a hawker, with his basket, and who had had some tough experiences in his service as a soldier in Spain. He formed one of the storming party at Badajos, and could describe the events of that terrible siege with so much energy and action as to make it all very real to my comprehension. He told us of the terrible death struggle he and his fellows had to make over the dead and wounded bodies of comrades in the moat, in order to cross bayonets with the equally brave and ardent French soldiers who were defending the breach; he spoke of the fiery heat of the day, and the excitement of the bayonet charge, having so worked upon his own brother, who was his front rank man, that he was foaming at the mouth in battle frenzy, as he rushed to the front, in advance of his comrades, to plunge his bayonet into one of the enemy. The old pensioner who was close behind him, seeing his danger, shouted to him in Welsh, "*Tendia, Twm!*" (Take care, Tom!) but, alas! the warning came too late, for no sooner were the words uttered than the gleaming point of a French bayonet, upon which he was impaled, protruded several inches through the back of his scarlet coat before the eyes of his horrified brother, and the body fell down among those in the moat, to be trodden on in turn by the rush of his comrades in that awful and bloody fray.

When I remember the stories of these old veterans, and the numerous deeds of personal valour, and the terrible hardships they suffered throughout the Peninsular and other campaigns, when both men and officers went through their work, as the every day duty of the soldier, with no expectation of being glorified in the dispatches sent home, I cannot help contrasting their modest endurance of hardship as soldiers, with the fuss and laudation which it is so much the fashion in the present day to bestow, and with the lavish distribution of decorations and crosses for every small achievement against African or Asiatic tribesmen. Can we wonder if these petty affairs serve to provoke the derision, rather than the admiration, of our Continental neighbours?

EARTHQUAKE.

About 1841, while sojourning at Ruthin for the purpose of recruiting my health, I passed through the severest shock of earthquake that I have ever experienced. Earth tremors, more or less serious, I have felt in England, in Sicily, in New Zealand, and in Japan; but that of 1841, the real nature of which I failed at the moment to understand, remains in my memory as by far the worst I have undergone. Lying wide awake in my bed in the dead of night, I suddenly heard loud rumbling sounds, as though scores of empty carts were passing on the hard road. All at once the bed under me began to creak and rock with a wave-like motion that almost threw me on the floor. The house, a very old one, with extremely thick stone walls, shook violently, causing glasses and crockery to jingle and crash ominously. The whole thing probably did not occupy more than a minute or two, though it seemed much longer, but the effect was so weird and alarming that it made me tremble and shiver in a cold perspiration. Strangely enough the idea of an earthquake did not occur to me at the time, the rumbling of empty carts, going past for coals, being a nightly occurrence. It was not till the next day, when the newspapers revealed the extensive damage done all over North Wales, that I realised the true state of the case.

TEACHING IN YORKSHIRE.

The monotony of enforced idleness for about a year and a half, wearied me much, and as soon as the state of my health would permit, I longed for suitable employment. Providentially, as it then seemed, an opening was proposed to me by my old Ackworth principal, Thomas Pumphrey, to fill a vacancy, as teacher, at the Friends' School at Rawdon, near Leeds. My total want of experience and of ability for such work would of itself have deterred me from thinking of undertaking such a post, but the suggestion coming from the quarter it did, together with my own anxiety for work, overcame all scruples. I applied for the situation and was accepted, and shortly entered on the, to me, novel duty of assistant teacher of a school of thirty-six boys. Here, in about my eighteenth year, I soon became a sort of factotum for the whole school, nearly all the teaching being left in my hands, together with the entire management of the boys in play hours, my duties never ceasing from 6 a.m. to 8.30 p.m. Then came my only chance for private study and self-improvement, and I constantly "wasted the midnight oil" in the study of the classics, French, and mathematics, feeling that my store of these equipments was, as yet, too slender to enable me to become a successful teacher.

After nearly three years of incessant drudgery, which told seriously upon my health, and discouraged by the wretched pay and poor prospects, at that day, of a school teacher's life, I welcomed a proposal from a young friend to join him in farming. My future life, however, was not in the ordering of Providence to be so spent.

About that time the late John Pease of Darlington, a well-known preacher in the Society of Friends, during a ministerial visit to Rawdon, finding I was disengaged, proposed that I should accompany him to Darlington to see his brother Henry, who was looking out for a private tutor for his son, Henry Fell Pease, then aged about nine years. I therefore went to Darlington with John Pease, and became engaged as private tutor.

Of all the men who have helped me and aided in the formation of my character, no one more deeply influenced my religious life than John Pease. Even when a schoolboy at Ackworth I was much impressed with his ministry, on those occasional visits which he paid to the School. There was something even in the rich, melodious tone of his voice, which we compared to a "silver trumpet," that was calculated to arouse and to fix the attention of the most careless of schoolboys.

On arriving at his brother's residence, direct from the bare and bleak premises of Rawdon School, my first view of Pierremont, with its noble tower and stained glass window, was certainly calculated to impress the imagination of one unaccustomed to such surroundings.

There could hardly be a greater contrast with the hard life I had led at Rawdon School, than the comparative leisure which I now enjoyed at Pierremont, with its beautiful grounds and various accessories, carriages, horses, etc. My pupil, too, was a very engaging boy, with a most endearing transparency and truthfulness of disposition, which adhered to him throughout his entire life. His father, being a widower, the boy was during the daytime constantly under my care, and when not engaged with lessons, we rode out together, or visited his cousins of the other families of Pease in Darlington, and joined in their games and pursuits. A mutual attachment sprang up between my pupil and myself, which in after life developed into a partnership in business and into a close life-long friendship, our relations, during many years, being much more those of brothers than of friends. His sudden and unexpected death in December, 1896, came as an overwhelming shock to me. Deep indeed was my sorrow on behalf of his dear widow and children, in the grief into which they were plunged, through the loss of a husband and parent so tenderly beloved; whilst the blank thus created in my own life, through the death of one whose affectionate friendship had played so important a part in it, abides ever with me.

A French Master, coming to Pierremont to give lessons to my pupil twice a week, gave me the opportunity I had long desired, of obtaining a conversational knowledge of French. He had been an officer of Napoleon Bonaparte's, and after the "*sauve qui peut*" of Waterloo, he had escaped to England and settled at Darlington. He was a genial, racy old man, full of anecdote ; and, as I retained him expressly only to speak in French, I was able in about twelve months to converse in French with considerable fluency. This acquisition proved of great use to me in later years, and led to my being engaged in many of the services which are related in this work.

His admiration of Napoleon Bonaparte often drew from the old soldier rhapsodies of hero-worship. Many were the stories we heard from his lips of the great battles in which he had fought under him, ending up with the disastrous stampede from the fatal field of Waterloo.

When my tutorial engagement was drawing to a close, I spent six months in charge of my pupil in the city of Bristol, where he had gone to continue his education.

At the termination of my engagement I went back to Darlington, and soon obtained my first commercial position, as Secretary to the Darlington Gas and Water Company. With this was also united the Secretaryship of the Stockton and Middlesbrough Water Company. The source of water supply was the same for both undertakings, the water being pumped from the river Tees, about two miles above the town of Darlington.

CHAPTER IV.

DARLINGTON NOTABLES: EDWARD PEASE, THE FATHER OF RAILWAYS—GEORGE STEPHENSON, THE FIRST RAILWAY ENGINEER—FIRST PASSENGER RAILWAY—HENRY PEASE—CLEVER CAPTURE OF RUNAWAY ENGINE.—WILLIAM E. FORSTER.

IT was a real pleasure to me, during my early life at Darlington, to be frequently invited, with my pupil, to his grandfather Edward Pease's house, in Northgate.

Opposite that historical old house, on the pavement, may still be seen the noted "Boulder Stone," of well-rounded Shap Fell granite, a travelled relic of the "Ice Age," weighing many tons. The surveyors of the highway made on one occasion all preparations to remove the boulder as an obstruction. On this action coming to Edward Pease's knowledge, the old man promptly appeared on the scene, claimed the boulder as his private property, and sternly ordered the officials to leave it in its place. Thanks to his promptitude, this remarkable relic of remote bygone ages is still preserved to the town.

As Edward Pease lived to be nearly ninety-two years of age, his reminiscences were probably those of the oldest inhabitant. For instance, he remarked on one occasion that he had known a man who had been born in the year 1700. There was therefore but one life between himself and the founder of Pennsylvania, William Penn, who died in 1718. On another occasion I sat beside him on the platform, when a learned antiquarian was lecturing upon the antiquities of the neighbourhood. Among these, he alluded to the large stone, and iron staple, to be seen in the ground in the horse-market in Darlington, where he said the barbarous practice of bull-baiting was formerly carried on, but that it had been discontinued for a century or more. Edward Pease exclaimed in a whisper to me, but loud enough to be heard by the lecturer, "Stuff and nonsense. I have seen it many a time when I was a lad." On another occasion, he mentioned standing in the Market-place, between five and six o'clock in the morning, holding an umbrella over the head of John Wesley, when delivering, as was his practice, one of his very early morning sermons in the town. Another of his curious reminiscences was that he remembered the Darlington Post Office being located in a one-storied cottage in the Tubwell Row, and when the old lady who kept it heard the postboy's horn, as he came on horseback from Northallerton over the stone bridge, she appeared in the front of the cottage with the whole of the letters of Darlington and district between her finger and thumb, ready to put into the bag on his back, as he resumed his journey northwards to Durham, etc. "And now," added the old man, "I have lived to see the day when a van with two horses is employed, in taking them several times in the course of the day to the Railway Station."

To myself, his most interesting reminiscences, however, were connected with George Stephenson, the eminent railway engineer. Edward Pease, who is known as the "Father of Railways," originated the Stockton and Darlington line, and obtained the assistance of George Stephenson, then a colliery engineer, in its formation.

Previous to his engagement to the Stockton and Darlington Railway, which brought him distinction as a railway engineer, and led to his subsequent selection, in a similar capacity, on the Liverpool and Manchester Railway, Stephenson had constructed the mineral line, about eight miles in length, from Hetton Colliery, in the county of Durham, to the shipping staithes on the River Wear at Sunderland. This line, one of the first to be worked by locomotive power, continues in active operation, and its trains of primitive "chaldron" wagons may still be seen running.

Having completed this undertaking, Stephenson called on Messrs. Backhouse in Sunderland, the bankers of the Hetton Coal Company, and through them obtained an introduction to Edward Pease, who had then taken initiative steps towards the formation of the "Stockton and Darlington Railway."

Stephenson thus became a frequent visitor at the Northgate house, and being a man of many resources, his company was very acceptable to the young people. One incident which would make an effective picture, was when he taught the two young ladies, daughters of Edward Pease, the art of embroidery. When Stephenson became a wealthy man, in order to evince his gratitude to his early benefactor, he sent his friend Edward Pease a magnificent gold watch, ornamented with diamonds. Edward Pease, however, being one of the plainest of "plain Friends," returned the watch, as he told me himself, thanking George Stephenson for his kind intentions, but saying he should be ashamed to carry such a watch on his person, adding, "If thou wants to remember me, send me a plain gold watch." The *plain* gold watch accordingly came, doubtless of the highest quality and workmanship, and containing an appropriate inscription. This watch I have frequently seen, and it remains as an heirloom in the family to this day.

It was through the persevering efforts of Edward Pease that this, the first public railway in England, was opened for traffic in the year 1825; and the locomotive No. 1, that was used in the opening ceremony, may still be seen in the large Central Station at Darlington. In 1875, some years after the Stockton and Darlington line had been amalgamated with the North Eastern system, the jubilee of the railway was celebrated in Darlington, when many railway notables from foreign countries as well as from England, were present at a banquet given by the North Eastern Railway Company, under the presidency of the late Henry Pease, M.P., who himself had taken part in the opening of the first railway in 1825.

Edward Pease had in his possession a relic of the Rebellion of 1745, when so many of the clansmen in Scotland arose in support of the "Young Pretender," Prince Charles Edward. The Duke of Cumberland on his march northwards, to suppress the insurrection, passed through Darlington, and his troops were encamped in the "Green Tree" field, which is behind the Friends' Meeting House in Skinnergate. When the Duke's soldiers had departed, a cavalry sword in its scabbard was picked up in this field, probably by E. Pease's father, and became one of the curiosities of the old house in Northgate.

Another relic of bygone days, which was sometimes produced for the amusement of the young people, was a lady's drab beaver hat, of good quality, a survival from the times of Edward Pease's grandmother, or great-grandmother. This relic was interesting, as showing the orthodox head-gear worn by women in the early days of the Society of Friends. The hat had a remarkably wide brim, and a very shallow crown, corresponding to some portrayed in existing pictures of early Quakers' meetings. In a high wind, the hat was usually tied down by a broad ribbon or handkerchief over the crown and under the chin, thus forming two pokes, front and back; the genesis of the more modern "Friends' bonnet" can be readily understood from this; all that was required was to draw in the poke at the back, and the evolution of the "Friends' bonnet" was complete, on Darwinian principles.

Decision, firmness, and tenacity of purpose were characteristics that were conspicuous in Edward Pease; an instance of this came once under my personal observation. The Directors of the Local Water Company, of which I was then Secretary, having endeavoured in vain to carry out some business transactions with him, requested me to endeavour to bring him round to their views. I waited on him and did my best, but signally failed in my attempts to change the old man's mind. Turning to me with a friendly smile, he said, "Go back to thy Directors, William, and tell them that I am steadfast and immovable." After this, there was nothing more to be said, and the Directors wisely considered the question as closed.

George Stephenson, after he had amassed considerable wealth, retired to Tapton Hall, in the neighbourhood of Chesterfield. He was greatly respected by the eminent statesman Sir Robert Peel, who was then a comparatively near neighbour, at Drayton Manor, Tamworth. Sir Robert occasionally invited Stephenson to meet scientific and other guests at Drayton. On one of these occasions the company included Dean Buckland, who was regarded as the most eminent geologist of his day; the noted lawyer Sir William Scarlett, the then Attorney-General, and others. At dinner the conversation turned upon certain geological theories which Dean Buckland had advanced, but with which Stephenson did not agree, they being contrary to his practical experience as a mining engineer. Dean Buckland, being a much better logician and master of argument, carried all before him, notwithstanding Stephenson's intimate knowledge of the facts. The latter, though beaten in argument, was not convinced. Next morning, Stephenson, in the course of an early stroll, met Sir William Scarlett on the Terrace. The conversation turned upon the arguments of the previous evening, and Sir William said to Stephenson, "Tell me your facts again, and we will resume the conversation of last evening at breakfast, and see whether we can beat the Dean." This was done, and Sir William, now master of the facts, easily upset the Dean's plausible theories, to the intense delight of Stephenson, who rubbed his hands with glee, and exclaimed in his rich Northumbrian brogue, which he always retained, "Oh, ! Sir William, what it is to have the gift of the gab!"

In the later life of both men, Edward Pease visited his friend at Tapton Hall, and observing in his forcing-house a style of growing cucumbers in glass tubes, a yard long, which was new to him, he asked George Stephenson whose idea it was. Stephenson at once replied, "My own. I can manage to engineer matter, Mr. Pease, though I canna' always engineer men."

The late John Dixon, C.E., of Darlington, the resident engineer of the Stockton and Darlington

Railway, who was George Stephenson's first assistant, related to me the following story:—

After the completion of the Stockton and Darlington line, in 1825, Stephenson celebrated the occasion by inviting all his assistants to dinner, at the "Black Lion" Hotel, Stockton-on-Tees.

The company was a lively one, and Stephenson honoured the occasion, as was then customary, with port wine. His after-dinner speech was prophetic, yet fell curiously short of subsequent realizations. He spoke to this effect—"What we have done to-day, my lads, is not merely to put the finishing stroke to this local line, but we have begun a work which will, in the long run, go forward over the whole country. Ye lads may live to see the day (though I shall not) when it will be possible to travel the whole length of England, up to London, by railway, in a single day!"

Stephenson did live, I believe, to see the railway communications completed from London to the North of England on the West Coast.

What would he have said, however, had he been told that the journey would be done in half-a-day, as at present? Might not even he have been as incredulous as were the "noble Lords" in committee, who doubted that his locomotive could travel at the alarming speed of ten miles an hour. "I knew all the time," said Stephenson, "I could drive her twenty miles an hour, but I durst not tell them so."

An incident in the early days of the Stockton and Darlington Railway, before the establishment of electric telegraphs, related to me by Henry Pease, may be worthy of mention as a characteristic instance of the presence of mind and prompt decision of north-country mechanics. A train of empty coal wagons was travelling some miles west of Darlington, towards the colliery district, when suddenly there flashed past at a high speed on the down line a runaway engine and tender, without anyone in charge of it, and, which had somehow got detached from its train. The driver of the empty wagon-train, knowing that unless that engine could be intercepted before it reached Darlington, and it were allowed to dash into the station at a high speed, a fearful accident must inevitably result, quickly decided upon his plan of action. He ran his empty wagons into the nearest siding, and, detaching his own engine from them, crossed, by means of the points, on to the down line, and put on full pressure of steam, with a view to capture the runaway. The latter, however, having got so long a start in the race, was by no means soon overtaken, but after a sharp "stern chase" of some miles, he succeeded in coming up to the truant; the question now was, how to get it stopped. Taking in his hand a strong chain, he stood on the front of his own engine and dropped the chain over the hook attached to the tender of the runaway, thus securing the captive by the chain to his own locomotive. He now quickly went back to his own platform, shut off the steam, screwed his hand-break hard down, and thus checked the speed of both engines so much, that he was able to clamber over the back of the tender, and reach the platform of the runaway, shut off the steam and screw down the brake. It was time; for when he looked up, Darlington Station was in full view, and thus a great catastrophe was happily averted, through the presence of mind and courage of this thoughtful and able man.

At a Board Meeting of the Directors the man was sent for, and asked to tell his story in his own way; this he did so graphically that the Chairman complimented him on his courage and good sense, and a practical proof of their estimation of the service rendered was voted to him. On a Director putting the question to him how he knew that his engine could stop the runaway, he replied in his north country dialect—"Bless you, sir, if you'd only give me a chääine long enough to go round this building, I could make her pull down the whoale consarn," meaning the railway offices of the company in Northgate; an experiment, however, for which no one was inclined to vote.

In the formation of my own character, and especially in reference to my subsequent devotion to the cause of Peace, I owe much to the late Henry Pease, M.P., of Darlington. He was one of the three members of the Society of Friends who, it may be remembered, undertook to seek an interview with the Czar Nicholas in 1854, in order to plead that the forty years' peace of Europe might remain unbroken. The two Friends who accompanied him were Joseph Sturge, of Birmingham, and Robert Charleton, of Bristol. The visit was one purely of peace and goodwill, and had no political significance whatever. It was amazing, however, what a storm of indignant abuse and obloquy the benevolent purpose of the Friends raised throughout this country. There was hardly a newspaper in the land that did not bitterly assail "the fanatical Quakers" for their presumption and their interference. In simple truth, the nation had gone mad, in its intense excitement against the Czar, and in its keen desire, in the language of the day, for a "brush with the Russians."

The public at large, however, little knew the sort of men with whom they had to do. With the calm, settled heroism of "the Quaker of the olden time," who faced scourgings, imprisonment, and even death, rather than abjure his religious convictions, the three Friends, quietly ignoring all the scurrility heaped upon them in the public prints, proceeded to carry out their resolution, and set forth on a wearisome and dangerous sledge journey, through all the severities of a Russian winter, to St. Petersburg. That their mission could result in reversing the Czar's policy, as the war had actually commenced, could hardly be expected, even by the most sanguine.

The Emperor Nicholas, however, received the

Friends kindly, shook hands with them, and gave them a full opportunity of delivering their message. He expressed much indignation at the tone of the English Press, implying, as Henry Pease believed, that it would not have been impossible, even then, for England to come to terms with the Czar, had the English papers adopted a more conciliatory tone. To blame the Friends, however, for the outbreak of the Crimean War, as many writers have since done, is an absurdity, which the slightest attention to the chronological order of events would have avoided. The Turkish fleet had already been annihilated by the Russians in the Bay of Sinope, in the Black Sea, on the 30th November, 1853.* Again, a further act of war had taken place, in the advance of two Russian army corps across the Pruth into Turkish territory, and as the three Friends did not start on their Peace Mission until the month of January, 1854, these dates alone suffice to show how groundless was the charge so persistently made against them, of having actually caused the outbreak of war.

One reason for alluding to these events is to show the influence which they exercised upon myself and my subsequent life. In many quiet evening talks which I enjoyed with my late friend Henry Pease, the deep religious feelings were evidenced which had prompted him to obey the call to undertake this

* "The Turks were the first to begin actual military operations. More than five weeks before the 'Massacre of Sinope' they fired from a fortress on a Russian flotilla. They crossed the Danube at Widin and occupied Kalafat, and fought, under Omar Pasha, with brilliant success against the Russians at Oltenitza."—McCARTHY'S "HISTORY OF OUR OWN TIMES."

Peace Mission. "If there is one cause more than another," he remarked on one occasion, "for which I feel I could even lay down my life, it is this cause of Peace and Goodwill."

Through these intimate conversations, my own youthful sympathies toward the same cause became enlisted, and, being fully convinced that there was a higher and nobler courage than the purely physical courage which had captivated my youthful fancy while listening to my grandfather's stories of "forlorn hopes" and human slaughter, it had become clear to me that the courage shown by these Friends was on an altogether higher plane. Theirs was true *Christian* courage, springing from the highest Source. My own resolve to devote myself, God helping me, and such leisure as I could command, to advocating the cause of "Peace on earth and goodwill to men," dates from the deep conviction resulting from these conversations with one so intensely in earnest on the question, as the late Henry Pease.

William Edward Forster, M.P.

Before coming to Darlington, and during my engagement at Rawdon, I became acquainted with the late well-known statesman, William Edward Forster, who had learnt his business of wool-sorter in the mills of Henry Pease and Co., at Darlington. When he resided at Rawdon he had not resigned his membership in the Society of Friends, and on Sunday mornings he regularly attended their meetings.

His powers as a public speaker had already marked him out for distinction, but his subsequent career as an orator and able administrator need not here be referred to. His residence in the village caused us at the school to enjoy the privilege of occasional visits from his father, the venerated William Forster, a minister in the Society of Friends, and well-known Abolitionist, whose life was ultimately laid down in the cause of the slave, in the Southern States of America. I well remember the kindly old man walking up and down in the garden, with his hand upon my shoulder, speaking words of sympathy and counsel, all the more appreciated by me because then so rare.

An amusing incident, connected with William Edward Forster, arises in my memory, showing that in spite of certain personal peculiarities, there was in him a deep-seated benevolence of heart. He and I happened to meet in a Friend's shop (B. Sowden's) in the adjacent village of Yeadon, and whilst we were conversing, a ragged child came in and asked for a "háporth" of meal. "Do you make háporths of meal, Benjamin?" said Mr. Forster. The reply was, "We are glad to make them háporths of anything, so long as they have the money to pay for it." This took place at a time of much distress among the operatives. Mr. Forster immediately gave the shopkeeper an order to load up the child with as much as she could carry, of meal, bacon, and groceries, and sent her home with a beaming countenance, staggering under the burden. After we had concluded our business we found on getting back into the main street, that the villagers, having heard of the transaction, had turned out of their houses, and were shouting their benedictions to Mr. Forster, as he strode rapidly past. His extraordinary length of nether limbs, together with his singular costume—his head being inserted through a "Spanish poncho" which flapped out straight behind him in the breeze—as he strode briskly along, to avoid the embarrassing cries of the people, formed a singular picture, which I regret I had not the power to sketch. I kept up with him with difficulty, and as we were passing out of the village over a stile, some urchins there shouted to us in their vernacular, much to Mr. Forster's amusement, "Heigh! canny man, what's the hurry? there's another day i' th' morn!" I seldom saw Mr. Forster later, for not long after, on his marriage with the daughter of Dr. Arnold, of Rugby, he removed to a new residence, which he had built at Burley in Wharfedale.

CHAPTER V.

RESCUE FROM DROWNING — DR. ADAM CLARKE'S DROWNING EXPERIENCES — JOSEPH PEASE, M.P. — MARRIAGE AND BUSINESS LIFE.

IT was in the Month of August in the year 1847, when I was 21 years of age, that an incident occurred which created some interest in the medical papers of the day, as a remarkable case of restoration to animation, after an unusual length of submersion, and also had a lasting effect upon the whole of my subsequent life. This event took place whilst I was tutor to the late Henry Fell Pease. We were staying at the seaside residence of the Pease family, at Marske near Redcar, on the Yorkshire coast, where we were frequently in the habit of bathing from the beach. One morning, I went down to bathe, accompanied by the late Edward Pease, second son of the late Joseph Pease, M.P., of South End, Darlington. I was but a moderate swimmer, and ventured too far, not knowing how strongly the current was setting out to sea. I was carried along imperceptibly, until, turning round and finding no bottom, I perceived how great was my distance from the shore. I felt no alarm, however, but set vigorously to work to swim back. In this I made little progress, owing to the strength of the current, which, whenever I stopped for rest, floated me further out to sea. Finding myself becoming exhausted, I shouted to my young friend Edward Pease, who was much nearer the shore, to cry out for help, or I should be drowned. But there was no help forthcoming. A man did at length venture in on a horse from the bathing machines, but his courage failed him when he found how deep was the sea where I was struggling, and how strong was the current. He then turned his horse's face to the shore, and left me to my fate, but had the good sense to gallop off for a doctor. By this time I was quite exhausted and was sinking fast, and in my struggles for breath, gulping much water. All hope of being saved was taken away when I saw the man on horseback abandon me, there being no boat nor any life-saving apparatus on the beach, or anywhere near. I sank in deep water, and have a distinct recollection of lying on the bottom of the sea with my eyes wide open, and seeing a faint green light shining from above. I had swallowed so much water, that it was impossible for me to rise to the surface, and I now fully realised that to me, Eternity was but a question of moments.

The rapidity of thought passing through the mind in such a crisis is intense. I seemed to pass in review much of my past life, and fancied the grief of my friends over my death, and even pictured them following my coffin to the grave. Being in full possession of my faculties, and quite convinced that my end was at hand, my last conscious thoughts were directed towards my Saviour, whilst earnestly praying for the forgiveness of my sins, and commending my soul to Him in the words, "Lord Jesus receive my Spirit." This was the last effort. The awe-inspiring crisis was over. The bitterness of death was passed. Whatever of suffering may be involved in the act of dying, all had been passed through. Still and cold, as in the grave, my body lay insensible in the deep, in stony, death-like unconsciousness.

Providentially, rescue was at hand, though all unknown to me. I knew nothing of what had transpired in the interim, until my restoration to consciousness in my bed-chamber, late in the afternoon. It was not until some time afterwards that I learned that two of the coastguardsmen, who had been on duty through the night, sauntered leisurely to the beach, and learned from the bystanders that I was drowning in the sea. One of them rushed into the water, fully clothed as he was, but finding that, owing to the roughness of the sea, he could not well swim, he came out and undressed himself. Both of them then swam out in the direction indicated, but were long in finding any clue to the position of my body. At length one of them, as he told me some time after, saw an arm in a wave. They swam immediately to the spot, and after diving, recovered the body, which they towed with difficulty ashore. Some of the bystanders remarked, "He is quite dead, poor fellow. His body is blue and cold." My brave rescuers, however, encouraged them to wrap me up in the horse-sheet on which our clothes had been laid, and bade them hasten up with me to the house. Here my dear friend Joseph Pease, who, providentially for me, was at home that day—a rare occurrence during the great financial crisis of 1847, the year of the Irish Famine—immediately put into requisition all the best known means for restoring animation. Two doctors presented themselves; and Joseph Pease decided promptly in favour of the one who proposed to adopt the established methods of restoring the circulation, as, in so critical a case, no experiments must be allowed.

They persevered for a long period before any signs of animation were perceptible. Their efforts were at length rewarded by some moanings and other signs of life, and late in the afternoon I opened my eyes to consciousness again, there having, seemingly, been a perfect blank of some hours in my existence.

The first object which attracted my gaze was the kind smiling face of Joseph Pease, who said with delight, "It's all right now, William." I was hardly able to speak, but begged that no more of that stuff (brandy) should be poured down my throat, which felt excoriated with the raw spirit administered.

My sufferings, for some hours on returning to animation, were extreme ; the system being full of water, I was unable to breathe, except in quick short pantings, accompanied with a most painful sense of suffocation. The pain in the head also, from the presence of vitiated blood, which had passed on to the brain without being oxygenated in the lungs, was most racking. Altogether, I felt as though I should die every moment for want of breath. Gradually, however, as the system was relieved of the sea-water it was gorged with, these feelings passed away.

I do not remember having suffered much physical pain in the act of drowning. There was much discomfort, of course, in gulping water instead of air, but possibly the distress and anxiety of mind overmastered all feeling of bodily pain. The real suffering, however, was on returning again to life. Fearing delirium, the doctor drew a considerable amount of blood from my arm, which I now think was a great mistake; it made me so weak, I was unable to raise my head from the pillow for three weeks.

Many persons took great interest in the case, on account of my restoration after so unusual a length of submersion. Among these was the late Earl of Zetland, uncle of the present Marquis, who had a country seat at Upleatham, near Marske. Having been informed about the case by his nephews—four of the Yeoman family, who had assisted in rubbing me during the process of restoration—the old gentleman took several opportunities, as soon as I was able to get out of doors again, of inquiring minutely into my feelings and sensations when actually on the point of drowning.

The medical men informed me at the time that the heart had undergone so severe a strain, that it might be permanently weakened, and would no doubt grow still weaker in later life. This will account, in part, for the heart-affection from which I have suffered for many years, and which compelled me ultimately to give up all public speaking, and to lead as quiet and unexciting a life as practicable.

The restoration of a man to life who has passed through all the varied experiences of the drowned, with a mind perfectly clear and collected, down to the last verge of conscious sensation, is an event so rare, that now, after the lapse of half a century, according to my present knowledge and estimate of such occurrences, I am constrained to regard it, in all its details, as an event of exceptional interest. When I reflect upon each step and circumstance of this deliverance, and mark how many links there were in the lengthy chain, resulting in complete and successful restoration, failing any one of which I was irrecoverably lost for this life, it would be against the deepest instincts of my nature not to acknowledge in it all the visible hand of a merciful over-ruling Providence. How else is the success of the efforts to restore animation to be accounted for, after so unprecedented a period of submergence? From any knowledge of physiology that I now possess, such a recovery, I should say, would otherwise have been a physical impossibility.

How often, in the passing years, I have queried with myself, Why was my life spared? Surely the great Giver of life has a purpose in view for every soul that He creates. "To every man his work." How have I fulfilled His wise purposes? To this and many such solemn questions I must frankly own that as an unprofitable servant I have not done "that which was my duty to do." One thing, however, has never failed me, amid all the vicissitudes of life; I have never doubted that Christ loves me. In every time of failure, or of disloyalty to Him, this has ever been, and still remains to be, the rock under my feet, the rock of my Salvation. To believe and trust in that all-conquering Love has of all the lessons of my life been the one best learned. It is a living reality. Though all else may fail, this Divine Love "never faileth." Thanks be unto God for His unspeakable gift!

I cannot pass away from this subject, without mentioning the sympathizing, motherly care I experienced from the late Mrs. Joseph Pease. She visited my bedside daily during my protracted weakness and slow recovery, saw to my every want being supplied, and, what was more precious to me, would sit by my side and talk to me, with a tender motherly sympathy, that often brought tears into my eyes. As soon as I was able to bear it, she took me out by her side in her own pony-carriage for many pleasant drives on the sands. Kindnesses like these, received in early youth, remain an ineffaceable memory, in a grateful heart, to the end of life.

The following extract from his father's diary has been kindly furnished by Sir Joseph Pease, Bart., M.P., of Hutton Hall, Guisborough. It will be seen to corroborate in essential points my own account.

Marske, 8mo. 10th (August), 1847, Tuesday—

"An alarm about 11 o'clock, that William Jones was drowning; and so it proved, but the great exertions of two of the "Preventive men" saved him and brought him safely to shore, and after *long protracted exertions*, we had the comfort of seeing him gradually recover.

How narrow the escape!—When taken out of the water I was ready to despair,—a great mercy truly!—thus spared so much sorrow, as we must have witnessed and felt!

Evening.—William Jones recovering, 12th—Good report of William Jones and his improvement."

Dr. Adam Clarke's Similar Experience.

Some years ago I met with the following account, from the pen of Dr. Stoughton, in the "Sunday at Home," of an address by Dr. Adam Clarke, the well-known Biblical Commentator, of his own drowning experiences, which interested me deeply, and which may be usefully compared with my own narrative.

"I would mention a visit paid to the City Road Chapel, in 1832, to hear the famous Dr. Adam Clarke preach for the Royal Humane Society. He preached from the words, 'Verily, verily, I say unto you, the hour is coming and now is, when the dead shall hear the voice of the Son of God; and they that hear shall live.' At the close he related an anecdote which, from that time to this, I have never forgotten, and which is here repeated in the words reported at the time.

"Referring to an interview with Dr. Lettsom, the Quaker, the preacher related this conversation: 'Pray, what does your experience, doctor Lettsom, teach you, respecting the state of those that evidently have been dead, and would have continued under the power of death, had it not been for the means prescribed by the Royal Society? Have you ever found any that were conscious of the state into which they had departed?'

"'I have never found one,' said he. 'Not of all those that have been revived, to your own knowledge, that were dead as to all human appearance, when the heart had ceased its pulsation, the lungs no longer played, the blood no longer circulated, and there was every evidence that the person was finally deceased?' He again answered, 'No!'

"'Doctor,' continued I, 'I have not been so long conversant with these matters as you have been, but my experience in things of that kind has led me to a different conclusion. I knew a person who was drowned, and that person to my own knowledge had a perfect consciousness during the whole interim, and declared many things concerning the state through which he passed.'

"'But was the person drowned?' said the doctor. 'Yes,' said I, 'completely drowned. I have no doubt of it whatever.'—'Had you the testimony from himself?' he inquired. 'I had, Sir.'—'Could you trust in him?'—'Most perfectly.' And then assuming an attitude he was accustomed to assume when making anxious inquiry respecting anything, he said, 'I should wish to have had the examination of that person.' I looked him stedfastly in the face, and said, '*Ecce homo! Coram quem queritis adsum!*' (Behold in me the very man whom you seek.) He arose immediately, and said, 'What were the circumstances?'—'I will tell them simply,' said I. 'I was a fearless lad, and I went on a fine mare of my father's to the shore of a river that pours itself into the Irish sea. As I was determined to have a swim, I rode the mare into the water, and we swam on till we got beyond the breakers entirely; but when we had got over swell after swell, and were proceeding still onward to the ocean, the mare and myself were swamped in a moment. I was soon disengaged from the mare, and as I afterwards found, she naturally turned, got ashore, and went plodding her way back to home. In a moment I seemed to have all my former views and ideas entirely changed, and I had a sensation of the most complete happiness or felicity, that it is possible, independent of rapture, for the human mind to feel. I had felt no pain from the moment I was submerged, and at once a kind of representation, nearly of a green colour, presented itself to me; multitudes of objects were in it, not one of them, however, possessing any kind of likeness or analogy to anything I had seen before. In this state how long I continued He only knows who saved my life, but so long did I continue in it till one wave after another—for the tide was coming in—rolled me to the shore. The first sensation when I came to life was as if a spear had been run through my heart. I found myself sitting in the water, and it was by a very swelling wave that I was put out of the way of being overwhelmed by any of the succeeding waves. How long I was submerged it would be impossible precisely to say; but it was sufficiently long, according to my apprehensions, and any skill I now have in physiology, for me to have been completely dead, and never more to breathe in this world, had it not been for that Providence, which, as it were, once more breathed into my nostrils and lungs the breath of this animal life, and I became once more a living soul, and at the space of three-score years, you have this strange phenomenon before you—the preacher before the Royal Humane Society.' The effect of this anecdote on the crowded congregation may be well imagined."

The reader will observe certain resemblances and some differences between the record of the experiences of Dr. Adam Clarke and my own. Both narratives agree as to feeling no actual pain, and as to the rapidity of thought and review of the past rushing through the mind, in the act of drowning. But the sensation of "complete felicity" of which he speaks, was wholly wanting in my case—the whole soul being preoccupied with the gravity of my position, and the certainty of impending death, no hope of deliverance being at hand. With regard to the representation "nearly of a green colour, with multitudes of objects in it," etc., which the worthy doctor describes, may not the simple fact be, that the daylight (as in my case) descending through the sea-water acquired this greenish tinge, the "multitude of objects," one may well conceive being due to an excited imagination in the desperate situation in which the young man found himself placed?

Then, on coming to life, I do not remember any such sensation as "though a spear had been run through my heart"; it may however be, that the dreadful sense of suffocation and inability to draw a full breath, caused me such prolonged agony as to overpower every other sensation.

Both records agree as to the hand of a merciful Providence being visible, both in the recovery of the bodies and in their restoration to life. Dr. Clarke distinctly avers that in his case, *death* had actually taken place, and that the body would not have been brought back to life "had it not been for that Providence which once more breathed the breath of this animal life into his nostrils and lungs."

In comparing the two records, my own total submergence appears to have been much longer than that of Dr. Clarke—and my restoration to life, unlike his, was with difficulty effected, after all that medical skill and long perseverance on the part of kind friends could do. If Dr. Clarke is right in judging himself to "have been completely dead," it would appear, *à fortiori*, that actual death, in my case, was even more certain than in his.

From that day to this, however, I have been unable to solve the mystery of the wonderful revivification of the body, or to throw any light whatever on the problem as to what becomes of the soul during the absolute blank of several hours in one's conscious existence, in the, to all human appearance, lifeless state of the body.

The Late Joseph Pease, M.P.

It will be observed how important a part was taken by the late Joseph Pease in the restoration of my bodily life. Under Providence, I owe my existence to his energetic action and patient perseverance, as without his prolonged efforts, hoping as it were against hope, the case might well have been abandoned as hopeless. No effort, no means, which could contribute to ultimate success, were overlooked by him, and now, after a lapse of half a century, I cannot but gratefully acknowledge the loving care and kindness which this true friend exerted on my behalf until I was again restored to consciousness.

Much might be said here about the public life and commercial undertakings of this eminent man, who was widely known as the first Quaker Member of Parliament. The limits of the old family woollen business could not for long cramp the energies of his enterprising nature. He soon threw himself with characteristic vigour into the railway project inaugurated by his father, and contributed largely to the success of the Stockton and Darlington Railway. Then followed, in course, the acquisition by himself and friends, of the Middlesbrough estate, upon which a town of some 80,000 inhabitants has been created. Among other great undertakings of Pease and Partners, were collieries and coke ovens in Durham, and ironstone mines in North Yorkshire, concerns which have helped largely in the development of the great iron industry of Cleveland.

After his death, his fellow townsmen, in recognition of his eminent services, which contributed so greatly to the prosperity of the district, erected a statue to his memory in the market-place of Darlington. The best monument, however, to the memory of Joseph Pease, is to be found in the schools, good cottages, and other works of philanthropy, wherever the workmen in the employ of his firm were congregated. It may thus be said of him, in a survey of South Durham and

North Yorkshire, as is said of Wren, the architect of St. Paul's—

"If you seek his monument, look around!"

It is not, however, so much of the genius and enterprise which largely contributed to the wealth and prosperity of the district, that I wish to speak here, but of the personality of the man, as it influenced me during many years. There was a noble presence in his tall, erect figure, equally graceful on horseback as on foot. The exterior was an indication of the internal capacity and power of the man. In whatever company or assemblage he was found, the leading part fell naturally, by common consent, to Joseph Pease. His fluent speech, his capacious intellect, his wide outlook, his grasp of affairs, added to his genial humour, his affability and courtesy, marked him out as one born to lead, and won for him the esteem of rich and poor alike.

It was in the home and the family circle, where I was frequently privileged to be a guest, that the genial, fatherly influence was seen at its best. In the drawing-room at Southend, Darlington, when the united family circle, consisting then of eight sons and four daughters, was engaged in various evening occupations, one of the daughters would frequently read aloud for the general benefit. The father, although busy with his vast correspondence, yet keeping one ear intent upon the reading, would stay his hand, and interject pointed remarks, or questions, as though he had done nothing else but listen all the time to the reader.

In his latter years, when failing sight ultimately faded into total blindness, it was affecting to see his venerable figure, with his hand upon the arm of his faithful secretary, Samuel Hare, proceeding with measured tread to his accustomed place in the Friends' Meeting-house. With advancing age came also a mellowness of Christian character, together with a fuller depth of spiritual power, which, with no decrease in intellectual clearness, rendered his Gospel ministry, rich as it was in Scriptural quotations, one that was specially appreciated and valued throughout the religious body of which he was so distinguished a member.

Marriage and Business Life.

In the month of August, 1853, I was married to my beloved friend Ann Sefton, at the Friends' Meeting-house in Stockton-on-Tees, and the home in which we first settled was situated in Coniscliffe Lane, Darlington. In a short time, as we both loved country life, I being then the secretary of the Water Company, we removed to a renovated farmhouse, pleasantly situated near the Water Works, on the Coniscliffe Road, and having a small farm attached to it. Here the first member of our family, Herbert Sefton-Jones, was born; our second son, Llewelyn, was born about two years later, after we had removed to North Terrace, in Darlington, and our third child, Dora, was also born there.

After the gas and water undertakings had been purchased by the town of Darlington, I resigned my position as secretary, and became connected with the Alum Works, situated near Guisborough, in Cleveland. My friend the late Robert Clapham of Newcastle, whom we had engaged as our consulting chemist, suggested to me about this time the establishment of sulphuric acid works, in order to utilise the large quantity of iron pyrites which was thrown away among the rubbish heaps, as a useless and noxious material, in the Cleveland ironstone mines. As this contained about 25 per cent. of sulphur, it was of the utmost importance that it should be separated from the ironstone, previous to the ore being sent to the calcining furnaces of the various ironworks.

After careful investigation, I came to the conclusion, that as the seam of pyrites existed in considerable quantity, entirely distinct from the iron stone, it could easily be separated, and a sufficient quantity obtained to make it worth while to erect works, in order to convert it into sulphuric acid on a commercial scale. With the assistance of Mr. Clapham, and in conjunction with the late Isaac Sharp of Middlesbrough, who became my first partner, two leaden acid chambers, with the needful burners and appliances, were erected at Middlesbrough about 1856. These works were gradually enlarged to meet the increased demand. My former pupil, H. F. Pease, now joined in the partnership, and later, Isaac Sharp withdrew.

The works subsequently were disposed of, about 1882, to a chemical company, who required a large quantity of sulphuric acid for the manufacture of aniline and other tar products, and they are still carried on, under the style of Sadler and Co., Limited.

During my residence in Middlesbrough I became Poor Law Guardian, Town Councillor, and a member of the Water Board. The Corporations of Stockton and Middlesbrough having purchased, for a very large sum, the undertaking of the "Stockton and Middlesbrough Water Company," much careful thought and investigation had to be given to the question of increasing and improving the water supply. Here my previous experience as Secretary of the Water Company was thought to be of advantage to the newly-formed Water Board. In addition to the pumping station on the Tees near Darlington, a gravitation scheme was ultimately decided upon, and a line of more than thirty miles of large water pipes was laid up to the Balder, in Upper Teesdale, thus making it one of the most important water undertakings in the country.

These water works have proved an enormous benefit to the Cleveland District, in which are situated many great industries whose consumption of water is on a very large scale.

CHAPTER VI.

FRANCO-GERMAN WAR—OUTLINE OF ORIGIN—STATEMENT OF RELIEF WORK—FRENCH OFFICIAL RECOGNITION OF THE WORK—MY CREDENTIALS AS REPRESENTING THE SOCIETY OF FRIENDS—CARDINAL MANNING—DANGEROUS MIDNIGHT DRIVE.

BEFORE proceeding to describe the work of relief undertaken by the Society of Friends during the Franco-German War, and how I personally became connected with it, it may be well, in the first place, briefly to recall its origin, and give a *résumé* of its principal events.

The declaration of war between France and Germany, in July, 1870, burst upon Europe like a "bolt from the blue." There had been certain rumours and premonitions in connection with the succession to the crown of Spain. The conciliatory attitude of Prussia, however, in the origin of the dispute, having removed all cause of quarrel, the sudden rupture of peaceful relations fell with a shock of surprise upon the whole of Europe.

It had been announced in July, 1870, that Prince Leopold, a scion of one of the two branches of the Hohenzollern family, was a candidate for the vacant crown of Spain. France would not endure what she regarded as a menace to her national independence, from a great military power—Prussia. The Ministers of the Emperor Napoleon III. officially declared to the Legislative Assembly, that France would not permit the throne of Charles V. to be occupied by a Hohenzollern.

Ever since the victorious campaign of Prussia against Austria in 1866, France and Prussia had vied with each other for the possession, equipment, and facile mobilization, of the best and largest military force, avowedly for defence, really for defiance. There stood out with terrible distinctness before the gaze of Europe the picture of two great nations armed to the teeth, watching one another with jealous eyes, and full of the conviction, that come what might of the original ground of quarrel, the time was close at hand when they would measure strength with each other.

In the meantime, the King of Prussia, in order to avoid a rupture with France, had caused Prince Leopold to withdraw his candidature for the Spanish throne. The Liberal party in the French Chamber, headed by Thiers, persistently opposed the war; the Bonapartists, on the other hand, fiercely pushed matters on; they refused the good offices of the other states of Europe, and, in shameful ignorance of the truth, they declared that everything was "ready to the last gaiter-button," and were only eager to begin.

In Paris the profoundest ignorance prevailed. Nothing was known of the real condition of the Prussian preparations. Equally little was known of the unfitness of the French Army for a great war; it was thought that it was strong and ready, whereas it proved to be ill-organised, ill-supplied, and without proper reserves. Bravery there was in plenty, but leading and management were absolutely wanting.

It was under these circumstances that France resolved to force on a war with Prussia. The desired pretext was not far to seek. M. Benedetti, the French ambassador at Berlin, was instructed to proceed to Ems, where the King of Prussia was taking the waters, and to demand that he should interdict the resumption of the Hohenzollern candidature at any future period. The King, having already complied with the first demands of France, viewed this exacting proposal as gratuitously insulting, and refused to hold any further communication with the French ambassador on the subject. A brass plate inserted into a stone is shown in the public gardens at Ems, where King William I., after this historic interview, turned upon his heels from what he regarded as the unheard of presumption of the French ambassador. Thus, on a mere point of etiquette, war was declared by France, and the challenge was eagerly accepted by Prussia. The French Prime Minister, M. Emile Ollivier, in a spirit of foolish bravado, declared in the Legislative Assembly that he entered upon this war with a "light heart."

So far as Paris was concerned, the war was highly popular; there were nightly demonstrations on the boulevards, and popular cries resounded of "*Vive la France*," and "*A Berlin, à Berlin.*"

In the North German Parliament the matter was treated in a more serious light; nevertheless proofs were not wanting, among the least thoughtful of the community, of a certain delight in the prospect of the impending conflict.

All North Germany was roused to a high pitch of enthusiasm in favour of war. The King, on his return to Berlin, received an ovation; dense crowds assembled nightly in front of the Royal Palace singing patriotic songs, and shouting, "To the Rhine, to the Rhine!"

Meantime, at the magic word "*Mobil*" (mobilize), telegraphed over all the land by the chief of staff, Von Moltke, the ever ready legions of North Germany sprang forward like hounds from the leash, being eager to cross the Rhine, and begin the attack upon the Eastern frontiers of France.

By August 2nd the hostile armies came into collision. The French *reconnaissance en force* drove the Germans out of Saarbruck on that day, and the Prince Imperial then underwent his "baptism of fire," a baptism into misfortune and sorrow. This was the *one* success of the French arms across the German frontier. On the same day the Germans were victorious at Wissembourg, and other victories followed in rapid succession in Alsace. The Prussians and their allies now closed in on Metz, and on the 14th and 16th of August great battles were fought.

Ultimately, after the hard fought contest on August 18th at Gravelotte, the French commander, Bazaine, was compelled to retreat upon Metz.

On September 1st there followed the great catastrophe of Sedan. On the 2nd, the Emperor, with an army of more than 80,000 men, was the prisoner of the King of Prussia.

This, however, did not put an end to the war. Paris was invested on September 19th, and after an obstinate defence, finally surrendered on January 28th, 1871, and an armistice was arranged.

Fighting was, however, resumed under the Dictatorship of Gambetta, who raised, with incredible efforts, raw levies in large numbers, who were sent to cope with the disciplined legions of Germany. It was a vain and useless sacrifice on a huge scale of human life and national treasure.

Finally, on the 10th of May, 1871, M. Thiers, by unwearied efforts, succeeded in getting a Treaty of Peace signed at Frankfort on the Maine, by which Alsace and a large part of Lorraine were ceded back to Germany, and a heavy money indemnity was to be paid by France towards the cost of the war.

A short time after the conflict had commenced, when the immense armies of both Powers were in occupation of Alsace and Lorraine, grave tidings reached this country of widespread distress brought upon the non-combatant population, and especially upon the peasants, by the devastations and requisitions of the all-devouring legions encamped in their midst.

The subject was taken up by various bodies of "Friends" in England, and amongst them, by the Durham "Quarterly Meeting" of the Society of Friends, of which I was then a member. It was frankly acknowledged that the case of these innocent sufferers presented no such obstacle to the benevolence of Friends as occurred at the time when the so-called "Patriotic Fund" was raised during the Crimean War. Conscientious objections to subscribe to any fund, which went chiefly to the relief of wounded and sick "*soldiers*," were felt by many Friends; but no such scruples intervened in regard to the suffering among the non-combatant population, and innocent women and children.

Commissioners of Relief.

The question thus appealed in a special manner to the Society of Friends. It was decided by the representative body of the Society in London, to raise a large relief fund, and to invite volunteers to undertake the work of distribution in France. Preliminary information being much wanted as to the extent and character of the distress, I was applied to (as having some knowledge of the country, and being familiar with the language) by two esteemed members of the representative body, viz., the late Thomas Harvey of Leeds, and the late Henry Pease of Darlington, and was requested, if willing and able, to proceed at once to France with a companion, on this pioneer service, and to report to the committee in London as to the extent and localities of the distress; also to suggest, as far as practicable, the best means of relief. My first companion in the work was Henry John Allen of Dublin, who had already visited the neighbourhood of Sedan, and was able to converse fluently in French. Feeling much reluctance to leave my wife and children at home, and to entrust my business affairs to the hands of others, I could only consent to go for a limited period.

The Relief Fund, as shown in the detailed statement published by the French committees themselves, finally reached the large amount of about £160,000, many of the English public having freely contributed, it being understood that every shilling of the fund would go to the objects of the charity, and the expenses of the commissioners would be defrayed privately, or by the Society of Friends. The operations of the commissioners embraced several departments in the east of France, and throughout the Loire district in the centre and west. The most important and beneficial part of the work was unquestionably the distribution of seed-corn to the peasants and farmers, whose losses had been greatest during the war.

Annexed is a statement of the total relief administered by the Society of Friends during 1870-71, confirmed by the various French committees of distribution, and taken from the official account entitled "*Rapport de la Répartition des Secours*," and dedicated by permission to the President of the French Republic, by James Long, M.A.

[*Translation.*]

SUMMARY OF SUCCOUR OF VARIOUS KINDS GIVEN TO FRANCE BY THE SOCIETY OF FRIENDS.

	Francs.
RELIEF TO AGRICULTURISTS.	
Seed Corn of various kinds	2,611,630
Agricultural Implements	82,947
Cattle	102,000
RELIEF TO THE POOR.	
Houses and Furniture	13,750
Food, Medicine, and fuel	257,250
Organisation of the work for the unemployed, Wages, &c.	50,525
GIFTS IN MONEY.	
To various localities	167,625
To 69 Communes round Paris	536,375

This relief, valued according to the current exchange in France at that time, amounted to a total of 4,055,071 francs, or about £162,000 sterling.

In the *Journal Officiel* of the French Republic, M. Drouyn de Lhuys (President of the Agricultural Society of France), writes under date of 31st October, 1871:

. . . "This Society has given to France, in less than one year, gifts exceeding in value four millions of francs. These figures are confirmed by a system of book-keeping as exact as that of a commercial house in the city of London. The eloquence of figures like these outweighs all eulogiums. The public gratitude is due to the generous men who have done so much for France."

The work obtained official recognition also on the part of the French Government, in the following terms, viz :—

"*Ministère de l'Agriculture et du Commerce, Cabinet du Ministère.*

"*Je suis autorisé par Monsieur le Président de la Republique et par le Conseil des Ministres, à transmettre à la Société Anglaise des Amis l'expression des sentiments du peuple et du Gouvernement Français. Puisse le souvenir de notre profonde reconnaissance, vivre chez vous, aussi longtemps que vivra chez nous le souvenir de vos généreux efforts.*

"*Le Ministre de l'Agriculture et du Commerce,*

"VICTOR LEFRANC.

"*Versailles, le 16 Novembre, 1871.*"

The following official credentials, in English, French, and German, of which a facsimile is annexed, were granted me by the representative body of the Society of Friends, attested by the signatures of Joseph Crosfield, chairman (or clerk) of that body; also of Charles Hoyland and Ernest Beck, secretaries of the "War Victims Fund," and dated London, 21st October, 1870:—

"The bearer of this document, William Jones, is sent out by the religious Society, known in England as the 'Society of Friends,' commonly called 'Quakers,' solely to give relief to the non-combatant sufferers through the present war. We, the members of the above named Society of Friends, believe all war to be contrary to the will and spirit of our Heavenly Father, as shown in the New Testament. But, moved by Christian love, we desire to alleviate, as far as may be in our power, the misery of non-combatants, irrespective of nationality, remembering that all are children of one Father, and that one Saviour died for all. We therefore entreat all to whom the bearer may come, to aid him in the fulfilment of this Mission."

Beside the official signatures of the Friends, it was deemed desirable to obtain those of some influential persons outside that Society, whose names might carry weight.

The first signature on the document bears the important looking seal of the city of York, which was placed upon it by George Leeman, M.P. (then Lord Mayor of the city), after I had addressed an audience in the Corn Exchange. He certifies as follows :—

"The bearer, William Jones, of the town of Middlesbrough-on-Tees, England, is well known in the County of York as a man of benevolence and integrity, as witness my hand and official seal."

Having been carried so long in my pocket, in the course of my various travels, and often pro-

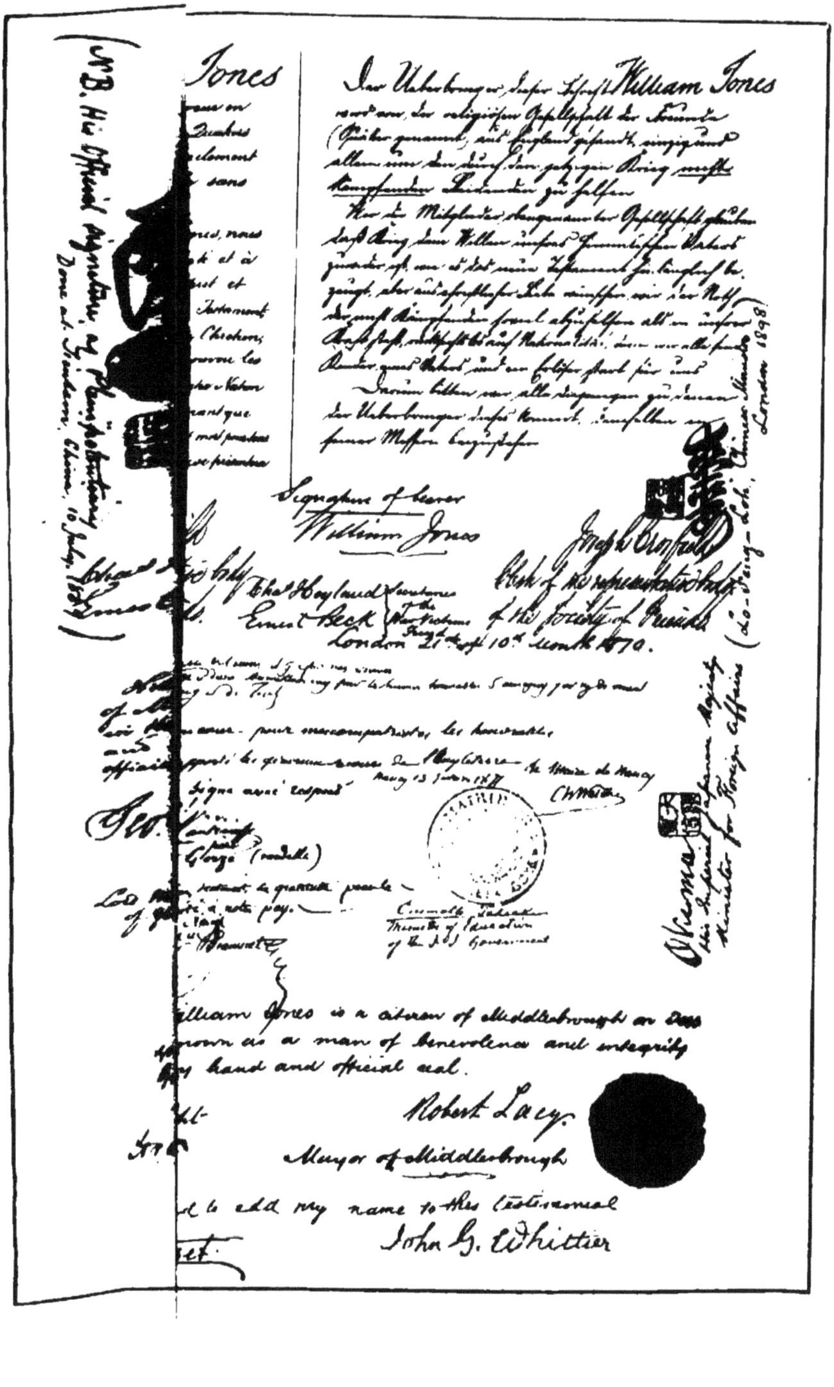

William Jones
Signature of bearer
William Jones
Joseph Crosfield
Clerk of the representative body of the Society of Friends
Thos Hayland
Ernest Beck
Secretaries of the War Victims Fund
London 21st of 10th month 1870.
N.B. His Official Signature, as Plenipotentiary
Done at Tientsin, China, 10 July, 1878
Lo-Feng-Loh, Chinese Minister London 1898
Okuma
His Imperial Japanese Majesty's Minister for Foreign Affairs
Le Maire de Nancy
Nancy 13 Juin 1877
Minister of Education
William Jones is a citizen of Middlesbrough
known as a man of benevolence and integrity
my hand and official seal.
Robert Lacy
Mayor of Middlesbrough
to add my name to this testimonial
John G. Whittier

duced in all weathers and in many lands, before a great variety of people, the parchment has naturally become much creased, and the seals lost or injured. This does not, however, apply to this noble seal of the ancient city of York, which, not being composed of sealing-wax, is wonderfully well preserved. For the purposes of my "Peace Mission," this was the *seal of seals*, by far the most influential of any of those upon the parchment. Often have I been amused in observing the effect of this grand old seal upon the mind of any Frenchman who could not read—and also upon the minds of some who *could* read.

In the opposite corner of the document appears the signature and seal of the Mayor of my own borough of Middlesbrough, bearing a similar endorsement :—

"The bearer, William Jones, is a citizen of Middlesbrough-on-Tees, and is well-known as a man of benevolence and integrity, as witness my hand and official seal.—Robert Lacey, Mayor of Middlesbrough."

The next signature upon my document, and one of the earliest which was placed there, is that of the late Cardinal Manning, who signed as Archbishop of Westminster, (the dignity he then held), with a cross, and then "Henricus E. Archiepiscopus Westmonasteriensis." The Cardinal was a good friend to our work, and to the cause of international peace and arbitration. He very cheerfully agreed to take part in a meeting which was held later in the Mansion House, London, with a view to raise funds to help us in the work of relieving the distress in France. He made an admirable and helpful speech on that occasion, when Sir Thomas Dakin, as Lord Mayor of London, occupied the chair, and also signed and sealed my document.

In conversation with Archbishop Manning, after the meeting, I suggested that if Cardinal Antonelli's signature, who was then practically acting as Pope, were attached to the document, it would have a powerful effect among all the Roman Catholic authorities in France. The Archbishop strongly advised me to go to Rome and call on the Cardinal, with that object in view. I said, "I fear he would not care to see an unimportant individual like myself, I feel afraid to intrude upon him." But the Archbishop replied, "He would be very glad to hear about your work in France." Consequently, I decided to go to Rome, on condition that the Archbishop gave me a line of introduction to Cardinal Antonelli. He sat down and wrote a note in Italian, in the Lord Mayor's Parlour, and requested me to let him know the result of my interview.

ENTERING UPON THE WORK.

When at Brussels, on our way towards Sedan, H. J. Allen and I were advised by the English Ambassador, Mr. Lumley, to adopt a *star* as our badge, in lieu of the "Red Cross," which, he said, unauthorised persons were wearing. His suggestion was adopted, and the star became the badge worn by all our fellow commissioners of the "War Victims' Fund." At Bouillon, near the frontier, we found Mr. Bullock, the Commissioner of the "*Daily News* Fund," who advised our breaking new ground in the neighbourhood of Metz. Accordingly, we proceeded by the frontier town of Longwy, and here, as we were entering a country in a state of war, we obtained an interview at the Castle with the Commandant. He was very friendly with us, and placed his endorsement as a "safe conduct" on our passports. Anxious to get on the ground as speedily as possible, we hired a conveyance the same afternoon, and, in spite of a storm which was brewing, set off in the direction of Briey. As we proceeded on our journey, darkness fell upon us, the gale became a terrible storm, and, to add to our discomfort, rain came down furiously. Our driver lost his way in the darkness of the night, and was unable to obtain any information, there being no response from any of the houses he inquired at, the people evidently being afraid to show themselves on account of its being war-time. We were in no small danger, too, from the falling of great poplar trees, which were frequently being blown down across the road, and were compelled to get out of our conveyance, to drag the horse and trap round these obstacles, several times in the course of the night. In this dilemma, our horse was suddenly stopped, in the dark, apparently by someone seizing his head. One's first thought was naturally of brigands, for what honest man, if he could possibly avoid it, would be found on the road on such a stormy night as this? I had been warned in London before starting, by a Frenchman, against such nightly visitants, and had been offered the loan of a pair of revolvers for my protection, which, of course, I had declined.

In the intense darkness of the night we were startled to hear, but could not see, someone feeling his way with his hands along the horse's body, up to the seat where we sat, and as he approached my side of the conveyance, I screwed up my courage to seize his hands, fully expecting to find a weapon in them. Such was not the case, however, and from the thick utterance of the man I judged at once that he was drunk. To find that it was nothing worse was a great relief. He began a story of his horse having being killed, and he wanted help to remove his cart from the road. We ordered him peremptorily to stand aside, not believing his tale. When we had driven about a kilometre further, we found that it was quite true. A poplar tree had fallen across the body of his horse which lay dead in the road, the cart was broken, and the wine casks upset and some of the contents spilled.

In the miserable condition in which we ourselves were, owing to the cold and wet, we could not stay to render him any help, but gave notice to the people at Briey, which we reached soon after, in order that they might send to his assistance. Before entering Briey, a difficulty of a new kind presented itself. We had now come within the jurisdiction of the German Army, and two sentries stepped out of their boxes at the roadside and peremptorily commanded us to "Halt," shouting, when we came within hail, "*Wer geht da?*" ("Who goes there?") We replied, "Two Englishmen, with authorisations from the German Embassy in London." Advancing towards us with their rifles and bayonets levelled, the sentries demanded our papers, which they examined by the light of their lanterns. Finding all in order, they presented arms and respectfully saluted, leaving us free to go into the town. At their recommendation, we went to the principal hotel, which was occupied by German officers. Right glad we were to get under shelter, in our famished and drenched condition, in the small hours of the morning.

CHAPTER VII.

BATTLE OF GRAVELOTTE—BURNING OF ST. PRIVAT—TYPICAL CASE OF DISTRESS—REVISIT TWENTY-FIVE YEARS LATER—USE OF MASONIC SIGN—GRAVELOTTE VILLAGE AND BATTLEFIELD—AMANVILLERS—ROUGH SURGERY AFTER THE BATTLE—WHITWELL ON THE DISTRESS—BURNING OF PELTRE—BAYONET FIGHT IN THE CHURCH.

WE commenced the relief work in the neighbourhood of Briey. Metz not having yet surrendered, we were not permitted to pass beyond the bounds of the villages occupied by the Germans. We found, however, ample work at St. Privat and other villages around the plain of Gravelotte. At St. Privat we were horror-struck with the work of devastation. Almost every house was in ruins, and the regiment of German soldiers quartered in it were living mostly in the basements or cellars. The church, a melancholy ruin, was knocked to pieces by shells from the battlefield, and had been set on fire by the explosion of a bomb.

The battle of Gravelotte, resulting in the defeat of the best soldiers, including the Imperial Guard, and of the ablest generals of France—and subsequently in their surrender after the siege of

Metz,—was the most stubbornly-contested of all the sanguinary conflicts of the war.

In this great struggle the French opposed 180,000 men to 230,000 Germans, and the loss of the latter in killed and wounded exceeded 19,000 men. The loss of the former is not known, but was probably less, for the French occupied selected positions, especially Canrobert's Division at St. Privat, which poured a murderous fire from a superior infantry weapon—the "chassepot,"—and from batteries of mitrailleuses, upon the Germans advancing across the open to storm the position. "St. Privat is the grave of our Prussian Guards" was the mournful remark I heard somewhat later from a German officer.

Imagination strives in vain to realise the fell crop of death scattered thickly over a battlefield so wide as this. The agonies from wounds and from thirst, the terrible mutilations beyond all hope of surgery, the vast array of the slaughtered, and the yet vaster multitude of widows and orphans, form altogether a picture of human suffering that no language can adequately describe.

TYPICAL CASE OF DISTRESS.

It was in the village of St. Privat that Allen and I came first into actual contact with the sufferings of the innocent victims of this disastrous war, as instanced in the persons of many of the small peasant proprietors. "No corn, no cattle, no horses, no hay, no straw, no food, absolutely nothing left but the clothes we wear," was said to us again and again. All had been destroyed, or devoured by the armed hosts of both sides, who had lived amongst them for months. Nor was this all, many of their houses had been battered into ruins by shells from the battlefield.

A typical instance of distress in an acute form, to which we made frequent reference afterwards in public addresses at home, arises before my memory. In one of the most shattered houses in St. Privat, my companion and I stopped to speak to a decent elderly woman, who was busy at a wash-tub. The front part of the house was much shattered by shot and shell. The windows were all gone, and in order to ward off some of the cold winds, a pile of stable manure was heaped up before the open spaces.

The woman's story, told with many tears, was very touching. "We, who were so happy before the war, living here upon our own little property, lost everything by requisitions, first from the French army, and afterwards from the Germans. Then, to crown our misery, came the great battle of Gravelotte, when our house was battered to pieces over our heads!"

Her husband had been compelled to load up his wagon with his own hay and corn, and follow in the transport service of the French army. Many weeks afterwards she heard indirectly that he had died of fever, far away in another part of France. The wretched men who are conscripted into the transport service receive scant attention in war-time from the military authorities, whose *first* care is over the "effectives," so-called, and the *second*, over their sick and wounded, so that when the poor transport men are struck down by fever or other dangerous maladies, it is often the case that no doctor can be spared to look after them, and they are simply left to die, or to struggle through as best they can.

The woman told me she now earned a pittance to keep herself and sick daughter alive, by washing for the German soldiers who were quartered in the village, and were kind to them. Whilst I was talking with her, Allen had penetrated to the back of the house, where he found the sick daughter in a wretchedly cold chamber, with insufficient clothing or bedding to protect her from the wintry weather, and the only apparent food for this poor consumptive patient was a piece of the black "ration" bread of the German soldiers.

Ah! This was indeed a typical home of misery! but, in our later experiences of the war, one that was, in some of its painful aspects, often repeated.

How the remembrance of homes like this, in which happiness will never be again known on this side of the grave, crowds on the mind, and utterly tarnishes and blots out all that men call *glory* in successful war, and leaves behind nought but its cold reality in the unspeakable misery and sorrow of its wretched victims.

An interesting relic in my possession is a piece of the melted bell-metal of the church of St.

Privat. The curé took my friend Allen and myself over the village, and to the ruins of the church. We noticed, on entering through the door, a mass of swords and bayonets fused together by strong heat, and a quantity of glittering bell-metal, a piece of which the curé gave me as a relic. He said that during the battle, his church, though much shattered by shells, was used as an ambulance, and the floor was thickly covered with wounded men. The weather being extremely hot, their cries for water were heartrending. This water he carried with his own hands from the village well, in innumerable bucket-fulls, and did what he could to assuage their great thirst. The battle raged all around furiously, and the cry was suddenly raised, "The church is on fire." A scene of confusion and alarm followed. He feared it would be impossible to remove the whole of the wounded men before the fire reached them. The people did their utmost, however, and carried as many as they possibly could into the houses in the village, many of which were also shattered by shot and shell. The flames raged furiously, and roared up the church tower, melting the bells, and the church became a total wreck.

Re-visit Twenty-Five Years Later.

Twenty-five years after these events, I revisited this scene of the war, accompanied by my wife and her sister. The old priest was still living, and, after a little explanation, remembered me in connection with the incident of the bell-metal. We found that an entirely new church had been erected upon a fresh site, and the houses in the village had been rebuilt and repaired, though they still showed marks of shot and shell. The priest took us round to visit the German monuments, or "Denkmäler," erected to the memory of their comrades who fell in the battle. He showed us the spot where the Saxon contingent suffered so severely during the fight. Pointing to the place, he said, "As they emerged above the ridge, they were met with such a withering fire from French chassepots and mitrailleuses that, it is stated, 8,000 men were put *hors de combat* in ten minutes." He also pointed out the wooded ridge, the Bois de Saulny, where Bazaine kept the Imperial Guard posted and inactive during the whole time of the battle. On my asking him why he did this, he shrugged his shoulders saying "*Qui sait?*" (Who knows?) "Possibly it might be want of ammunition: but if those fresh troops, the flower of the French army, had been launched upon the Germans, wearied with the long fight, anyone can see how different the result might have been." The old man told me how, recently, the present Emperor of Germany had sent for him to Metz, and placed a decoration on his breast for his services to the wounded, both French and German. "But," I said to him, "you don't wear it." He replied, "*Non, monsieur, je suis prêtre,*" meaning I suppose that it would be inconsistent with his sacred office to wear a warlike decoration.

My comrades Thomas Whitwell and Dr. Spence Watson had to pass through a somewhat rough experience when they followed H. J. Allen and myself to Metz. They entered, as we had done, into French territory, from Belgium, by the town and fortress of Longwy, but neglected the needful precaution, on entering a country in a state of war, of obtaining from the Commandant of the Garrison a "safe conduct" for the journey. At Longwy they were arrested by *gens d'armes* sent by the Commandant, were taken as "prisoners of war" at the point of the bayonet to Longwy-Haut, and were marched up the parade ground, in front of the Castle, where the Commandant was reviewing his troops.

The Commandant, having received the previous evening news of the surrender of Metz, eyed the two Englishmen furiously, refusing to look at the passport tendered him by Dr. Watson, and in his rage, stamped on it with his boot. He would listen to no explanations, but charged them with being "Prussian spies," and muttered threats as to what he would do to them. The situation was alarming enough, but during this outburst of passion Whitwell gazed steadily into his face, hoping to catch his eye, and give him the Masonic sign, having the impression that he was, like himself, a Freemason. His first attempt failed, but after an interval, he caught the officer's eye full, and noticed that he took the sign. The Commandant came round past the soldiers, and told the two gentlemen to walk into the Castle. They preceded him there, and he followed and closed the door. When he and Whitwell came to hand-grips with each other, the officer recognising, perhaps, that Whitwell was a Mason of a superior rank, was now profuse in his apologies, and most effusive in his professions of cordial friendship; in short, as Watson, who was astonished at the change in the Commandant, observed to me soon after, "These two bearded fellows hugged and kissed each other in the most ridiculous fashion." The lion had become a lamb all at once. Having explained to them how the news of Bazaine's treachery, in surrendering Metz to the Germans, had provoked him to uncontrollable fury, he now amply made up for his fault by doing all in his power to facilitate their journey to Metz, and endorsed their passports with his "safe conduct," as he had previously done for Allen and myself.

The whole story, when freshly told to us in the course of a day or two, intensely interested and amused my companion and myself. Watson, when commenting on this curious incident, said that one of the first things he should do when he reached home, after this wonderful instance of its usefulness, would be to become installed as a "Freemason."

On a long slope leading down from a wide plain stands the important village of Gravelotte.

It was one of the places which figured on our lists among the earliest as needing relief. The first visit paid there by my companion and self was on one of the dreariest and most drenching days of that wettest of autumns, and about three months after the battle of the 18th of August.

On entering the village one of the first things to arrest our attention was the foul, inky-looking fluid streaming down the open gutters at the roadside. On tracing this upwards to its source, we discovered that it was the drainage of the battlefield, which owing to the heavy rainfall thus found its way down the slope, and through the main street of the village. After this it caused no surprise to learn that there was fever in almost every house in Gravelotte. Having an introduction to Dr. Laseron's deaconess-nurses, some of whom were still in charge of a hospital for the sick and wounded, we called on them, but after learning something of the condition of things around, concluded to make no stay for the time being in Gravelotte.

Later on, we became familiar with the roads which cross the scene of the battle in various directions. Thus when visiting the distressed villages on and around the plain, and wishing to return to Metz before total darkness set in, on more than one occasion, when taking a short cut across the field of slaughter, the horse's foot has suddenly plunged into one of the many shallow graves, with which some parts were thickly strewn, and one became unpleasantly aware of the fact by the sickening odours which were almost overpowering. In the burning heat of August, after the fight, the dead bodies of the fallen soldiers were hurriedly buried, and a few shovelfuls of earth thrown over them. The succeeding heavy rains of October had in some cases washed off the thin covering of earth, and laid bare to view these ghastly uncared-for remains.

Gruesome stories were told by some of the villagers how night was made hideous by the howling of wolves. These ravenous animals were intent on gorging themselves upon the neglected corpses, retreating before daylight to their distant lairs in the Ardennes about forty miles away.

As soon as the Germans had established their authority in the province, large burying parties were told off to collect the corpses from all these shallow graves, which would otherwise have materially interfered with the cultivation of the land, and to give them proper burial in certain selected spots. Afterwards a number of "Denkmäler" or monuments were erected, in memory of those who fell in the battle.

AMANVILLERS.

Among other villages which required assistance from our stores in Metz was Amanvillers, which is situated on the plain of Gravelotte, and which has now a station on the line between Metz and Paris.

It was visited in December, 1870, by Dr. R. Spence Watson and myself. At the Presbytère we endeavoured to ascertain from the curé what were the needs of the village.

While in the house our horses were left hitched up at the front door, Dr. Spence Watson having incautiously left his waterproof riding-coat upon the saddle ; on our return to the horses, the coat was missing, having been appropriated by some thief in our absence. This was a lesson to me ever afterwards during the war in France, as, wherever we went, this plundering spirit prevailed among the people.

As no article of the kind could be procured nearer than Paris, and as the weather continued to be very rough and wet, the loss of the waterproof was serious.

Even in the matter of feeding our horses it was necessary to stand by the manger until the horse had eaten up his corn, otherwise it was almost certain to be appropriated for some one else's horse. It was rather hard, on returning from a long ride on wet cold nights, to be unable to leave the foul stables until the animals had been fed, when we were longing to change our wet clothing and to satisfy our own hunger ; but, as the horses were in every-day use, it was essential to see that they were properly attended to.

The house of the curé of Amanvillers having been used as an ambulance during the battle of Gravelotte, we heard from him some gruesome stories of what occurred under his own roof on that day.

Looking at me, he said, "On that couch where

you are sitting, they laid a young French sergeant, both of whose arms had been broken by the explosion of a bomb, he having thrown up both hands to protect his face. The surgeons were amputating his limbs with *kitchen knives*, and without any anæsthetics. The poor fellow's screams were heartrending, and he died soon after the operation." What stronger proof could there be that the French organisation was utterly defective.

So far from being ready "to the button of a gaiter," as Marshal Lebœuf had glibly responded to the Emperor's inquiries, it proved in the hour of need, that the surgeons were unprovided even with sufficient surgical instruments and anæsthetics.

All the floors of the curé's house were covered with tell-tale stains of a dark hue.

My friend John Bellows, on a subsequent visit, saw two men on their knees, engaged in vigorously scrubbing the boards.

The curé asked him, "Do you know what they are doing?" He replied, "I can guess."

Strange to say, after a quarter of a century's scrubbings, when my wife and I visited the house in 1895, several of the boards still retained the indelible dark stains of blood.

The old curé told Dr. Watson and myself that surgical operations were going on in every room of his house during the battle, and that blood was flowing to such an extent from the upper rooms, that it ran down the stairs, and out through the front door into the street.

He further informed us that when the German doctors visited his house after the battle, they found every article of bedding in the house to be so saturated with blood that they ordered them to be carried out into the public street and burned, in order to avoid the outbreak of any epidemic.

He told us also, that immediately after the surrender of Metz, a large number of disarmed French soldiers were massed in the field opposite his house, and were kept there under a guard for several days, without shelter of any kind, so that many were unable to rise from the ground, and perished miserably from cold and wet, before they could be despatched in train-loads to German fortresses. Such a contingency might be unavoidable from the German point of view, seeing that the number of prisoners of war suddenly thrown upon their hands exceeded 170,000 men, to transport whom all at once was impossible.

RELIEF COMMISSIONER WHITWELL ON THE DISTRESS.

"Metz, November, 1870.

. . . "Could some of the English public see the look of the poor peasants in the villages round Metz, as they tell us of the loss of their all, '*ni foin, ni paille, ni pommes-de-terre, ni blé, ni pain,*' and taking the thumb-nail between the front teeth, biting it and flinging the hand out towards you, the poor mother adds, '*rien*'! The houses had all the wood burnt, the glass shivered out of the windows, the doors destroyed; and, looking round, you see the bare

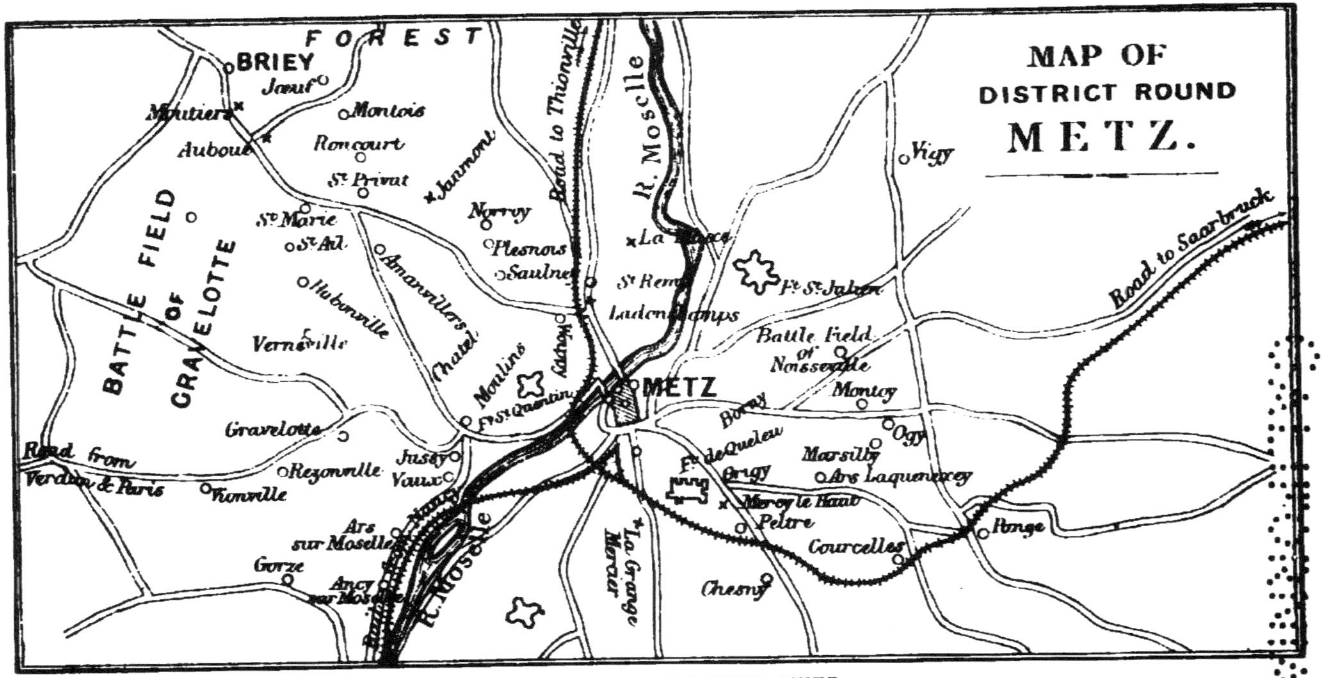

MAP OF DISTRICT ROUND METZ.

floor, and the children crying within—outside the dark wintry sky and coming storm. The spectators of such misery would not, for a moment, hesitate to bear a willing hand to help.

"The distress is heartrending. I have to-day made out our plans for feeding the villages, sixty in number, where the people are starving; and I find that we shall next week, when we open the depôt here, have of actually destitute starving people, nearly 8,000 souls. . . . I am not an amateur at this kind of work, being accustomed to Ragged Schools, to distribution of coals and soup in winter, and the sight of what we in England call great suffering. I say that nothing in our own country, at a time of depression in trade, or in winter, or in other ways, has ever struck me so forcibly as riding over this country, beaten down with the trampling of many feet, and ploughed with the wheels of artillery, the land lying waste and unsown, the houses wrecked on every side for miles, and the sad, hopeless, pinched look of men, women, and children. I say that nothing has impressed me more forcibly with the evils wrought by this accursed war, and the thousands of poor souls that will, in spite of all that we can do, be swept away by want, disease, and death."

Peltre: Bayonet Fight in the Church.

When re-visiting Metz, accompanied by my wife and sister in 1895, one of the points of greatest interest to them was the village of Peltre, distant about five miles, to which we took a drive one fine afternoon. The pathetic story of the burning of the Convent of the "Sisters of Providence," in 1870, which had often been related by me in my Peace lectures, made my companions naturally desirous of visiting the scene.

I found the whole place rebuilt and repaired beyond recognition, a handsome chapel having been erected on a new site. The contrast between these new erections, in a beautiful light stone, was very great, as compared with the calcined, roofless ruin, which I remembered in 1870. Only one of the inmates, now an elderly "sister," was a survivor of the events of the war, and remembered the previous visits of Whitwell and myself. She took us over the premises and related some of the details of the burning of the convent. The only point that was new to me, was that the German General had considerately given the "sisters" a "safe conduct" on the night of their flight, so that they might pass through the German lines with all their scholars, numbering about one hundred.

On looking back to the circumstances of our first visit, I remember how aghast we felt on finding every one of the substantial stone-built houses in the village abandoned, and burnt to a calcined ruin. Ninety-two houses were thus destroyed in a village of 500 inhabitants. We had rambled on into the precincts of the convent, which told the same story. On looking round what had been a beautifully ornamented chapel, now roofless and blackened, we picked up as souvenirs a few pieces of the rich stained glass from the shattered windows. Whilst thus engaged we were suddenly confronted by a lady, one evidently of some authority, as she rather haughtily demanded our business ; this we promptly explained, with all politeness. When she understood that we were not Germans but Englishmen, who were occupied in relieving the distress in Metz and neighbourhood, and had come as far as Peltre to inquire into their needs, she was mollified, and a pleasant smile came over her expressive countenance. Instead of giving us her story, however, which we had asked for, she walked deliberately away and disappeared. Not knowing exactly what was the right thing to do, after waiting a while, we followed in the same direction. Suddenly we found her behind some projection that had screened her from our view, on her knees before a large crucifix, which had been thrown down, broken in pieces, and was stained with human blood. In sympathy with her, though brought up in a simpler form of faith, we stood uncovered, reverently waiting the end of her devotions.

When she arose, she said with a cheerful smile, "Now, gentlemen, I can tell you our story ; I was the Superior of the Convent, which was the home of a large number of sisters, and a boarding school for more than 100 young girls. Being a large establishment, 200 German soldiers were quartered upon us. Well, we did not complain, but fed them, and worked for them, and did all we could to make them comfortable." Then, with an impassioned tone, pointing to the burnt, roofless chapel, she said with bitterness, "*Vous voyez, Messieurs, leur reconnaissance!*" (You see gentlemen, their gratitude!)

Proceeding with her story she said, "It was in the dead of night, after we had all retired to bed, and were sound asleep, that we were rudely awakened by thundering knocks at the front door. I hastened down and asked what they wanted. Some Germans shouted that they had orders to clear all out of the house in ten minutes, and to set it on fire, for which they had petroleum and combustibles ready. Picture to yourselves, gentlemen, my consternation! *Ten minutes!* to rouse 100 girls out of their first sound slumbers, to dress them, and turn them and all the sisterhood out into the dark lonesome night, with no roof over their heads!"

Overcome by her feelings, she stopped and wrung her hands in bitterness, exclaiming, "Oh! the cruelty of men,—Yes, of *men*! towards innocent women and children."

Anxious to hear the rest of her story, I inquired, "Well, madame, what did you do? What became of you?" She continued, "I was in dread, lest any of our young charges should be left in their beds, and become a prey to the flames; but we were not allowed to linger, the work of destruction was already beginning, so we took our mournful journey towards the wood, *que voila*!"

pointing through the now unglazed window. "After a while, on emerging from the darkness of the wood, we observed the whole heavens were red and lurid, and on looking back we saw flames bursting through the roof of our beloved home below. Ah, mon Dieu!" she exclaimed, "the agony of that moment, when we saw our beloved convent a prey to the devouring flames, and we, wretched wanderers, had not where to lay our heads. Oh! the bitter tears we shed on that never-to-be-forgotten night!"

After more in the same strain, I learnt that she did finally succeed in getting all her charges safely into temporary homes.

It may be asked why all this vindictiveness fell so heavily upon Peltre, and upon the innocent inmates of the convent? The Germans alleged its necessity as an act of *reprisal*, this being the mild term generally used by warriors, when *revenge* would more suitably describe the deeds done.

Peltre being situated on the railway from Metz to Saarbruck and Germany, a large commissariat store for the supply of the besieging army was established there; this invited frequent raids from the starving French army in Metz. But the crowning act, which drove the Germans to the resolve to burn down the whole place, was that in which a number of their soldiers had been *butchered*, without quarter, in a desperate bayonet fight, *inside the chapel* of the convent.

Some of the details of this fight we gleaned

afterwards from other sources. Very early in the morning of Sunday, the 30th of September, 1870, before the sun was up, the French General Lapasset was ready with his brigade, together with six pieces of artillery. They marched out of Metz under cover of the embankment alongside the line, with a battery of mitrailleuses. The Germans were surprised, but soon the rattle of rifle-fire rang out from one side or the other. A portion of the French force pushed rapidly towards the village, where the Germans were immensely outnumbered, and ran to the convent, whose walls were already loopholed for defence. Then, under a deadly fire, an entrance was forced by the pursuing French soldiers.

Now commenced a horrible sight for these poor peace-loving sisters. Strange beings invaded their peaceful sanctuary, which echoed with the yells and shouts of excited soldiers, bent upon carnage and death. Their church became a charnel-house, the very sanctuary ran with blood. The *House of Mercy* became the *House of Vengeance*, for there was *no mercy* there! The Germans craved no quarter, and the French gave none, and flight was impossible.

When it comes to brave men crossing bayonets with each other, they know that one of them *must* inevitably go down. In the white-heat of a life and death struggle, the demon of cruelty takes full possession of the infuriated combatants, overpowers every humane feeling, and drives men to commit deeds of vengeance, which in the quietude of their home life they would shudder at as impossible. Thus the ruthless slaughter continued until the last brave German was done to death.

Such was the *morning sacrifice* perpetrated in the early hours of that bright smiling Sunday, within the walls of a temple dedicated to a God of love and mercy!

The Germans maintained that this butchery was inexcusable and unfair by the laws of war; hence their determination to make an example of Peltre, with the utmost severity of retaliation. How bitter would be the irony, if the ensigns of these vengeful warriors, *professing* to be enlisted under the banner of Christ, were inscribed with the great words of His Gospel, "*God is Love!*"

CHAPTER VIII.

WAR SCENES — SIEGE AND SURRENDER OF METZ — TRIUMPHAL ENTRY OF GERMANS — FAMINE AND SMALLPOX — MY EXPERIENCE OF RE-VACCINATION — VACCINATION IN THE FRENCH ARMY—BLACK TYPHUS IN RAILWAY WAGONS—PATHETIC STORY OF A YOUNG DOCTOR—SUFFERINGS OF ANIMALS.

MARSHAL BAZAINE, after his defeat at Gravelotte, marched his whole army down towards Metz. There being already a strong garrison under General Coffinière within the city, Bazaine's army took up its quarters in the first circle of villages surrounding it. Nearly half the army, however, remained under canvas, on the banks of the Moselle. This ground was dry and healthy in August, but in October, when we first visited the camp, the autumnal rains had converted it into a swamp, poached into a sea of mud by the wheels of artillery and the trampling of cavalry.

The besiegers, under Prince Frederic Charles, now closed in their lines, and occupied a circle of villages extending to a distance of five to nine miles from Metz, outside those of the French army, thus forming a "ring of steel," closing every avenue to Metz, and holding Bazaine's whole army within their grip. The investment by the Germans at every point was so perfect, that in the words of one of their officers, "not a mouse can go in or out without our permission."

The siege lasted from the date of the battle of Gravelotte, on August 18th, until the surrender on October 28th, 1870.

There was no bombardment of Metz—the guns of the formidable forts which crowned the hills around kept the besiegers at a distance. The officer in command of the German battery at Ars-sur-Moselle told me, "We have never fired a ball into Metz yet!" Throughout its warlike annals, Metz, "the impregnable," though it has yielded at various times to famine, has never surrendered to force.

As soon as the preliminaries of the surrender of Metz were arranged, we were permitted to pass through the lines leading down to the camp of Marshal Bazaine. Many thousands of the men, for whom there was no room in the villages, were encamped near the Moselle, under the small shelter-tents usually carried by French soldiers, called "tentes d'abri." These afforded but little shelter during the continuous rains and cold winds of the stormy October days and nights, and consequently the condition of the men was miserable in the extreme. Having had, as they told us, for some time but half a biscuit and a small piece of horse-flesh per man per day, hunger-bitten and fever-stricken, many of them were a prey to that scourge of armies everywhere, dysentery; also smallpox and typhoid were raging in their midst. And no wonder, we thought, as we looked around on their damp and squalid surroundings. They were lying on the bare earth, which was so moist as to leave a cast of their persons and beards on it, with but one filthy blanket for covering, whilst the ground around the camp was flecked over with hundreds of decaying noisome carcases of horses, thus forming a perfect breeding ground of every foul and hideous disease.

It was a marvel to us that any of them were able to go about at all, in the ghastly famine-stricken condition which they presented. Their clothes ragged and filthy, their beards plastered with mud, their eyes sunk, and their cheeks hollow, they presented the most forlorn and dejected pictures of misery and suffering our eyes had ever beheld. Strange to say, the one thing the lack of which they most complained was salt, resulting no doubt from the bad horse-flesh diet, which, without salt, had become utterly loathsome to them. Next day, when my friend and I came amongst them, with our pockets full of salt, the men were so ravenous for it, that they almost tore the clothes off our backs, in their fierce eagerness to obtain a few grains.

As we could do nothing to relieve a weltering mass of misery like this, it remains in one's memory as one of the most painful reminiscences of the war; harrowing indeed it was to look into the eyes of thousands of our fellow-men in extreme want and suffering in their worst forms, and yet feel utterly powerless to alleviate the wretchedness of the myriad victims of disease, hunger, and cold. The whole of the army under tents being disarmed, it had a strangely ominous look to see wagon after wagon, each drawn by four horses, piled up with French "chassepots," and led away in charge of German soldiers.

In the village of Ars-sur-Moselle every house was crowded with soldiers. Night had come on and it was with the utmost difficulty that we succeeded at last in finding a bed, in a small cabaret or inn, filled to the attic as it was with soldiers. The bed thus kindly(?) given to us was in a dark and dirty little back room, and the sheets were ominously warm, with an odour far from pleasant. Thankful to get our heads under shelter anywhere, we could not be fastidious, and asking no questions, we were soon sound asleep. When morning came round we learned to our dismay that two soldiers ill with smallpox, had just been taken out of this very bed, and we had slept in the same sheets! Is it any wonder that about a fortnight afterwards, the normal period of incubation, my companion, H. J. Allen, developed symptoms of this dreaded disease, and had to be carefully nursed, under much difficulty, within the city of Metz?

His uncle, Richard Allen, who had been telegraphed for, soon arrived from Dublin, bringing his niece, Miss Ellen Allen, with him, to nurse her brother. So assiduous was this young lady in this labour of love, so constant in her sisterly watchfulness, night and day, by the bedside of her beloved brother, that her own health was soon undermined, and taking the infection from him she rapidly succumbed, and fell a victim to this terrible malady. Her friends, consisting of all our little company then in Metz, had the sad and mournful duty of following her remains to the cemetery at Plantières, about two kilometres from the city, where a headstone may still be seen over her grave suitably commemorating her death.

During our stay in Metz, in 1895, my wife and I paid a visit to the spot where she is interred. We found it well kept and in excellent order. As we stood there and observed the wreaths which had recently been placed on the grave by kindly hands, there was something extremely touching in the sad reminiscences which the reading of the simple "Friendly" inscription called up:—

ELLEN ALLEN
OF DUBLIN, IRELAND,
BORN SECOND MONTH 7TH, 1828,
DIED AT METZ
TWELFTH MONTH 21ST, 1870,
OF SMALLPOX CAUGHT WHILE
ATTENDING HER BROTHER IN THE
SAME ILLNESS.
O GRAVE, WHERE IS THY VICTORY?

We learnt from the "*gardien*" that on the completion of a quarter of a century, the German

Government voted considerable sums for the national celebration of the victory of Gravelotte. So all the monuments, or "*denkmäler*" of the war, together with the graves of those who had perished therein, were afresh decorated at the cost of the Government. In these special attentions, the grave of Ellen Allen had not been overlooked. The Military Governor of Metz had sent two workmen to clean and renovate the headstone and inscription, which looked like new, and on the anniversary day a large wreath of oak leaves, bound with broad ribbons of the national colours, had been placed on the grave. In addition to these official attentions, another wreath of heather and yew had been placed there by a *voluntary* Association called the National Patriotic Society. These reminiscences are to be kept up annually.

How strange it all seemed! That the most powerful military Government on earth should thus solicitously care for the grave of a gentle unassuming Quaker maiden, who had sacrificed her own life, in her unselfish devotion to her beloved brother, stricken down by a dangerous illness, whilst on a mission of peace and goodwill. Would that the pen of a Whittier had perpetuated in immortal verse this peaceful "*denkmal*" of this manifestation of sisterly love in the midst of the troubles and alarms in war!

SURRENDER OF METZ.

The 29th of October, 1870, was a red-letter day in German annals, the day when Metz opened its gates to admit the beleaguering hosts which surrounded it, who made a grand triumphal march through the city. Having obtained permission from General Stiehle, chief of Prince Frederick Charles's staff, whom we interviewed at Corny, Allen and I presented ourselves early in the morning at the principal gate of the city, and entered with the German army. The Marshal, Prince Frederick Charles, accompanied by a brilliant staff of Chiefs and Generals, their breasts glittering with stars and decorations, headed the procession. Bands of music, waving banners, flashing bayonets and glittering helmets of myriads of horse, foot, and artillerymen, in an almost endless procession, glorying in all the "pomp and panoply of war," constituted an impressive demonstration of the might of *human* power, rarely if ever equalled.

The spectator, seeing this demonstration only, would have gone away having realised but little of the grim realities of war. Let him cast his eyes down the side streets, and scrutinize the dense throngs of French soldiers, disarmed, dejected, ragged, diseased. Many for whom there was no room in the overcrowded hospitals had their faces covered with the loathsome eruption of smallpox in a virulent form, and were parading the streets, to the danger of all passers by. Let him further take in the fact that all the hospitals and barracks, and many of the churches, were filled with sick and wounded men, whilst numbers more were quartered in private houses, until the city had become one vast hospital. Let him consider what this enormous mass of human misery, this waste of human life and property, meant to the citizens themselves, to their country, and to humanity at large. Let him realise the contrast, more or less conspicuous in every war, between the triumphs of victory on the one hand, and on the other, the unutterable wretchedness, misery, and woe of its victims. Haunted, thenceforth, by the recollection of gruesome experiences like these, all that men call the "glory of war" will have vanished for ever from his soul, leaving nothing behind but its unspeakable horrors.

How severe the famine was in the city may be understood from the fact that Allen and myself were unable to get any food, or to buy any bread, or even a biscuit, during the whole of the first day, and we had to leave the city and return at night to our quarters at Ars-sur-Moselle, in order to obtain food and shelter.

The Germans, however, with their usual forethought, had whole train-loads of provisions waiting a few miles from the city, which were promptly brought in and distributed among the starving citizens of Metz.

In these days, when the efficacy of vaccination as a protection from smallpox is so much questioned, I have sometimes referred to my experiences at Metz as a proof of the good done by re-vaccination in my own person. Before leaving England I had taken the precaution to be re-vaccinated, and although subjected to precisely the same infection as my friend Allen, who had not taken the same care, I remained free from the malady. The wound in the arm, however, where the vaccine lymph had been introduced, became very painful, swelling up like a great carbuncle. The place was long in healing, and, it being on the bridle arm, the constant friction on horseback caused so much irritation that it became inflamed and angry from the wrist to the shoulder. In fact, had it not been skilfully dressed every night by my friend Whitwell, who was as good as a surgeon, I should have been compelled to return home invalided. Whether this was the effect of the vaccine lymph and the small-pox virus in my system contending for the mastery, I leave for doctors to decide. The simple fact, however, that after being re-vaccinated I did *not* take the smallpox, when surrounded by infection, has weighed with me more than any amount of adverse theories. The wide-spread prevalence of smallpox in its most loathsome form among the famine-stricken soldiers of the French Army, notwithstanding the fact that vaccination is compulsory in the case of every recruit, did not appear to us at all surprising. The scanty and unwholesome food, and the squalor and filth of their environment, in those wretched shelter tents, under which these poor fellows had lain so long in the camp outside the city walls, were quite enough to account to us, who had been eye-witnesses of their sufferings, for every form of loathsome disease to which so many of them were a prey. Although this alone would account for the prevalence of smallpox in Metz, there is another fact, which has only recently come to my knowledge, that has an important bearing on the case, namely, that at that epoch the regulations as to vaccination in the French Army were grossly neglected.

A brief quotation may here be permitted from a work published by Dr. Leon Colin, the Physician-General of the French Army, on the smallpox epidemic during the war, which was quoted by Lord Playfair in a speech in the House of Commons, June 19th, 1883. He tells us that the levies, hurriedly called up, were unvaccinated.

"Raised in haste and placed in the field without time for re-vaccination, they were exposed to the attacks of this epidemic. The consequence was that during 1870 and 1871 no less than 23,489 French soldiers died of the disease. The smallpox followed the German camps also, but only 263 of their well-vaccinated soldiers died."

A small percentage truly, out of more than a million of Germans who were called into the field! I am aware that these statistics have been much questioned, but as they have recently been practically verified, they may be accepted as, at least, approximately correct. Surely these figures speak for themselves as to the efficacy of vaccination!

Black Typhus Epidemic.

Those of us who arrived first in Metz, heard grave stories of the terrible condition of the French soldiers, who had survived the hardships of the siege. In order to know the truth of these accounts, I determined, early one morning, to visit the "Grande Place," which is associated with one of the most tragic scenes of the whole war. This great square was packed with railway-wagons belonging to the Eastern Railway Company of France, brought within the fortifications in order to save them from falling into the hands of the Germans. During the siege, these wagons were converted into field-ambulances, into which a number of helpless black typhus patients were carried from the military hospitals,—a necessary precaution, doubtless, considering the dreadfully infectious nature of this most fatal malady.

Attempting to enter the square, I found it guarded on every side by German sentries, who presented the bayonet and shouted, "no entry"; it was "*strengst verboten*" (strictly forbidden). Wishful, however, to verify the stories I had heard, I persevered in walking outside, as near to the wagons as I was allowed to go, and, in some cases where the sliding doors of the wagons were open, I was able to see the wretched sufferers laid within on straw. One glimpse of those worn, livid faces, from whose lips piteous moans were heard, sufficed to impress the dreadful vision on my brain, never to be effaced as long as life lasts. The livid hue seemed, in some instances, to be overlaid by a yellowish efflorescence, the effect of which was ghastly in the extreme; even now as I write, the remembrance of it sends a cold shudder through my frame.

THE GREAT PARADE GROUND AT METZ.

Part of the 320 Railway Vans forming the temporary typhus fever hospital at Metz, adjoining the Caserne du génie, which was crowded with wounded French. The tents in the park also filled with sick. The Hill in the background is Fort St. Quentin.

How many of these gruesome receptacles were there in the square? John Bellows, in his excellent pamphlet, "The Track of the War Around Metz," states that there were 320 of these railway-wagons containing black typhus patients. Each truck had accommodation for at least six men, so that there must have been about 1,800 in all! His description is further confirmed by a sketch, taken from a local photograph, published at the time, of the wagons *in situ*.

I lingered long about the spot, in order to see if anything were being done for the relief and comfort of these poor dying wretches. But, so far as I could see, or learn, there was no one to hand them even so much as a cup of cold water to quench their raging thirst. Death, no doubt, was inevitable in every case smitten with this awful malady. How utterly sad and depressing to stand face to face with a mass of dying humanity like this, in the last throes of mortal agony! What an awful scene in a Christian country, almost under the eaves of temples dedicated to a God of Mercy. Alas! that a multitude of our fellow-beings should thus be cast aside, forsaken, abandoned to die, "like beasts that perish!" Such is war! Yes, war, as carried on in the lifetime of many of us, by nations claiming to be in the first rank of Christian civilization! How true the dictum of a soldier of great experience (General Sherman, U.S.A.), "War is *cruelty*; and you *cannot* refine it!"

On returning to Metz, after my visit to the valley of the Saar, I learned from my friends who had remained in the city the sequel of this pitiful story of the victims of black typhus. It was to this effect. After a certain lapse of time, a detachment of German soldiers entered the "Grande Place," in order to remove the dead for burial. A large quantity of quick-lime was brought in wagons, and thrown from long-handled shovels over the corpses in the trucks. The bodies were then swung by the legs into the wagons, carted away into the fields outside the walls, and thrown promiscuously into huge trenches prepared for their reception. The soil was at once shovelled over them.—"Tools," as Byron bitterly protests, "the broken tools, which tyrants cast away." Among the bodies thus unceremoniously huddled into the trenches, was that of a young doctor, who had volunteered to attend on the sick men in the railway wagons, and who had himself fallen a victim to the fatal malady.

The pathetic story of this youth of twenty-two, which I afterwards heard from my friend Whitwell, who had it from what he considered to be a reliable source, deserves mention as a remarkable instance of magnanimous self-sacrifice and courageous devotion to duty. He was a medical student of American nationality, unknown to me even by name. He had served in the French army as a surgeon throughout the campaign, and had been shut up with it during the siege of Metz. When the black typhus patients had been conveyed out of the hospitals into the railway-wagons in the "Grande Place," and no surgeon or nurse was found willing to be shut up entirely with them in the square, he volunteered to go alone into the enclosure to undertake this dangerous duty. As a medical man he knew perfectly well that he was taking his life in his hand, in thus devoting himself to the care of these men, who were dying of the most terribly infectious of all forms of fever. All that one pair of hands could do to relieve their sufferings, he did for them, by night and day, literally handing them the "cup of cold water, in the name of a disciple"; for it is to me inconceivable that any lesser motive could possibly induce a youth of twenty-two to undertake so dangerous a task, than "the love of Christ constraining him."

Naturally, in a short time the fever seized him in that hot-bed of disease, and ended his brave young life. Buried, undistinguished, among the heaps of corpses thrown indiscriminately into the trenches—no "storied urn or animated bust" reared over that nameless grave, to commemorate his noble self-sacrifice in the service of his fellow-beings—he remains, in my memory and in that of my companions who knew the story, to be distinguished, as the *one true hero* of the Siege of Metz.

Sufferings of Horses.

I have alluded to the mass of dead horses which lay around the French camp outside the walls of

Metz, the poisonous effluvia emitted from these carcases being, no doubt, one main cause of the dreadful diseases existing among the soldiers.

I refrain from enlarging upon the sufferings of horses that are wounded on the battlefield, simply because I have not personally seen them, but one knows too well how the agonies of the wretched animals are often aggravated by their vain struggles to raise themselves upon their broken limbs, whilst they sometimes endure the additional tortures of hunger and thirst for hours, or even for days, because there is no one to give them the final "*coup de grace.*" There were horses in Marshal Bazaine's camp still alive at the end of the siege, which were kept probably for food, but, being like the men themselves, famine-stricken, they were in condition little better than living skeletons. We noticed a group of these fastened to some stunted pine trees, which had not only gnawed off each other's manes, but also the resinous bark of the trees within their reach, a plain proof of the severity of the pangs of hunger they endured, for, under ordinary conditions, the smell and taste of pine bark are utterly loathsome to a horse.

In a country where the forage was so severely requisitioned for army use, as was the case around Metz, there was naturally a grievous loss from hunger among the ordinary farmers' horses. Cattle were generally slaughtered for beef, but the horses, being generally deemed unsuitable by the Germans for army purposes, were simply left to die. One of my friends and myself were invited by a farmer to see his horses in the stable. There were fourteen of them, all in a weak and emaciated condition. "Take any of them, or all of them, if you will," he said, "as I have nothing to give the poor animals." All we could do was to urge him to put them out of their sufferings. Horses were a complete "drug" in Metz, the prices ranging from five up to one hundred francs, according to condition. As cavalry horses they were of no use to the conquerors, being far too light for the ordinary German horse-soldier.

In Belgium I had purchased one of these discarded cavalry horses, a light and weedy-looking Arab from North Africa, whose ambling paces were specially easy for a lady. I left careful instructions for the animal to be properly cared for, and to be forwarded by rail to Antwerp, and shipped thence by the first steamer for Middlesbrough. These instructions, however, were utterly neglected, and the poor beast died within a day or two of being landed in England. When first captured, he was roaming in some woods near Sedan, some time after the great battle. Having evidently had little or nothing to eat, he was in the condition known to horsemen as "tucked up," resembling in appearance more the form of a greyhound than of a horse.

Had he lived, I intended to have given him a summer's run on my farm at Ayton, as he was somewhat of a curiosity in his way,—a light "flea-bit" grey, his long tail nearly reaching the ground, and he had his cavalry number branded on his hoof. There was a bullet lodged in his thigh, and one of his nostrils was slit with either a sword or bayonet thrust. All I could preserve of him, by way of keepsake, was his poor hide, which really was hardly worth tanning.

These African "Arabs," though so slight looking, are said to be capable of great endurance.

An instance of this was mentioned to me in a hotel at Namur, in Belgium. On the Sunday succeeding the battle of Sedan, which I believe was fought on a Thursday, there came into the courtyard a wounded French officer, more dead than alive. His horse had carried him through from the battlefield, a distance of about 90 miles, going slowly onward, by night and day—the injured man being unable to dismount—until they arrived, both in a condition of extreme exhaustion, at this hotel. Here the officer was lifted out of the saddle, every care was bestowed upon him, so that he soon began to recover from the effects of his wounds. What became of the horse I did not learn. The animal which had carried his rider so faithfully certainly deserved to be duly cared for.

The treatment of draught animals, as well as the tortures endured by horses wounded on the battlefield, are aspects of modern warfare that have not received the careful consideration they deserve from all lovers of animals.

Persistent and united protests on their part would

doubtless lead to a more humane system of treatment by those responsible for the care of such animals in war-time. In 1883, in a Peace address given by him in Westminster, I heard the late John Bright, M.P., descant feelingly upon the cruelties that had been inflicted upon the camels which were employed in the transport service in the last Afghan campaign, when, in consequence of overloading and over-driving, no less than sixty thousand of these animals perished miserably!

It ought not to be beyond the resources of humanity to provide a remedy against wholesale cruelty, and fearful waste like this!

CHAPTER IX.

BOMBARDMENT OF STRASBURG—INTERVIEW WITH COUNT BISMARCK—RELIC OF STRASBURG—FRENCH PRISONERS AND DEATH SCENES AT TREVÈS—SUNSET ON THE MOSELLE—HOSPITAL AT DUSSELDORF.

UNDERNEATH the seal of the city of York, on my commission, appears the signature, and seal (now effaced), of Count Bismarck von Bohlen (cousin of Prince Bismarck), Lieutenant-General, and first Governor General of Alsace, who signed the document at Strasburg, 14th February, 1871. He expresses the wish that God's blessing might follow our endeavours to relieve the distress.

Allen and I had proceeded to Strasburg, where, for the first time, our eyes rested upon the awful sight of a bombarded city.

The whole of one quarter was levelled to the ground, not a house being left standing; the streets had been wiped out, and encumbered with mounds of rubbish. During the eleven weeks of the bombardment, some of the terrified inhabitants had, as they informed us, lived in the basements, the upper floors being laid down thickly with mattresses, to prevent the shells, which fell night and day, from bursting through upon their heads below. What wonder that numerous deaths had occurred through sheer fright!

This was the condition of affairs in the city when we entered, in search of Count Bismarck, by whom we were courteously received at his head-quarters, the Hotel de Paris.

I had two interviews, at different times, with Count Bismarck, and found him very sympathetic and helpful in our work. On my second visit, he kindly invited Whitwell and myself to his head-quarters, and we attended church with him on Sunday morning, Whitwell walking side by side with the Count. Although a man of ample proportions, and 6ft. 2in. in height, Whitwell looked small beside the commanding figure of Count Bismarck, as they marched in front of me towards the church, the Count with his military helmet, and with his sabre clanking on the pavement as they went along, looking even more than his full height of 6ft. 4in.

We afterwards dined with him at his head-quarters, and spent the afternoon in discussing the plans connected with our work, and in answering his numerous inquiries about the Society of Friends and their principles. He also told me he had a son who was a young officer in the army then investing Paris, and begged me, as a father, when in the neighbourhood, to look up that young man, and give him good paternal advice.

I took the opportunity of informing Count Bismarck of the very strong feeling which the French in Metz and the neighbourhood entertained against being annexed to Germany. Of this I was able to give him many instances, from my own personal observation.

Count Bismarck said, "We know all about this feeling. Nevertheless, you are aware that these people are of German origin, and 200 years ago they formed an integral part of the German Empire; what we intend to do is to re-Germanise them, and make them as loyal to Germany as they are to France now."

"How will you do that, Count Bismarck?" I asked, having my doubts on the subject.

He replied: "We shall bring up their young children in our German schools; we shall take all their young men and pass them through the drill of our great German army. It may take us half a generation to effect the desired change, but if you are able to come back to this country in about fifteen years, you will find these people as deeply loyal to Germany as they now are to France."

I accepted his statement with considerable reservation. However, I was able, in about fifteen years after that date, to return to the two provinces, and, after numerous consultations with old friends in Metz, Strasburg, and other intervening places, I again came to the conclusion that Count Bismarck was mistaken, and that there was as yet no substantial change in the sentiments of the people. I was also informed that

SIEGE OF STRASBURG.

the whole of the representatives of the annexed provinces in the German Parliament, numbering about twenty, were irreconcilably opposed to Prince Bismarck and his policy.

Being much impressed by this state of things, I determined to go as far as Berlin, in order to discuss the matter with Count Bismarck again; but, upon inquiries made in that city, I found, unfortunately, that he had gone to his estates far away in Silesia, and I did not feel authorised to follow him to his retreat.

What I wished to have said to this courteous nobleman, was, "You may remember, Count Bismarck, a conversation we had fifteen years ago, at your head-quarters in Strasburg, when you expressed the opinion that in 'half a generation' the people of the annexed provinces of Alsace-Lorraine would become as German in their sentiments as they were French then. After careful inquiry during my recent visit there, what do I find? That the feeling against the German rule is as strong and bitter, apparently, at this day, as it was fifteen years ago!"

I may further confirm this by the results of another brief visit to the cities of Metz and Strasburg, ten years later, in 1895, at the time of the celebrations of the 25th anniversary of the battle of Sedan, when I found that the information given me by *Germans* was certainly to the effect that the people were contented and settled down under German rule. On the other hand, *French* people informed me directly to the contrary—that there still existed an entire want of good feeling and a smouldering discontent under the German ruling authority, with a strong desire to return to France.

The lapse of time since the war has doubtless wrought considerable change in the sentiments of the present population of Alsace-Lorraine, who dread nothing more than the recrudescence of war around their peaceful and prosperous homes. One contributing cause to this change of feeling has been the gradual absorption of a considerable element of German settlers, who have emigrated from the Fatherland, and now occupy many rural homes which were deserted by their former inhabitants, who refusing to become German subjects, proved their loyalty to France by abandoning their beloved Alsatia, and settling on French or Algerian soil.

Relic of Strasburg.

Among my relics of the war is a piece of German shell, with which is connected an interesting coincidence. I obtained possession of it after the bombardment of Strasburg from a bookseller in the city, with whom I was friendly. He told me that, one morning, during the bombardment, he noticed, from the corner of his street, that the golden cross, at the top of the spire of the Cathedral, had fallen out of the perpendicular. He at once sought the sacristan, and together they ventured up to the top of the spire, which is at the giddy height of about 430 feet. Climbing the last fifteen or twenty feet outside the spire, they found a piece of a shell embedded in the masonry, just below the cross. He brought the piece away with him and —for a consideration—handed it over to me, as a souvenir of the bombardment of Strasburg.

The circumstance had pretty much passed out of my memory, when, some two or three months later, following up on horseback the German armies, in the west of France, I put up for the night at a small inn in a country town. The house was crowded with German Artillery officers, and as there was a lack of sleeping accommodation, we sat up all night. I listened attentively to their various stories of the campaign, and my interest was quickened when one officer began to relate, how when he was in command of a battery near Strasburg, the General, Von Werder, came early in the morning to his battery, and ordered him to get the range of the Cathedral. He was surprised, as hitherto they had used every effort to spare it; but the General said he had given notice, in writing, to the French Commandant, Von Uhrich, that if he persisted in using the tower as a position of war, by posting his spies there, who signalled to their sharp shooters where to pick off German officers, he would treat it accordingly and fire upon it. The officer continued: "The spies were still there, so the General waited until I had got the range. My first shot was considerably short; the second missed the construction; but in the third I got the accurate range. I observed through my glass that the shot struck the Cathedral spire just below the cross, which fell over at an angle of about forty-five degrees."

I had followed this conversation with much interest, and here put in a word which made all utter exclamations of surprise. "Captain, I have a piece of your identical shell." "*You!* How did you get it? Quite impossible." I simply related the story told to me by the bookseller. "Oh," he said, "he has given you a piece of a shell with a lot of studs diagonally placed in it, I suppose?" I said: "No, Captain, I have not been all these months mixed up with this war, without learning the difference between a French and a German shell. My shell has short parallel bars on it, and if complete would terminate in a time-fuse." At this he dropped his incredulous attitude and exclaimed, "*Donner-Wetter!* My identical shell! Have you got it with you?" "No, I left it in England when I went home last Christmas," I replied. He was sorry, because, as he said, he would have given a good deal for it, as the *first shell* which struck Strasburg Cathedral. He continued, "The best use you can make of it is to let all your friends at home see it, and tell them what a triumph it is of the accuracy of German Artillery practice." What is remarkable in this narrative is that I should, months afterwards, unexpectedly meet with such a coincidence, as proved the accuracy of the statements of the bookseller in Strasburg.

Trêves on the Moselle.

In carrying out our commission to relieve distress wherever we found it, irrespective of religion or nationality, I undertook to go by Saarbruck, down the Saar valley, in which we had been told that distress existed owing to the passage of immense bodies of troops. With a young German as companion, I visited many of the villages in that valley, and found that, though there had been distress, it was of a temporary character, relief having been sent to them from Germany. I proceeded, however, by the railway down the Moselle, as far as the city of Trêves. At the railway station there, I witnessed, one Sunday, another phase of the results of war. Train loads of French prisoners were arriving during the whole day, in open trucks exposed to the weather. As the railway then terminated at Trêves, these prisoners, or as many of them as were able to march, were sent forward on foot to different fortresses in Germany. It was an intensely busy scene at the railway station. Many of the respectable inhabitants of Trêves were occupied the whole day in administering bread and meat and warmed wine to the hungry French soldiers, in literal fulfilment of the Scriptural injunction, "If thine enemy hunger, feed him, if he thirst, give him drink." Proceeding into the station-yard, I witnessed the disembarking of the men out of the railway trucks. Many of them were suffering very severely from dysentery, others from various chest diseases; the weather had become intensely cold, and they had been exposed many hours to its severity. Some of them were utterly helpless, and were being lifted out over the sides of the trucks, in the strong arms of the German Landwehr guard, into the charge of their comrades below, and were thus carried, in a helpless condition, into the station, where the Good Samaritans of Trêves were attending to their necessities. My companion and I joined in the work of distribution, in the course of which I had several times during the afternoon offered food and warmed wine to a young Frenchman, belonging, as I recognised by his uniform, to the Alsatian dragoons. He was extremely ill, and was seated in an armchair. Thinking he refused refreshment from the hands of Germans because they were the enemies of his nation, I pressed him to take it from me, as an Englishman who loved his people, and had been engaged in relieving the distress in and around Metz. All my persuasion, however, availed nothing. He steadfastly refused to partake of food or drink. Later on in the day, making one last effort to relieve him, I put my hand under his head and gently raised it, begging him to take a sip of the warmed wine. With one last supreme effort, he opened his eyes and looked at me wildly, and exclaimed, "*Mon Dieu*, let me alone to die!" The truth now flashed upon me. I was in the presence of death. His eyes were glazing over, and in a few minutes his spirit had departed. I felt utterly overcome, the piercing glance of his dying eyes going like a dagger to my heart. Outside, at the door, was a cavalry guard of young "one-year volunteers," ready to escort the prisoners on their journey into captivity in Germany. These young men, not having yet been engaged in the war, were dressed in new uniforms, and mounted on excellent horses. As I looked at them and conversed with one with whom I had a little acquaintance, I could but mentally contrast these volunteer warriors, in all the vigour of young manhood, with the poor fellow inside the station, whose tragic death I had just witnessed. The outside company I could only compare to the raw material, and the war-worn youth inside, of about the same age, to the *finished article; finished* indeed by the cruel exigencies of war. This individual case needs but to be multiplied by tens of thousands in order to help us to realise one of the worst phases of the terrible realities of war.

Whilst still under the painful emotions which all the tragic scenes of the day had made almost overwhelming, especially the last touching incident of the young dragoon's death in the railway station, whose dying glance I could not forget, I made my way alone down to the river side, and wandered along the wooded banks of the Moselle, beautiful even then, in mid-winter.

> "A gold and purple sunset
> Flowed down the broad Moselle,
> O'er hills of vine and meadow lands,
> The peace of twilight fell."
>
> —WHITTIER.

With a sad and heavy heart, I pondered over the scenes among which we had been living and working; the burnt and ruined villages, the famine-stricken people, the diseased and wounded men, the tears of the widows, the cries of the orphans for bread, as, pinched and blue with cold and hunger, they had stretched out their hands imploringly toward us. Recollections like these came with overpowering effect upon me in this absolutely quiet solitude, far from the haunts of men, whilst my thoughts naturally reverted to my native land and to the dearest spot it contained—my own home, far away among the Cleveland Hills of Yorkshire, where my wife and children were dwelling in comfort and safety. The thought that our island-home was mercifully preserved from the foot of the invader and from all war's desolations came like a benediction over me, in this "peace of twilight," and my soul was uplifted in thankfulness to God for the unspeakable blessing of His protecting love and care extended to my native land.

Never did the words of the prophet Isaiah appeal more forcibly to me, "Thou wilt keep him in perfect peace whose mind is stayed on Thee, because he trusteth in Thee."

In connection with these thoughts arose the query, what of the gorgeous ceremonials and grand "Te Deums" that had been celebrated with imposing pomp and magnificence in the cathedral of Notre Dâme in Paris, over the victory of Saarbruck? And what, on the other hand, of the effusively pious telegrams of the German Emperor despatched to Berlin, where, with all the sanctions of religion, to the accompaniment of loud huzzas and salvoes of artillery, the Great Being, whom they styled the "God of Battles" (a god unknown indeed to New Testament Christianity), was loudly extolled for the "crowning mercy" of Metz? Oh, the bitter irony of all this! When, at this very moment, tens of thousands of men, in the prime of their young manhood, were lying prostrate with disease, many were lingering in agony from wounds, whilst the whole war-ruined country around was ringing with the lamentations of innocent sufferers in their devastated homes. Was it for ruthless deeds like these, in which they had been the principal actors, that men, professing to be followers of the "Prince of Peace," were singing these loud pæans of triumph in His name?

Oh, Christianity! what glaring inconsistencies are perpetrated in thy name! How is it possible to believe in the reality and genuineness of such conventional praises, when *both parties alike* are claiming victory over the other, as a proof of the Almighty being on their side? It may well be asked: Can this indeed be the religion of Christ, or is it not downright presumption, closely akin to blasphemy?

As my thoughts turned towards Him who said He came not to destroy men's lives, but to save them, the words of a heathen poet came appropriately to mind, "Unhallowed is the sound of loud thanksgiving over slaughtered men!"

Military Hospitals.

Being upon German territory, I took a short trip down the Rhine to Dusseldorf. In our journeys around Metz we had found great need of accurate maps, which were not to be obtained anywhere within the limits of Alsace-Lorraine. The most reliable maps of France were those published by the German Staff, with which all their officers with the army in France were supplied, so that they were able to find their way about the country without difficulty, and, if occasion required, could immediately check any local guide who attempted to mislead them. Of these excellent maps I obtained a supply at Dusseldorf.

Another object I had in view was to visit the large well-organized hospitals at Dusseldorf, in which many of the sick and wounded from the field of Gravelotte and the siege of Metz were being admirably cared for. My credentials were a sufficient introduction, and I was courteously invited and conducted through all the wards. It would serve no purpose to dilate here upon the great variety or the terrible nature of the wounds or mutilations received on the battlefield—many of these were such as would render life a burden to the sufferer until its final close. Two cases in particular have impressed themselves indelibly on my memory. They will suffice to illustrate the strange unlooked-for variety of battle-wounds.

Let the reader take his stand by my side at the foot of a neat iron bedstead, in a large well-ventilated ward, filled with similar beds. Just before our earnest gaze is the handsome face, of extraordinary pallor, of a youth of some twenty summers, whose wound, a rifle-shot through the lungs, is evidently proving mortal. Paroxysms of vomiting are forcing his life-blood to well-out freely through his lips. He lies prostrated and apparently unconscious through exhaustion. Suspended over his head hangs the "Iron Cross"—the much coveted distinction won through personal valour. Alas! what avails now the prized decoration, when life itself is fast ebbing away, in the near presence of death—the power before which all earthly distinctions fade! There is a touching pathos over the whole scene, that fills one's heart with a mournful and sympathetic interest, and renders it difficult to tear oneself away before the fast approaching end arrives.

The other case alluded to was of a wholly different kind. In another ward I came upon a man standing in a partially stripped condition, having some dressing applied by the surgeon to his side, which I noticed was black from the shoulder downwards. On my inquiring about his wounds, the surgeon said, "He has not a scratch upon him, but the man has suffered intense pain in the system of nerves all down his side. This discolouration that you see is from the effect of the concussion or windage of a cannon-ball, which passed close to his body without touching him, and yet, strange as it may seem, was the cause of prolonged suffering." I had heard before this of hair-breadth escapes,—here was one indeed in a very literal sense!

When leaving the hospital, I was conducted to an outer court, where a large wooden annexe for the accommodation of further patients had been erected. It was a roomy, airy structure, the temperature being little, if at all, above that of the outer atmosphere, in the cold winter of 1870-71. Some of the patients were actually shivering in their beds, although their warm top-coats were laid over the bedclothes. I remarked to the surgeon, that the extreme cold must be very prejudicial to the sufferers. He answered, "You will be surprised when I say, that the proportion of good recoveries is considerably larger in this cold, airy annexe, than it is in the wards of the adjoining hospital." How far the theory of bacteria and microbes was understood in surgical operations in 1871, I am unable to say, but undoubtedly the comparative immunity from these—the bane of all military hospitals at that time—had much to do with the quicker recovery of the patients in the amply-ventilated annexe.

Returning to Metz, I reported my efforts to relieve distress, whether found in France or Germany. In reality, though there had been suffering, owing to the passage of immense armies through the Saar valley, especially in the district of the Eiffel, our help and pecuniary assistance were everywhere declined, on the ground that Germany was supplying the need. Thenceforth, accordingly, our relief was entirely confined to

French territory. As several other "Friends" had now arrived to join our little party at Metz, lodgings were secured for the company in the Rue Poncelet, and a large warehouse adjoining was hired as a store for potatoes and provisions. The distressed villages, within a radius of ten miles, were arranged in groups, from which lists of all really destitute cases were sent in to our store in Metz from the Mayors, or other responsible persons. A regular system of weekly supplies of food and clothing—blankets, potatoes, flour, bacon, bread, etc.—was organised throughout the whole district. About sixty villages were thus relieved, every precaution being taken to administer the relief wisely.

Leaving our friends to continue this beneficent work, we who came first into the field, that is Dr. Spence Watson, T. Whitwell and myself, prepared to return to England for Christmas, 1870, leaving poor H. J. Allen under good care, to be nursed through his attack of smallpox. The means taken happily proved effectual in his case, and he made a good recovery.

Speaking of this period, John Bellows says, in his "Track of the War around Metz," that "out of twelve of our number who were at Metz when I arrived, or who came while I was there, eight have been ill, five of them with smallpox, and one, Miss Allen [as before mentioned] died of this dreaded malady."

These facts speak for themselves of the risks which were incurred by our little company.

CHAPTER X.

T. WHITWELL ARRESTED — RETURN TO ENGLAND— MEETINGS IN AID OF THE RELIEF FUND — BACK TO METZ — COUNT VON DONNERSMARCK, PREFECT OF METZ—"SAFE CONDUCT"—FIVE DAYS IN A HORSE-BOX— VERSAILLES — PRINCE BISMARCK — COMMUNARDS IN PARIS—DR. NORCOTT AND THE COMMUNE.

SHORTLY after I had left Metz by rail for England, Thomas Whitwell drove, in a hired trap, to Thionville, in order to take train there, intending to reach Kendal in time to join the family gathering on New Year's Eve. At Thionville, a box of relics which he was bringing home unfortunately caused him trouble. The Prussian sentries demanded what the box contained. "Only old relics," replied Whitwell. "Have you any chassepots?" "Yes," was the straightforward answer; whereupon the box was forced opened, and the chassepots produced. "You will have to see the Lieutenant about these," said the guards, "as we have strict orders to intercept all French firearms." The Lieutenant was called, and notwithstanding all Whitwell's pleadings of ignorance of the order, notwithstanding the protecting document which was given him by Count Donnersmarck, the Prefect of Metz, and in spite of the fact that these were merely *relics*, he was peremptorily ordered to return in his conveyance, in charge of an armed officer, to be incarcerated in the military prison of Metz.

On reaching Metz, Whitwell, through his tact and courtesy, succeeded in persuading his guard to drive first to the Prefecture, to the great astonishment of his friend Count Donnersmarck. Having told his story, in the expectation that the Count would at once order him to be set at liberty, he was rather downcast, when the latter, after a hearty laugh at the ridiculousness of the situation, exclaimed, "Dat is goot, dat is rich, you a *Quaker* sent to prison for bearing arms!" and then seriously informed Whitwell that it was not in his power, as the *Civil* Governor, to give him his freedom, or he would willingly do so. "You are not my prisoner," he said, "but the prisoner of the military authorities, and only the Military Governor, General Von Löwenfels, can give you your liberty."

Thanking Count Donnersmarck for his courtesy, Whitwell returned in no very cheerful mood to his guard, and was driven direct to the gloomy military prison, where an officer's cell and bed were his fate for that winter night.

After being immured there for about twenty-four hours in solitary confinement, John Bellows, having heard of his imprisonment, at once obtained leave to visit him, and hastened to the prison. "Oh, William," said Whitwell to me some time after, when relating this story, "dear John Bellows' face shone like the face of an angel; I was delighted to see his pleasant smile as he entered my cell." Through John Bellows' efforts, Whitwell was promptly brought before the General and his officers, who made a show of sternness, though probably enjoying the joke, and then set him free. Whitwell then asked, "I suppose I may now take away the box of relics?" "Certainly not," sternly retorted the Military Governor, "you know it is against military orders."

Leaving his box in their custody, Whitwell lost no time in starting again homeward by rail, and by dint of travelling night and day, succeeded in reaching his father's house near Kendal in time to join the family circle on that eventful New Year's Eve.

Home Again.

Thankful to reach England once more, safe and sound, we all stood greatly in need of a period of rest and relaxation, and our business affairs also needed our close personal attention. But soon after the Christmas and New Year's season was well over, under pressure from the Central Committee in London, funds being urgently needed to carry on the work of relief in France, Dr. R. Spence Watson, Whitwell, and I, undertook to visit about twenty-five of the principal centres throughout Great Britain, with a view to lecturing and obtaining more money. At a public meeting held in Devonshire House Meeting-house, London, presided over by the late John Hodgkin of Lewes, addresses were delivered by Dr. Spence Watson and myself. A description of the uncultivated condition of the arable land around Metz, through want of horses and implements, having been laid before the meeting, it was resolved, on the motion of the Chairman, to send out a steam plough, with complete cultivating apparatus. This was successfully carried out, somewhat later, under the charge of my late friend John Dunning, C.E., of Middlesbrough-on-Tees, and notwithstanding the prejudices which had to be encountered, and many groundless fears, lest the plough-shares should strike unexploded shells embedded in the ground on the battlefields, and so cause much damage, good work was done, and a large area brought into cultivation, which would otherwise have been wholly unproductive; thus the season for sowing was saved. Ultimately the steam ploughing apparatus was handed over, after the war, for a very moderate figure to the "*Comice Agricole*" of Metz, to be employed for the future benefit of French agriculture.

Shortly after our return, at a large meeting held in Leeds, addressed by Dr. Spence Watson and myself, the sum of more than £500 was raised in the room for the relief fund.

In the city of Edinburgh we had the advantage

of being supported, in a large meeting presided over by the Lord Provost, by the late eminent Dr. Guthrie, whose eloquent appeals proved an effective help. But perhaps the most influential gathering before which we appeared, was that held in the Mansion House, in the city of London, presided over by the Lord Mayor. This meeting, held in the daytime, was largely composed of city merchants, to whom Thomas Whitwell and I briefly stated the case for relief. This was the occasion referred to elsewhere, when the late Cardinal Manning gave efficient help in advocating our cause.

Pioneering in Central France.

The funds at the disposal of our Central Committee being materially increased, it was resolved to recommence the work of distribution of seed corn and potatoes, on a larger scale, in the distressed districts of France. The work had been carried on to some extent by our Commissioners in the Eastern Departments, but as in the vicissitudes of war there had been much fighting, and marching and counter-marching of armies in the central and western Departments, where consequently heavy losses and damage had been sustained by the farmers and the peasant proprietors, it was resolved, after a preliminary investigation had been made, to organise the distribution of seed corn throughout the war-ruined district, from the city of Orleans westward.

Whitwell and myself were again pressed into this pioneer service of making the needful arrangements with the authorities, and of organising committees of distribution in the chief centres of destitution.

For this purpose, we first proceeded to Brussels in search of suitable saddle horses, which were scarcely to be obtained at any price in France. Assisted by the late W. Sheldon, then director of the Brussels tramways, we soon obtained two serviceable looking animals—an old English weight-carrying hunter for Whitwell, and an active Belgian trotter for myself. This beast carried me well in all respects but one, and that a most serious one, in our long ride of about one thousand miles up and down rural France. He had the *one* vice which I dreaded most in a horse, he was a *rearer*, and twice I narrowly escaped being crushed by his falling over with me.

On our return to Metz, Whitwell and I found our colleagues in the work of relief had established themselves in very superior quarters, the house being, in fact, one of the best in the city. The proprietor, M. Simon, a Jew banker, found it to his advantage to have his grand apartments occupied by the Friends' "War Victims Commissioners," in order to avoid having German officers quartered on him. At first I felt almost ashamed to mount the grand white marble staircase, and to tread the highly polished parquetry floors, booted and spurred, and accoutred in stout riding costume as I was.

Interesting as this mansion was, and in every respect superior to our lodgings in the Rue Poncelet, what most interested me there was the lady of the house herself. Mme. Simon showed by her conversation that she was eminently gifted, highly intelligent and cultured. After we had become a little acquainted, there was nothing she enjoyed more than to get me into a corner of the drawing-room, and in her exquisite French, try to "draw me out" on some of the problems of the day, especially on the invasion of her country by the Germans. On this subject she betrayed intensely bitter feelings. When I mildly asked her to moderate her vehemence, and hinted that the war had up to the present been conducted by the Germans with more consideration for both persons and property than any previous war of which I had heard or read, she retorted sharply, "But what about the robbery of our country?"—referring to the annexation of Alsace. Then, in a voice vehement with passion, and which still seems to ring in my ears, she continued, "*Mais, monsieur, nous sommes Français et nous* MOURRONS *avant d'etre Prussiens!*" (But Sir, we are French, and we will *die* rather than become Prussians.) "These are merely your own sentiments, Madame?" I queried. "They are the sentiments of every one of my country-women throughout Alsace and Lorraine," she rejoined. This incident was one of several adduced by me to Count Bismarck Von

Bohlen, in proof of the intense feeling of the people against annexation to Germany, during our interview with him at Strasburg.

Whitwell and I did not stay in Metz longer than was needful to get our authorisations put in proper order, and to make the necessary preparations for a long campaign on horseback, in following up the contending armies through Central France, where the conflict under Prince Frederick Charles and General Chanzy was still raging. We expected to be absent for a month or more, and to be very much cut off from communication with our friends, because the railways and telegraphs were either suspended altogether or monopolized by the Germans.

By far the most useful document that was furnished to us by the German authorities, during our stay in the neighbourhood of Metz, was the "safe conduct" handed to us at the request of his uncle, Count Bismarck Von Bohlen, by Count Henckel Von Donnersmarck, the Prefect of Metz. The original document, which is in my possession, is written in German, and bears the splendid signature of Count Von Donnersmarck. The translation is as follows :—

Metz, 1st Nov. 1870.

"Messrs. William Jones and Henry John Allen are commissioned in the name of an English Benevolent Society, to bring charitable gifts into the territories visited by the war, and principally in the neighbourhood of Metz. As they have duly legitimised themselves through the certificate of the North German Embassy in London, dated 21st of October, I request all the military and civil officials, and especially the railway officials, to allow these gentlemen to pass freely, and to the best of their power to protect and assist them.

"(Signed) THE PREFECT,

"HENCKEL VON DONNERSMARCK."

TO VERSAILLES IN A HORSE-BOX.

At a later date, namely, on February 16th, 1871, the document was endorsed by the orders of the Commander of the 8th Army Corps, granting to Thomas Whitwell and myself a Government van and free passage over the railway to Versailles, with all necessaries for ourselves and two horses. In this van we were shut up with our horses for five days and five nights, in extremely hard wintry weather. Unfortunately, the horses had been placed in the van transversely, instead of longitudinally; consequently at every rough shock from shunting, which happened at all hours of the day and night, we were kept in constant fear of the horses being knocked off their feet, and falling upon us as we lay on the straw beside them.

In the daytime I made it my duty to forage for provisions in the neighbouring villages, or, failing this, to purchase from the German soldiers (who had generally ample rations served out to them) excellent "*Erbswurst*" (peas sausage) and other comestibles. My friend Whitwell had brought with him a Russian cooking-furnace belonging to his canoe, and having had much experience in the culinary art, produced not only tea and coffee, but savoury soups and sundry other dishes. These, for safety, were usually cooked within a large tin bucket, so as to avoid setting the straw on fire in case the furnace were upset, when our van was shunted.

One stormy snowy winter's night, as our van stood in a siding, the sliding door was roughly pushed open, and two German soldiers, with their hoods over their heads and thickly covered with snow, attracted no doubt by the light inside, attempted to enter. We at once showed them our papers, and told them we were classed as "*zwei offiziere*" (two officers). Generally this was quite sufficient to send away intruders, as German soldiers are extremely respectful to their officers; but on this occasion, whether it was the storminess of the weather that impelled them, or whether they did not hear our remonstrances, pushing their bayonets in front of them into the horse-box, and making us step back to a respectful distance, they clambered in, and after shaking off the snow, planted themselves on the straw beside us. We jocosely bargained with them to turn the bayonets round, and "hold the fort for us"; otherwise it was almost a question of life and death, unless we could keep the van to ourselves. Whitwell at once set to work to make them each a canful of strong coffee, and after they had consumed it, we found we had a couple of very pleasant companions—two of the "Landwehr"—old soldiers, who had been through the Austrian campaign.

Whitwell engaged in conversation with one of them, who had asked him for a copy of the "British Workman," in German. He found him instead, a copy of the Gospel of Luke, and commending it to him with his winning smile, said, "Here's something '*auf ewigkeit*'" (for eternity). The man's eyes glistened, as he found it was a copy of the Gospel, and repeating, "*Ach! so, auf ewigkeit*," lay down on the straw to read it. Meanwhile, the other soldier fell to my lot. Producing a pocket-book containing a number of photographs of his wife and children, he dwelt upon each one very lovingly, and when he came to the last of all, he remarked, "This little one I shall never see again. She has died while I have been here in the war." And tears followed each other down the rough bearded face.

I said to him, "I see, my friend, you have a father's heart. Would you not rather be at home with your family, than be engaged in slaughtering your fellow-men here?" "*Ach! Gott!* Don't speak of it. I pray God every day of my life that we may have even an armistice, so that I could go home and kiss my wife and children." These noble fellows were but specimens of hundreds and thousands of their class to be found in the ranks of the German army, who, whilst doing what they believed to be their duty, manfully, in defence of their country, had an intense yearning in their hearts for the conclusion of the war, in order that they might return to their daily occupations and their own peaceful homes.

After the fifth night of our tarriance in the horse-box, we arrived, past midnight, at Versailles; and, utterly wearied of our horse-box life, I resolved, if possible, to obtain a civilised bed to sleep in that night. However pleasant a companion a horse may be, you find out, after being shut up with him for five nights, that he is anything but a pleasant bedfellow, and you sigh longingly for clean sheets! Leaving Whitwell in charge of the horse-box, I set off immediately into the town, to find out the Quartermaster-General of the German army. From him, or one of his assistants, who had already gone to bed, but obligingly rose to give me what I wanted, I obtained orders for quarters for us both that night, and set off back with glee to my comrade in the horse-box.

On reaching the station, however, I found all in darkness, and searched in vain for the train. After stumbling about the line in the dark night for some time, I found a railway employé, who told me the train had gone round to the other bank of the river, which he said was across the town, a long distance off. Hiring this man as my guide, we proceeded to the other station, and, after a long tramp through the darkness, entered the yard. Here a new difficulty presented itself, the station being strongly guarded by Bavarian troops. As soon as we came into sight they shouted to us for the *password.* There being no guard at the station at which our train had arrived, I had omitted to ask the Quartermaster for the password, so after trying in vain one or two passwords that I had known at Metz, such as "*Ein Guter Freund*," the Bavarian sentries shouted furiously, "*Nix, Nix*," (No, No), "*Halt, da!*" Hereupon, my French guide abandoned me to my fate, and I heard his wooden sabots clattering on the pavement for a long distance away. I held out my papers and called to the sentry that I had just got orders from the Quartermaster-General for quarters that night, and begged him to look at my papers, advancing towards him all the time. Perceiving my intentions, he levelled his rifle menacingly, and I heard the ominous click of the trigger of his needle-gun, as he shouted, "Halt! Another step and I fire." As his rifle now covered me, I was brought up sharp within a few feet of him, and dared not advance an inch. Being terribly exhausted with fatigue and want of food, I was ready to drop into the snow at my feet, and began to wonder how long he could hold his heavy piece in that horizontal position.

After what seemed to me an age, he slowly raised his weapon and uncovered me. In a moment I made a rush, and was at his feet, throwing myself down on some corn sacks behind him. As he did not offer to disturb me, being at the last extremity of fatigue, I dropped asleep almost as soon as my head was laid on the sacks.

How long I slept I do not know, but was with difficulty awakened by a very rough shaking from somebody who stood over me. As soon as I could collect my senses, I found it was my friend Whitwell. Wearied at last with waiting for me in the horse-box, he locked it up, and determined to go in search of me, and found me as described, sound asleep under the verandah of the station upon the corn sacks, on an extremely cold, snowy night.

The Bavarian sentry, when asked how it was that he said nothing to my friend about a password, when he had been almost on the point of running his bayonet into me because I did not know it, replied, "It does not need a password to *come out* of a place. It is when you go in *from outside* that a password is required. You did wrong to come in, *and you know it very well.*" *So I did*, and concluded the less said the better.

We then set off into the town of Versailles, in the early hours of the morning, in search of the quarters mentioned upon my order. It was not easy to find the place in some obscure street, when there was no one, not even a policeman, visible in the city. At last we found the *cabaret*, or public-house, we were in search of; and after thundering at the door, a man came cautiously, opening it an inch or two, and asked our business. The moment, however, he heard us talk of *quarters*, he attempted to close the door in our faces; but I had taken the precaution to slip the toe of my heavy riding boot into the crevice, so that he could not shut us out. After a short parley, in which we told him we were not Germans, but Englishmen, engaged in relieving the distress of his countrymen, and were willing to pay for the accommodation, he opened the door and allowed us to sit in his warm kitchen, and immediately proceeded to find us some food, of which we stood very greatly in need. He told us that his house was crammed with German soldiers, and he had not a room to put us into. We replied we would stay contentedly where we were, in his comfortable *salon*.

Whilst we were having our supper he returned with a cheerful face and said, "Gentlemen, I have managed to find you a bed." Following him upstairs we found in a small room a bed, still warm, out of which, I have no doubt, he and his wife had just risen, to make room for us. Here we slept the sleep of the wearied, until late in the afternoon.

When we arose, we went in search of two of our own countrymen, who were in favour with the German Headquarters' Staff, namely Lord Odo Russell and Captain Hosier. By their kind help we obtained suitable accommodation for ourselves and our two horses, which would otherwise have been almost impossible in Versailles, crowded as it was with German cavalry. They also assisted us in obtaining proper authorizations for our further journeys in the parts of Central France occupied by the German armies.

Having, through the good offices of our countrymen, secured all we required, we refrained from presenting the introduction given us by Count Bismarck to his cousin, the Imperial Chancellor, whose whole time, we were well aware, was very closely occupied with high affairs of State. On more than one occasion, however, I had the pleasure of seeing both Bismarck and the Emperor William I. in front of the Prefecture of Versailles,—a plain building which the Emperor had selected for his headquarters.

Here, day by day, after breakfast, one might see a horse in charge of an orderly promenaded in front of the Prefecture, and after a time the tall and massive figure of the Emperor would appear, and, though at the age of seventy-four, he would spring into the saddle with the agility of a man of half his years; then, without ceremony, he would simply ride away on his war charger, an erect, stalwart, soldierly figure, to visit the besieging army.

Some historic associations connected with the antecedents of the Emperor William I., gave a special interest to these glances at his person before the Prefecture. I pictured him mentally, as he appeared before the humble cottage which was his headquarters at Donchéry, on the Belgian frontier, where, after the victory of Sedan, the fugitive French Emperor, Napoleon III., broken down in health, and disheartened by defeat, presented himself before his conqueror, handing him his sword in token of surrender. King William received the dejected fugitive with chivalrous courtesy and kindness, returned his sword, and assigned him one of his own palaces, Wilhelmshöhe, in Hesse Cassel, as his future residence.

Certain events in King William's boyhood must have left a deep impression upon his mind. At the age of fourteen he had been summoned to the bedside of his mother, Queen Louise of Prussia, who was dying of a broken heart owing to the miseries brought upon her unhappy country by the harsh treatment experienced from their conqueror, Napoleon Bonaparte. Terrible as the sufferings of her people were, they were much aggravated by his unfeeling and cruel behaviour towards the Queen herself. William was then an intelligent boy, quite capable of understanding the calamity, in all its bitterness, which was thus inflicted upon his fatherland, his family, and his own beloved mother.

How wonderful are the unforeseen transformations which time often brings round! Just sixty years later, how marvellous the change of scene which took place in the obscure village of Donchéry! Another Bonaparte, himself an Emperor, appears as a suppliant for mercy at the feet of William, elevated as he was then to the dignity of King and Conqueror. How much nobler, however, and more generous, was his attitude towards the avowed foe of his country, whose future destiny was now completely in his hands.

Whilst very far from admiring all the acts of William I., I have always regarded this special incident in his career as a proof of a magnanimous and forgiving disposition.

PRINCE BISMARCK.

Bismarck was unquestionably a great man, perhaps the greatest of all of his *special type* of statesmen, for centuries past. Differing totally from our own eminent statesman, Mr. Gladstone, who believed in the supremacy of moral ideas, in bringing about the permanent profit of mankind, Bismarck restored brute force to the position of prime factor in the policy of nations, and cynically avowed his reliance upon *blood and iron*, as the means of establishing national rights.

One result of his life is the present heavily armed condition of Europe. This curse of militarism, which is all but certain to bring about another great and disastrous war, is directly due to Bismarck's powerful influence upon the political ideas of the Continent of Europe. How far his marvellous career, and the triumph which he achieved as the creator of the modern German Empire, brought real happiness into his own life, may be gathered from the candid statements recorded by his secretary, Dr. Moritz Busch, the Boswell of Bismarck's "table talk." He tells us that the Prince sometimes in a low and moody state of mind would soliloquise aloud in this tragic strain: "Nobody loves me for what I have done. I have never made anybody happy, not myself, nor my family, nor anyone else. But how many have I made unhappy? Had it not been for me, three great wars would not have been fought; eighty-thousand men would not have perished; parents, brothers, sisters and widows would not have been bereaved and plunged into mourning. That matter, however, I have settled with my Maker. But I have had little or no joy from all my achievements; nothing but vexation, care and trouble."

Prince Bismarck seems to have realised to the full, the truth of the words of the "Preacher,"—"All is vanity and vexation of spirit." A man may achieve his highest life-purpose in this world, and yet find it bring "no happiness, neither to himself nor to anybody else." Does not the real secret of the matter lie in that terrible retrospect of the "eighty thousand lives," which "but for me" (to use his own words) "would not have perished," and of the multitudes of "parents, brothers, sisters, and widows, bereaved and plunged into mourning." Hardened, indeed, would be that soul that could be wholly unmoved at the thought of being the acknowledged cause of such wide-spread and lasting sorrow and suffering. It can hardly be doubted that Prince Bismarck felt the grievous weight of this burden when he uttered the sad and mournful note which Dr. Busch calls "moody."

Paris in the Hands of the Communards.

During our tarriance at Versailles, Whitwell and I entered Paris on horseback, having no knowledge that the city was then entirely in the hands of the Communards. Approaching Paris on the south side, we were allowed to pass without question through the gates, and proceeded a considerable distance towards the heart of the city, neither of us being familiar with this particular quarter. We were greatly struck, however, with the number of men in blouses and military caps, going about the streets with rifles in their hands; and the further we advanced the more numerous they became. Some of the streets were lined with their rifles, piled as far as we could see, and the men were standing in groups, evidently sharply criticising every passer-by. I overheard one group say that we were a species of "Uhlan," and mentioned this to my companion. He at once reined up his horse and said, "There's something wrong here. It is not safe to proceed. I don't like the look of these men, they may take a pot-shot at us." I then said, "If you will take charge of my horse I will dismount and speak to them." Approaching a group of a hundred or more, I saluted with my politest French bow, and asked them kindly to tell me whether we were on the right road for the Hotel de Ville, where we had understood George Moore of London had been distributing provisions after the siege. None of them deigned to give me an answer.

As they looked suspiciously and scowlingly at me, one of them, induced by curiosity, came to examine our badge—a star—upon my left arm. I asked him if he knew the meaning of the star. He gave a significant French shrug, muttering that he knew nothing about it. This gave me the opening I wished for, to tell them something of the work in which my comrade and I had been occupied, in distributing relief, and making arrangements for the distribution of seed corn among the distressed farmers of France. As soon as I mentioned the word Metz some of them eagerly shouted, "Were you in Metz?" I replied that I had entered in with the German army under Prince Frederick Charles on the day of surrender. Their next question was, "And did you see Bazaine?" I said, "Yes, later on, I saw him going under an escort of German soldiers to the railway station, some of the populace of Metz shouting and hooting him on the way." At this point their excitement became intense, and they all shouted, "*A bas Bazaine; traitre! cochon!* (Down with Bazaine; traitor! hog!)

When their excitement had subsided, their suspicions being allayed and all appearing to be friendly, I again took off my cap, bowed politely, and bade them good morning, as we were going on to the Hotel de Ville. At this point, one of them threw up his "*casquette*," shouting, "*Vive les Anglais!*" I asked the man who had been examining the star on my "*brassard*" to walk with me to my horse. On the way down I said to him, "Why did you look so suspiciously at us as we rode quietly past?" His answer was, "*Ma foi, monsieur*, we didn't know what to make of you—we should never have challenged you if you hadn't been armed."—

"Armed!" I exclaimed with genuine surprise, "Where did you see any arms?" (We were, it is true, a sort of nondescript cavalier, equipped in short riding jackets and boots, with a broad strap and haversack over the shoulder; fur caps, and our star both on the arm and on the front of the cap.) Again he said, "*Ma foi, monsieur*, if you had no pistols what were the holsters on your saddles for?" Here I may explain that we rode on two English cavalry-officer's saddles, which Dr. Spence Watson and Whitwell had brought with them from England, as being superior to any they could get in France, the saddles of course being provided with holsters, which up to that moment I had never considered dangerous. "Oh, it was the holsters that made you think us armed," I exclaimed. "Come along, and you shall see my arms." When we reached the horse, I asked him to undo the straps of the holsters, in one of which he found a little horse corn, and in the other a few religious tracts, which had become tattered and ragged during our long ride. These he held up between his finger and thumb, and with a scornful smile called to his companions, "*Voila, ses pistolets!*" ("These are his pistols!")

I thought we had come off well from a group of such forbidding looking characters, and said to myself, in the words of good old Isaac Watts, "Here's a lesson for me." In future avoid all *appearance* of evil; not only do not carry arms, but avoid even holsters designed for pistols.

After a short time in the city, we learned that the Communards had mercilessly shot two Generals of the regular army, had taken captive the Archbishop of Paris (who was afterwards shot in the prison yard), and were also laying hands on every available man, and compelling him to fight on the barricades.

DR. NORCOTT.

Whilst Whitwell and I were in Paris we made the acquaintance of Dr. Norcott, an Irish surgeon, who had settled in the city. He had previously rendered valuable help to a party of our "Friends" who had entered Paris immediately after the siege, bringing with them a large quantity of provisions for distribution among the famine-stricken population. This work went on until the outburst of the Commune, when the depôt was closed, and the "Friends" returned to England.

Norcott proved very useful to Whitwell and myself. Through his help we were able to obtain sundry articles, which, owing to the shops being generally closed, could not otherwise have been purchased.

He took such a fancy to our riding-costumes that he insisted on having us photographed in a group with himself. It was no easy matter to find a photographer, but through his local knowledge, he succeeded in finding an operator in a back street. Here the group which appears on opposite page was taken.

Dr. Norcott was an able man, with a very

NORCOTT, WHITWELL AND JONES.

captivating presence and genial disposition. He had succeeded in thoroughly ingratiating himself with the Chiefs of the Commune, and was so implicitly relied on by them, that they even entrusted him with authority to sign passes for persons who were granted the rare privilege of quitting Paris during the reign of the Commune. It was with a pass signed by Norcott that Professor Beljame was allowed to leave the city, carrying with him the precious manuscripts of that unique gem among dictionaries—"Bellows' Pocket French and English Dictionary." These manuscripts, which were under revision by Professor Beljame, had been shut up in Paris during the siege, causing my friend Bellows, who was then at Metz, much anxiety, during the bombardment of the city by the Germans. A shell had, in fact, burst not many metres from the place where they were kept. Professor Beljame's anxiety was naturally in the first place for his wife's safety. His next thought was the security of the manuscripts, which he now took to the centre of the city, *out of range*. Dr. Norcott's pass put an end to all further care with regard to these documents.

As none of the Chiefs of the Commune durst make their appearance at Versailles, they availed themselves of Dr. Norcott's services as an intermediary between themselves and the Government. Norcott gave to Whitwell and myself an interesting account of one of the most delicate of his missions to Versailles. It was to endeavour to induce President

Thiers to agree to an exchange of a leading Communard named Blanqui, for the Archbishop of Paris, Monseigneur Darboy, who had been captured and detained as hostage in the fortress of Mazas.

Norcott pleaded in vain for this exchange of prisoners. Thiers was obstinate, and when Norcott assured him that the life of the Archbishop was at stake, he shrugged his shoulders and cynically remarked, "The old fellow has lived long enough!"

When Norcott returned and reported the ill-success of his mission to the Chiefs of the Commune, they ordered the removal of the Archbishop from Mazas to the prison of La Roquette. What occurred there; somewhat later is a matter of history. The venerable prelate was brought out of his cell, and set against the wall in the courtyard of the prison, facing a firing-party of soldiers. Here the good man was seen calmly standing in the attitude of blessing his murderers, when the fatal shots were fired.

Dr. Norcott gladly availed himself of permission to visit the Archbishop during his incarceration, and did all that lay in his power to minister to his comfort, bringing him chicken and other suitable food, and endeavouring to cheer him in various ways, in his gloomy prison. But to save his life, alas! was beyond his power.

From his frequent association with the Communards, Dr. Norcott had many narrow escapes. Among other incidents, was that of his being the last person to ascend the Vendôme Column. Being told that it was to be overthrown, Norcott ventured once more to the top of the column, which dominated the whole city. Here he observed ropes attached to the summit, and hanging down into the hands of the crowd bent upon the work of destruction, in the square below. He hastened to descend the steps, but had not proceeded far down, before he felt the whole structure swaying and rocking from side to side in an alarming manner. Rushing with difficulty down the remaining steps, he just succeeded in clearing the foot of the column, when it fell with a tremendous crash, and was broken to pieces on the flags of the Place Vendôme.

The destruction of the Vendôme Column, which has since been restored, was akin to other acts of vandalism committed by the Communards while Paris was in their power. The burning of the Hotel de Ville, the Tuilleries, and many other noble buildings, seemed to have had no higher motive than a spiteful determination, on the part of these misguided men and women, from sheer wanton delight in causing ruin and desolation, to destroy whatever tended to ornament and beautify the city.

Among the many curious coincidences of my life, not the least interesting was that of meeting Dr. Norcott again in 1888, seventeen years after our intercourse in Paris, in the city of Melbourne, Australia, where he had gone to reside for the benefit of his health. Having observed my name upon a bill announcing my lecture, he found out where my wife and I were staying. Afterwards, at his hotel, he gave me his copy of the group of Whitwell, Norcott and Jones, my own having been spoiled by mildew.

It may readily be conceived that the renewal of intercourse with this bright-minded, genial Irish gentleman, was as agreeable as it was unexpected.

CHAPTER XI.

WESTWARD FROM ORLEANS—NIGHT RIDE OVER BATTLE-FIELD—EFFECTS OF THE CONSCRIPTION—DESTRUCTION OF CHATEAUDUN—THOMAS WHITWELL: A CHARACTER SKETCH—REARING HORSE: DANGEROUS ACCIDENT—SOME FRENCH SIGNATURES TO MY COMMISSION.

QUITTING Versailles, it took us three days to perform the journey of about 100 miles on horseback to Orleans. Before approaching this city, we lingered over several battlefields, where a short time previously the French General, Aurelles de Paladine, had kept at bay the Bavarian Army under Von der Tann. The French boast, with some degree of truth, that Von der Tann's army would have been annihilated had not the Duke of Mecklenburg arrived with 40,000 troops, liberated from the besieging army around Metz, after it had surrendered. Von der Tann, it was said, had fought fifteen battles, and his army corps of 35,000 had dwindled down to 5,000 "effective bayonets."

After gleaning all the information we could in Orleans, with regard to the districts that were most devastated by the marching and counter-marching of immense armies, we set off on horseback westward, in the track of the war, visiting *en route* Beaugency, Blois, Tours, Vendôme, Châteaudun, St. Calais, and Le Mans. About a thousand miles, as estimated by Whitwell, including the Metz district, were covered by us in traversing the intervening country in various directions, calling at almost every town and village, gleaning information and organising in each centre committees of distribution.

The information being telegraphed to London, the Home Committee sent out in swift steamers cargoes of seed-wheat, oats, and potatoes to Nantes and other ports of the Loire. These cargoes consisted of the best English spring-wheat that could be purchased in Mark Lane, and the finest Scotch oats that Leith market could supply.

How gladly these donations of seed corn were received and appreciated by French farmers everywhere, may be gathered from a speech made by the Minister of Agriculture at Havre, after the completion of our work of distribution.

His words, as then reported, were to this effect (I quote from memory): "No relief that could have been offered to our agriculturists could have been more acceptable. It was an entire change of seed, which every farmer could accept without loss of *amour propre*, and was a real agricultural boon to France. Our peasants will take their children to see the English wheat growing in their fields, and will tell them that the seeds sent in our hour of distress by our English friends, were not *bare grain*, they were the seeds of kindness, the seeds of goodwill, and they will produce a crop of international friendship and of gratitude towards the kind donors, so long as memory lasts." "Yes, gentlemen," the Minister continued, "these noble deeds of our English friends will do more to cement the good feeling and peaceable relations between our two countries, than if England had spent ten times the money upon her ironclad fleet."

I may here add that, later on in the year, an unexpected result from this seed-corn distribution came under my notice in Liverpool. A merchant told me in conversation that in the autumn of 1871 a late harvest in this country, and short supplies from America, were causing the price of bread stuffs to rise rapidly, when there arrived most opportunely cargo after cargo of wheat, in fine condition, from the Loire, this being the district of France to which our donations of seed had gone, so that the advance in price was checked, and millions of money were saved to the people of this country, in the price of food. The fulfilment of the words of our Lord in Luke vi. 38, "Give and it shall be given unto you, good measure, pressed down, shaken together, and running over, shall men give into your bosom," on an international scale like this, is surely worthy of note.

NIGHT RIDE ACROSS BATTLEFIELD.

Among the French signatures on my Credentials

is that of a gentleman for whom I had great esteem and regard, and who kept up a correspondence with me for some years. He says, "*Je signe avec le même sentiment de gratitude, pour les bienfaits que peuvent faire, la Societé à notre pays, Le Maire de Naveil, Wm. de Beaumetz.*" His son, M. Dujardin de Beaumetz, was at that time one of the most eminent physicians in Paris.

I stayed three days in the house of this gentleman at Naveil, near Vendôme, forming committees for the work of distribution over a wide area of country. At the close of the third day I was anxious to proceed further west, to the town of St. Calais, to keep an appointment with Whitwell. We had parted about two weeks before, he going north to Châteaudun, etc., while I turned south, in order the more rapidly to collect information as to the districts needing help.

M. de Beaumetz wished to keep me another night, saying he would gladly let me go in the morning, and did his best to dissuade me from undertaking the lonesome ride to St. Calais, a distance of about 25 miles, after dinner that winter's night. I insisted, however, on keeping my appointment with Whitwell, who I knew would be very anxious on my account, as the time appointed for our rendezvous had already expired.

M. de Beaumetz came with me to the stable-yard, and when my horse was brought out, ready saddled, about 9 p.m., he again earnestly begged me to stay the night, and said, what he did not like to tell me before, that in his capacity of Mayor of the district he was aware of certain bad characters who had picked up arms on the battle-field, and who frequented the road for the purpose of plunder, or even murder, being made desperate by the loss of their property through the war. I felt all the seriousness of this news, and queried with myself how far I was justified in undertaking so risky a journey alone at night, as my thoughts naturally turned towards my wife and children at home.

Requesting M. de Beaumetz to allow me a few minutes for reflection, I took a turn alone round his garden, by the light of a full moon, earnestly seeking for Divine guidance as to what course was the best for me to pursue. Presently I returned to M. de Beaumetz, saying in a cheerful manner, that I felt it right to go on, notwithstanding the information he had given me. He said he had done his best to restrain me from going into danger, he could do no more but pray that God would preserve me. I thanked him, bade him adieu, and mounted. My horse having had three days' rest, and good feeding in his stables, trotted merrily along the hard road on that brilliant moonlight night. The road was level and straight as though ruled across the country, for ten or fifteen kilometres at a stretch, the shadows of the poplar trees planted by the side of the road, crossing it at regular intervals. When I came to the battlefield of which he had spoken, I was naturally anxious about those dangerous characters he had warned me of, and kept looking over my horse's shoulder at the black shadows of the trees, lest there should be anyone hiding behind them; but for the whole length of the journey, which took me about five or six hours, I did not meet a single human being, or a living creature of any sort, and arrived at St. Calais in the early hours of the morning, March 7th, 1871.

Here a fresh difficulty was experienced. I had no idea where to find Whitwell, never having been in the town before. After riding about for some time, I fixed on what appeared to be the best hotel, rode into the stable-yard, and rang the bell. Presently an ostler appeared. I asked him if there were any English gentlemen in the house. He did not know. I then asked if there were any strange horse in the stable. He said, "Yes." I accompanied him into the stable, and by the light of his lantern saw the well-known form of the old English hunter which my friend Whitwell rode. This was enough for me. I entered the house and went to bed, requesting that Whitwell should be informed in the morning of my arrival. He came to my room after breakfast, while I was still asleep, and rousing me up, expressed his delight that I had turned up that morning. Had I failed to do so, he would have ordered his horse out, he said, the first thing after breakfast, and started off in search of me, fearing that something serious had happened to me by the way.

DISTRICT ROUND ORLEANS.

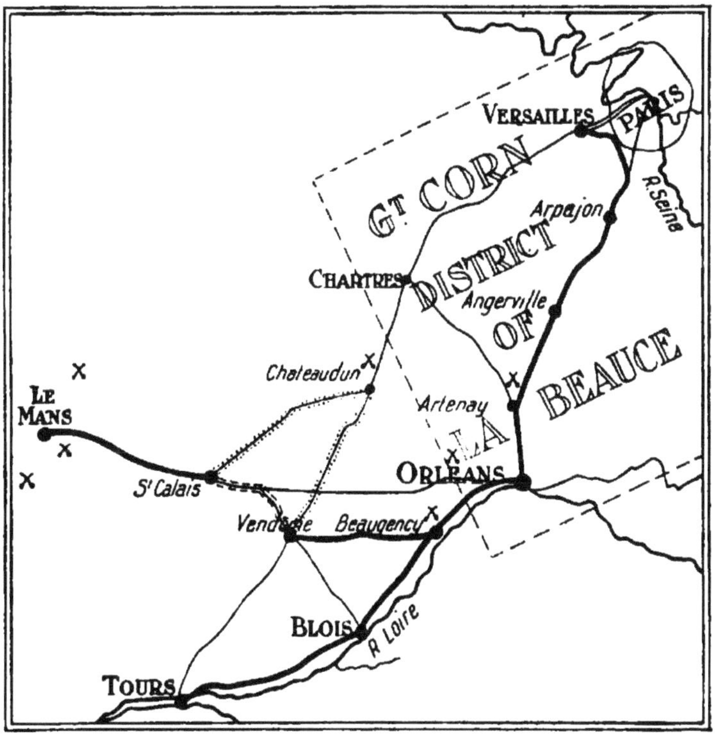

PART OF COUNTRY TRAVERSED BY T. WHITWELL & W. JONES.

Route
by T. Whitwell
by W. Jones

How glad I felt that I had followed the impression so clearly made on my mind, that, as I had always experienced protection so far during the war, it would be wrong for me to doubt that the same providential care would accompany me during the lonesome night journey through the supposed dangers of the road to St. Calais. I felt very thankful that all had ended so well.

The Conscription.

Whilst engaged on these lonesome horseback journeys in various parts of the Loire district, an example of the effects of conscription, in a way that was novel in my experience, came under my notice. Having lost my bearings whilst crossing an extensive wood, on emerging into a high road, I rode for some distance in order to ascertain my whereabouts. Presently I came upon a detachment of French soldiers, who appeared to be preparing to bivouac. I approached an artilleryman, who was seated on his gun smoking his pipe. The politeness and intelligence with which he answered my inquiries induced me to prolong the conversation, in order to obtain all the information he could give me about the movements of the French army. Having answered my questions, he suddenly extended the palms of his hands toward me, exclaiming, "Look at my hands, Monsieur."—"Well," I said, "they are hard and black enough, if that is what you mean!"—"Precisely," was his reply. "Just imagine, I am a watchmaker by trade, and was a highly-paid workman, having learnt my business in one of the best shops in Paris. But now, after handling these big guns and heavy shells for so long a time, I have lost my delicacy of touch, and can never go back to my proper business—in short, I am a ruined man." He resumed his pipe, puffing vigorously as though to dispel his melancholy feelings. In parting from him, I grasped his horny hand and said, "Yours is certainly a hard case. I hope there are not many men in a similar position?" "You are mistaken, Monsieur," he replied, "there are more than ten thousand men in the army of the West alone, taken from the light trades of Paris, whose case is much the same as mine."

Mention has already been made how heavily the burden of the conscription falls upon fathers of families, as in the instance of the two German "Landwehr" soldiers, who entered our private horse-box on the railway between Metz and Versailles. Here, in the case of the French watchmaker, who had lost all "the delicacy of his touch, and was a ruined man," was an altogether different illustration of the manifold ways in which the oppressive laws of conscription bear harshly upon the working classes. Did our working men in England but fully appreciate the happy immunity enjoyed by them in this free country from the evils of the conscription, they would resist to the very utmost any attempts, under whatever plea of necessity, to put round their necks the slave collar of the conscript, and to snap the lock.

Is there a possibility of compulsory military service being established in England? The question a few years ago would emphatically have been answered in the negative. Even yet, possibly, the well-known repugnance to Militarism in any form, among working men in the North of England, may be thought sufficient under any circumstances to ward off the danger.

Times are however changed. A new temper even among the British democracy has been created by the enormous additions of territory to our Empire during the past few years.

The real danger lies in the general laxity and indifference with which schemes of rampant imperialism have been allowed, unrestrained by public opinion, to go on adding continually to our national responsibilities. How great the danger may be, in the new acquisitions of ours with their ill-defined boundaries, of collision with other Powers, may be judged from the Fashoda incident in the Soudan.

Here then is the point requiring to be jealously watched by the leaders of our people—and by every true lover of his country. Why should men imbued with ideas of imperialism be allowed to load our country with responsibilities which in plain truth it is no longer able to bear? The "Jingo" spirit will not be backward in finding pretexts for clamouring for further military forces. Backed by a subservient press, the outcry will be raised—"The Empire is in danger," and then more British troops must be raised at any cost! If ever a law of compulsory service be hurried through the legislature, it will be under the influence of some such panic as this.

Surely if there be any force in these suggestions, it were wise on the part of the people to act promptly and firmly against further aggressiveness, upon the maxim that "eternal vigilance is the price of freedom."

CHATEAUDUN.

While we were together at St. Calais, Whitwell gave me some graphic details of his recent visit to Châteaudun. He protested indignantly against what he deemed the unjustifiable proceedings of the Prussians in shelling and burning this small unfortified town, for no other crime than manfully defending itself against invasion. I annex an extract from one of his letters written at the time, relating the exact particulars of the incident as he had ascertained them from the inhabitants themselves. How far their statements may have been exaggerated or otherwise, I have no information to enable me to judge.

Extract from T. Whitwell's letter.

"March, 1871.

"This ill-fated town, Châteaudun, has suffered terribly. I have visited Thionville, Bitsche and Strasbourg, all bombarded and more or less destroyed, but then these were regular fortresses, and the houses were burnt on account of the fortifications.

"Châteaudun, a town of 5,000 inhabitants, has a very fine castle, belonging to the Duc de Luynes. The town is open, and has no fortifications; but on the approach of the Prussians, the inhabitants threw up barricades, which were occupied by 500 *Franc-Tireurs* and about 800 *Gardes-Mobiles* of the town. Prussians, 15,000 strong, with 24 cannon, ranged themselves round the town, and bombarded it for six hours, burning fifteen houses. They then stormed the barricades, and began to burn down the town by hand.

"This 'pious' work was personally directed by German officers of high rank. It continued all night, and next day was conducted by patrols, who, with matches, petroleum and tar, managed to burn, in cold blood, 235—yes, *two hundred and thirty-five houses*,—burning therein, and thereby, twelve sick persons, unable to leave their beds!

"The Secretary of the *Comice Agricole*, himself sick at the time, told me that the Prussians lighted his bed under him with matches, and forced him out into the street. All this, in revenge, because the townspeople, in defending their town, killed some 2,000 Prussians, including some thirty officers.

"I have the printed statistics of the affair, which is unsurpassed in the history of this war for systematic and cold-blooded cruelty; for not only were the houses, especially all the shops and all the commercial part of the town, burned, but I was told by the wife of the Mayor, Mdme. L., who is connected with families in England and Ireland, that, in many cases, torches were put into the hands of the people themselves, and then, at the point of the bayonet, they were forced to fire their own houses!

"By this means 147 families, numbering about 600 souls, are utterly ruined, and have to be daily fed by the town. Beyond one flour-mill and one blanket factory, the place is for the most part agricultural. There is but little employment, owing to the absolute dearth of horses to till the soil. The land around is entirely corn-growing, and all the crops, except a little rye, are frozen.

"Some clothes were sent from Tours to the town, but were at once seized by the Prussians; so great was the sack and pillage, that they took from the Mayor's house all his shirts, trousers and boots, and all of the latter that belonged to his sons. In all cases the *works* of the timepieces were taken; these have been pillaged everywhere by the soldiers, and sold to a party of Cologne Jews that follow the Prussian army everywhere. Every cupboard and chest of drawers were rifled and smashed in. The losses in the town were estimated at £200,000.

"But little rebuilding has yet been done, as the money was wanting; but to help this on, and to assist the many starving families, I left with the 'Société de Bienfaisance' 2,500 francs (£100), which will be wisely expended as way may open. The above 600 needy people were in addition to the poor people previously in the town."

From St. Calais we proceeded together on horseback to Le Mans, a handsome old city with a grand Cathedral, being the capital of the Department of Sarthe. We found it occupied by a strong force of German soldiers, who, as we learned from the Mayor, notwithstanding the Armistice, were still levying heavy requisitions upon the inhabitants.

At Le Mans we felt that the service we had proposed to do was so far completed that we could now leave the actual work of distribution of seed corn, etc., to those who were about to follow us into the field. Each of us had also sent to our Committee at home, full reports of the local Committees and other arrangements which had been made in our respective districts.

As the railway, since the Armistice, was open again for ordinary traffic, and having no further need of my horse, we concluded to dispose of him, and hand over the proceeds to the authorities, for the benefit of the destitute poor of Le Mans. I took an affectionate leave of my friend Whitwell, and proceeded, as rapidly as I could travel, towards Rome.

Thomas Whitwell.

As I may not have occasion for further reference to my dear friend and companion, Thomas Whitwell, I wish here to record my testimony to his sterling character, both as a Christian man of business and a good citizen, taking a full share of civic responsibilities and philanthropic duties.

His previous responsibilities included, among other things, the founding of the local Volunteer Fire Brigade of his town, of which he was the captain, and his unremitting care over the Y.M.C.A.'s throughout the north of England. He was also a member of the Alpine Club, and literally had "paddled his own canoe" on many of the rivers of England and of the Continent.

Closely banded together as we had been during a considerable portion of the work in France, I had every opportunity of studying his character. Under every contingency, rough and smooth, he showed always the same cheerful, self-reliant nature; and however unfavourably we might be circumstanced, even when sharing at night the floor of a railway station as our dormitory with a lot of noisy, unruly soldiers, he was not afraid to let his loyalty to his Lord be seen, and conducted his private devotions as calmly and thoroughly as though he were in his own chamber at home. The act was characteristic of the man.

By men of all creeds and of no creed he was alike beloved and respected, for they saw in him something which constrained them to acknowledge that religion does not consist in word only, but in life. A remark once made to me by a careless, irreligious, young fellow, may suffice as an example of this feeling. He said, "I don't believe in your creeds, but I *do believe* in Tom Whitwell." It may, therefore, be well understood that when we parted for a time, at his suggestion, in Central France, in order the more speedily to get the needful information in a district devastated by war which we had hitherto traversed together, my heart sank within me as I turned my horse's head away to enter upon a lonesome journey in the depth of winter. He had been to me a tower of strength on all occasions of difficulty, and the lack of his cheerful companionship during my solitary rides and lonely evenings in a strange land was a loss often keenly felt by me.

The circumstances of his death, which occurred in 1878, were so tragic and painful that a brief allusion to them here may be admissible. T. Whitwell was well known in the Cleveland district as a civil engineer, and as the inventor of some valuable improvements connected with blast furnaces. In his own iron works at Thornaby-on-Tees he had adopted a foreign patent heating furnace, connected with which was a deep ash-pit, on a level with the furnace fire-bars. Something having on one occasion gone wrong in the fire-place, he descended the iron ladder into the ash-pit, which was about ten feet deep, with his foreman, to investigate the cause. Suddenly there occurred an explosion, with an outburst of heated gas and scalding steam, and the two men were caught in the pit, the only exit from which was by means of the small iron ladder in one corner. Blinded, and almost suffocated by the steam, even in this agonizing moment, his calm fortitude and noble self-denial were conspicuous, as, remembering that his foreman had a family, he called out, "You go out first, John."

T. Whitwell was just able to follow him to the surface, but alas, the scalding steam had done its work. Neither of them survived more than a few hours.

On hearing the news, I hastened from Middlesbrough, with one of his brothers, to his house in Stockton, where I learned that his condition was hopeless, and that he was unable to see anyone. Hearing his groans in the room above, I turned away in grief and sorrow, and proceeded to the Cottage Hospital of Middlesbrough, in search of a trained nurse to attend to him. He died the same evening, August 5th, 1878, aged forty. The funeral, on August 9th, was a deeply affecting occasion. Thousands of people, moved to sympathy by his tragic death, crowded the streets, while multitudes of mourners assembled to pay the last tribute of respect, and show the esteem in which they held one who, endeared to all who knew him, had thus been cut off in the prime of his manhood, and in the midst of his active and useful career. I have attended many funerals of leading "Friends" in the North of England, but never have I witnessed so large a concourse, nor one in which every class of the community showed such evident marks of sorrow and respect, as at the funeral of Thomas Whitwell.

A Rearing Horse.

To return to our journey in Central France. Soon after Whitwell and I had parted company, when riding alone towards a French village, an incident occurred, which might have had very serious, or even fatal results. I mention it here, as an illustration of those unforeseen dangers to which a solitary traveller is exposed, in traversing a country in war-time. Late one afternoon, when it was beginning to be dusk, I heard the sound of a band of music in front, as I was approaching a village—in the district east of Vendôme. My horse heard it too, as I saw by the ominous way in which he pricked up his ears, wagging them backward and forward in a manner that boded no good, given, as he was, to the vice of rearing.

My first thought was to dismount before the music approached; but I hesitated, because of the difficulty of the feat, owing to the high bundle of wraps strapped on behind the saddle. Whilst I hesitated, the Advance Guard of the German regiment, which was on the march, came up. It was now too late to attempt to get down, so fearing we should have a scene when the band came up, I resolved to sit firm and do my best to prepare for the event. After a former occasion when the beast reared dangerously, Whitwell had bought for me a stout Malacca hunting-crop, which I still keep as a memento of him. He had also given me instructions to hit the horse a thwack with the butt-end, between the ears, just as he started to rise on his hind legs. Unfortunately the animal, being evidently an expert in the art of rearing, was too quick for me. In a moment he made an instantaneous spring into the perpendicular, as the clanging music went by. As both hands were in instant requisition to hang on by, my obstinate steed never got what he so richly deserved, "a well directed punch on the head." I had gauged the situation beforehand, and decided upon the only course possible, so as to avoid the danger of his falling over *backward* upon my chest. To the left was a deep wide ditch, to the right, the soldiers were marching past with fixed bayonets. I flung my whole weight to the right, preferring the hard road to the ditch.

The infantry opened their ranks wide. We came down, horse and man together, with a heavy crash upon the road. Two German soldiers did instantly the right thing, seeing my leg was fast under the horse, they jumped to his head and held it down, to prevent his injuring me in his struggles to get on his feet.

Meantime, the Colonel of the regiment, who was in the rear, seeing the commotion, had ridden rapidly up and dismounted. He at once issued his commands in German, telling his men to raise the body of the horse a little, while his head was kept down, and then to draw my leg out very gently, for fear of broken bones. This was done while I laid stunned from the violence with which my head came in contact with the hard road. Had it not been for my thick sealskin cap, the shock was enough to have caused concussion of the brain. The Colonel, after telling his men to lift me carefully on to my feet, turned to me and asked, to my

FALL FROM REARING HORSE.

surprise, in good English, "Are you hurt?" Feeling first at my collar-bones, ribs, etc., I replied, "No bones are broken—only I am stunned."

Evidently relieved, the kind Colonel smiled and said, "Well, you did make my men *skedaddle*, worse than a charge of French cavalry" (mine being a cavalry charge of a novel and unexpected kind). At which I could not help smiling too, and exclaiming, "Oh! Colonel, where did you pick up that Yankee word 'skedaddle'?"—"*Ach mein herr*," he rejoined, "didn't I command a German regiment in America in the war between North and South? Now," he said, "what more can we do for you? Shall we lift you on your horse again?" Promptly came the answer, "No, thank you, I have had enough of him, for to-day at least." "Well, I cannot let you go quite alone. I will send a couple of men with you to the village." I thanked him; he saluted, mounted and rode off, as noble and genial an example of the German officer as any I had met with in any part of France.

On approaching the village, I dismissed my escort with a few francs, telling them the French people would receive me much better without them. For a day or two I was unable to mount my horse, owing to pain in the side, which was much bruised and remained discoloured for weeks afterwards. This, however, was a trifle compared with what might have been, had I been laid up in a small rural town in the centre of France, with broken limbs or internal injuries, without medical skill and no friends within reach. That I had much cause for thankfulness in these immunities was, naturally, my sincerest feeling.

Mention has already been made of some of the autographs inscribed on my Commission. Among the French signatures, the first is that of the Bishop of Nancy and Toul. Whitwell and I called upon him, with a view of obtaining his influence among the clergy of his diocese, to render us every assistance in the distribution of relief. Nancy did not suffer in the war like Metz. Being an open city, it had not been besieged, and had literally surrendered to a "couple of Uhlans." Consequently the local distress was not serious, but there was much dissatisfaction at the heaviness of the requisitions imposed upon it by the Germans.

The Bishop writes in a cramped hand (the whole of which I have not been able to decipher to this day) that he approves highly of our charitable thoughts, but has reserves with regard to the *doctrine* expressed in the document, meaning, I suppose, the expression that "Friends" believe "all war to be contrary to the will and spirit of our Heavenly Father, as shown in the New Testament." He was a man in the prime of life, full of energy and vigour, and as he wrote the foregoing words, he emphasised them with a vigorous blow of his fist upon the table, saying, "I want my revenge upon these Germans, you understand."

He asked me if I had been to the village of Fontenoy and heard of the atrocities committed by

Prussian soldiers there. I told him I was at Fontenoy the day before, but the inhabitants did not mention any atrocities that had been committed ; on the contrary, they said the German soldiers had taken them by the hand and drawn them out of their houses, allowing them to take whatever they pleased with them, as the German authorities had decided that the village must be burned. This was an act of reprisal for the blowing up, by Garibaldi and his "Red Shirts," of the railway bridge, on the line of the Eastern Railway of France, communicating with Germany, the keeping open of which was essential to the existence of the immense besieging army before Paris.

On my remarking that what the Germans had done in France could not be compared with the cruel conduct of the French in Germany, under Bonaparte, the Bishop became angry, and declined to write anything on Whitwell's document, and somewhat hastily showed us to the door.

A little below his signature there is another, forming a curious contrast to that of the Bishop. It reads thus : "*Sans restriction ! je signe avec respect et reconnaissance éternelle*" (Without restriction ! I sign with eternal respect and gratitude.) "*Vautrain, Agriculteur, à Gorze (Moselle).*" This is a characteristic French expression, and evidently intended as a rebuke to his Bishop, towards whom he expressed no very kindly feeling. His reference to the Bishop and his clergy as "*Ces abominables écclésiastiques*" was more vigorous than polite.

The Mayor of Nancy also signed, and added the official seal of the Mairie, "*Je remercie, de tout mon cœur, pour mes compatriotes, les honorables gentlemen, qui nous ont apporté le généreux secours de l'Angleterre. Le Maire de Nancy, Ch. Welche.*" (I heartily thank, on behalf of my countrymen, the honorable gentlemen who have brought us the generous relief from England.—The Mayor of Nancy, Ch. Welche.)

CHAPTER XII.

INTERVIEW WITH CARDINAL ANTONELLI IN THE VATICAN —CASUAL MEETING WITH THE POPE.

PROCEEDING, shortly after leaving Whitwell at Le Mans, to Rome, the visit to the Vatican became my first object. Being received by Cardinal Antonelli's Secretary I showed him my credentials, which contained Archbishop Manning's signature ; these he stated he would at once lay before the Cardinal. The promptness of his return, with the message "The Cardinal will see you now," greatly surprised me. Passing through the ante-room, I found numbers of apparently important personages, who were waiting for admission, as, following the Secretary, I was shown at once into the cabinet of the Cardinal Secretary of State. He rose, took me by the hand, and greeting me affably, asked if I spoke Italian. I replied, "Not enough for serious conversation." He remarked, "As I am not strong in English, are we on common ground in French?" My reply was, "I hope so." This point settled, our conversation was conducted entirely in French.

In explanation of my call, I proceeded to relate some details of the condition of the city of Metz, of the surrender of which I had been an eye-witness, and of the work of relief among the peasantry of France, during the war which was then in progress. At this point the Cardinal stopped me, and gave an entirely new direction to the conversation, saying he should probably hear, through the clergy, of the work of relief going on in France, but in the limited time at his disposal, he would gladly hear from me something about my own religious body, the Society of Friends. This was a turn in the conversation, for which I was wholly unprepared. I endeavoured, however, to make the best of the new character with which I was thus unexpectedly invested, by a man of the conspicuous ability of Cardinal Antonelli, viz., that of a responsible representative of the views and practices of the "Society of Friends." In response I said, that if His Eminence was pleased to ask questions upon any matters connected with our Society, upon which he desired information, I would do my utmost to satisfy him with perfect frankness and candour. He remarked, "Several of your Friends have from time to time seen 'His Holiness,' but you are the first who has come to see me personally, and I am grateful for your visit."

It was now my turn to be interviewed. The Cardinal, inviting me to place myself beside him on the sofa, I rose from the seat I had been occupying near the door, and crossed the floor of the cabinet, inwardly wondering what my friends at home would say, if they saw me seated side by side with the virtual ruler of the whole Roman Catholic world. A deeply interesting *tête-a-tête*, lasting over half an hour, ensued.

The Cardinal, being an Italian gentleman of the old school, than whom no more courteous being exists, his manner was so thoroughly kind and genial, that all feeling of reserve was taken away, the charm of his bearing and his smile causing me to feel quite at ease in his presence. Let me add also, that the Cardinal's mode of speaking the French language was in itself a pleasure to hear; his voice mellow and soft, together with his perfect knowledge of the idioms of the language, caused his French enunciation to sound like pleasing music to the ear. How vague his notions were, in regard to the Society of Friends, was evident from some of his first questions. For instance, he asked if my friend and I had been sent out "two by two," after the manner of "the seventy disciples of Christ," on works of benevolence, adding, "The seventy, you know, correspond to our Conclave."

"What! of Cardinals?" I exclaimed, with a smile at the incongruity of the thought, adding, "We have no Cardinals, no Hierarchy, no distinction in fact between clergy and laity. We are simply 'Friends' or 'Brothers'; all are on an equality in our Church." (Such, at least, I flattered myself, is our theory.)

Some further inquiries rapidly followed as to

how our ministers were appointed and maintained, also with regard to the preaching of women; the answers leading incidentally to the subject of silent spiritual worship. Speaking generally, he appeared to take a deep interest in the religious principle specially held by the Society of Friends, with regard to the indwelling and perceptible guidance of the Holy Spirit in the regenerated soul.

We did not get into really *close quarters* in the discussion, until he started a subject on which his questions were most searching, and betrayed the liveliest interest. Our conversation was then substantially as follows :—

Cardinal Antonelli : "I understand that in your meetings for church affairs you have no President, and that you never decide any questions by vote. Is that so?"

W.J. : "Practically that is so. One of our number is appointed as 'clerk,' (in French, *secrétaire*) of the meeting. His principal functions are to ascertain the 'evident sense' of the meeting, or the general consensus of opinion, upon the various matters under consideration, and to register its decisions in suitable minutes."

Cardinal Antonelli : "I am deeply interested in knowing how this can be done without a vote; for so far as I know, your practice is quite unique in the Christian world, or in the annals of church history."

I here explained, at some length, the workings of our meetings for "discipline," or church government, and the method of gathering the "sense of a meeting," by the "clerk," according to our usual practice; also how the minutes, when made, were submitted to the approval of the meeting—for adoption, or for amendment, as the case might be.

Cardinal Antonelli: "But suppose questions of great importance were to arise; questions which might even be *vital* to your existence as a church. How could the opinion of the meeting be correctly ascertained, and a satisfactory decision be arrived at, in cases like these, unless the sentiments of each individual church-member were plainly manifested by a vote, or its equivalent?" Then, after a pause, turning to me, "Have *you* ever done this?"

W.J.: "Yes, whilst acting as 'clerk' to what we term a Quarterly Meeting, which is composed of several smaller sectional, or Monthly Meetings, questions came up for decision which were of grave importance, though none, within my remembrance, that could be described as *vital* to our existence."

Cardinal Antonelli: "Ah! Now we have got down to a man that has done it! I am all attention" *(Je suis tout oreilles).* "Pray, my friend, tell me how *you* did it."

The question for a moment puzzled me, as I mentally asked myself, "How *did* I do it?" Never before had the difficulty been thus pointedly presented to my mind. Custom and habit, from youth up, in the Society of Friends, has enabled us, I suppose almost intuitively, to arrive at the result, without so much as a thought of the difficulties which our method of procedure presents to outsiders. To those who have never witnessed, in our meetings for Church affairs, the mutual concessions, the bearing and forbearing, in the spirit of that charity which thinketh no evil, it may doubtless appear strange that, on questions which cause a wide divergence of opinion, a sufficient degree of unanimity is ever obtained to be accepted as the deliberate judgment of the meeting; at the right moment, however, the "clerk" generally sees his way to record the decision, as the "evident sense of the meeting."

Cardinal Antonelli is by no means the only person I have met with who has confessed his difficulty in understanding the Quaker method of deciding questions, not by majorities, but by that which in the view of "Friends" constitutes the "weight of the meeting."

The explanation given in answer to the Cardinal was to the effect, that it was not always the length of speeches, or their number, that influenced the decision of the "clerk" in discussions of importance, but that due regard was paid to the sentiments of a minority, if such minority were constituted, as is sometimes the case, of the more experienced, and the more spiritually minded among the members present. In a tone of surprise, he exclaimed, "What! have *you* done that?" I hoped I had said nothing amiss. Then, with the acumen and tact so characteristic of him, he pressed on me the yet deeper question, "Tell me, my friend, how did you *know* who in the meeting were the spiritually minded? I should hesitate very much to decide who were, and who were not spiritually minded among our people, or in our conclave" (*i.e.*, Roman Catholics). "*Je n'oserais pas, Monsieur*" (I should not dare to do so). Feeling myself like clay in the hands of this intellectual giant, reputed to be the astutest diplomatist of his age, I begged a moment for reflection, and then replied, "Do you think, Cardinal, there can be any mistake in a matter like this, when we have the explicit rule of Christ, the Head of the Church Himself, to guide us, 'By their *fruits* ye shall know them'? In forming your judgment of a man's character, do you judge him by his words only? Do you not look to the testimony of his life, and where you see the evident fruits of the spirit, may you not safely conclude that such a man is spiritually minded?"

Whilst admitting the appositeness of the reply, he still maintained that I did not "touch the fringe of his difficulty"! Discouraged at the smallness of the result of so searching a cross-examination upon Quaker doctrines and practices, I rose to take my leave. "Are you in a hurry?" he asked. "Not at all," I replied, "but uneasy at occupying your valuable time, while personages of importance are waiting in the ante-room." "If that is all, pray be seated," he rejoined, placing his hand in a kindly manner on my knee. "I may never have another opportunity of seeing you or any member of your Society, and I *want* this information." Then, with a significant gesture, pointing to the door, he added, "*Qu'ils attendent*" (Let them wait).

Recognising something here, deeper than mere curiosity, a genuine thirst for information, on what evidently was to him a deeply interesting phase of church government, I resumed my seat. Question followed question, with a power and skill, tempered with refined courtesy, which, whilst taxing my own resources to the utmost, far from causing any unpleasant feeling, served only to deepen the admiration and regard I felt for the capacious intellect, the genial kindly heart, which could thus throw off all reserve, and enter with the freedom and familiarity of an intimate friend, into questions closely touching the sacredness of the inner life.

At last, when he stood up to intimate that our interview was ended, I said he would observe that the leading ecclesiastic of the Roman Catholic Church in England (Dr. Manning) had signed my credentials, in which were set forth the sentiments held by the Society of Friends in regard to war, namely, that it was contrary to the Divine Will, as revealed in the New Testament, and I ventured to ask the Cardinal, whether the Church of Rome admitted this to be the Biblical view of war. He paused thoughtfully for a moment, and then said, "That this is New Testament teaching, we should not deny; whether we have, or have not, always acted consistently in the matter." I bowed gravely, accepting his remark without comment. It was hardly to be expected that one in the dignified position of a "*Cardinal*," should have been more frank when speaking of any possible shortcoming of that which he regarded as the one true Church.

Desirous of possessing his name on my credentials, which he had perused with interest, I told him how much I should value his autograph as a souvenir of our pleasant interview, and of the great kindness with which he had received me.

With a smile, he replied, "I will sign it with pleasure, but let me place my name under that of a *good* man. Where is Archbishop Manning's name?" Under this, in a very fine Italian hand, contrasting with Manning's bold signature, he then wrote, "J. Card. Antonelli." Interesting and unique phenomenon! The approving sign-manuals of the two foremost princes, in their day, of the Roman Catholic Church, side by side upon a purely Quaker document.

The concluding incident, as a further proof of Antonelli's kindness of heart, should not go unmentioned. On my reaching the door, to leave his cabinet, he begged me to wait a moment *("Un instant, mon ami")*. Then, advancing to my side, he placed his arm through mine, and escorted me through the crowded ante-room, every personage there being most deferential, and bowing repeatedly as we passed through the apartment to the head of the great marble staircase. Here, on my bidding him adieu, the Cardinal held my hand between both of his, and cordially thanked me for my visit. "You have cleared up some things," he said, which have long been an enigma to me." This felt cheering and encouraging. I *had* succeeded, then, after all, in removing something more than "the fringe of his difficulty." Suddenly I remembered how on that very spot, when his secretary came to call me into the Cardinal's presence, a heart-sinking feeling came over me as I put the question to myself, "What right have I to intrude upon this great man? Have I any '*concern*' (as we 'Friends' say) to see him at all?" But when the Cardinal so heartily expressed his grateful thanks for my visit, it was borne in upon me that the "concern" appeared to be the other way; the real desire was doubtless on his side to see me, and this it was that so facilitated this memorable interview, with all its free and intimate conversation.

The Cardinal proceeded to close the interview in a hushed voice and deeply impressive manner, which touched me to tears. "You and I, my friend, will probably never meet again on earth, but I hope and trust we shall meet hereafter above. Adieu, may God go with you and bless you." We looked silently into each other's eyes for a moment; then, with a grasp of hands and another "adieu," we separated finally

Before my next visit to Rome, Cardinal Antonelli had departed this life and his place in the Vatican knew him no more.

I have often looked back upon this, which I regard as the most interesting personal interview of my life, and of which I am unable to give an explanation which quite satisfies even myself of the "how and the wherefore" of it all.

When I call to mind the earnestness of Cardinal Antonelli, and the searching nature of his questions during our conversation, no other suggestion occurs which serves to throw light upon his attitude towards me than that, at that moment, whatever his antecedents may have been, a *higher influence* was mutually felt, drawing us closely together in heart and soul. During the parting moments, at the head of the Vatican stairs, whilst holding my hand between both of his, the tenderness and kindness of his every word and action made one realise impressively, that in spite of differences in position and creed there was a real bond of sympathy between us.

In my conversation with Cardinal Antonelli, I had asked him whether he thought "His Holiness" would not feel interested in hearing some details regarding the war in France. He expressed a doubt, owing to the Pope's state of health, but said if he could arrange an interview, he would send me word to my hotel. I received a letter from him on the next day, stating that he had not been able to arrange an interview. But after leaving the Cardinal, and going down the marble staircase, I unexpectedly obtained a sight of the Pope, Pius IX.

On the staircase I found my Italian "Cicerone" in a state of great excitement, urging me to hasten down, as the Pope's guard were angry with our lingering on the stairs, which "His Holiness" was about to ascend.

I told the man to hasten down and I would follow. The Captain of the Guard rushed up the stairs and began to remonstrate with me. I asked him if he was not a German. He said, "No, a German-Swiss." I then told him in German, that I had recently come from Metz, where I had seen the great German army enter in triumph under Prince Frederick Charles. He listened for a few moments, thus giving me time, as we slowly walked down together, to meet the Pope on the stairs. I saw him, carried by four bearers in scarlet, in his sedan chair, from which he alighted at the foot of the marble staircase, which the old man slowly ascended. I passed close by him, and thus had a very good view, but no word of salutation took place between us. With his mild aspect and benevolent countenance, arrayed in a white flannel costume, edged with scarlet, and a very broad-brimmed hat, he reminded me of some good old "Friend" of former times.

CHAPTER XIII.

SICILY—SULPHUR MINES—BRIGANDAGE—CAPTURE OF MR. ROSE—EFFECTS OF MILITARISM—THE PELLAGRA.

AFTER the interview with Antonelli, I resumed my journey towards Sicily. The firm of chemical manufacturers at Middlesbrough, of which I was the managing partner, having, through the recommendation of the late eminent engineer, Robert C. May, C.E., of London, recently become lessees of a sulphur mine in Sicily, it became needful for me to visit the island to make all arrangements connected with taking possession, and with the management of the mine. Proceeding *via* Naples, I embarked in the mail steamer for Messina, and thence by rail, *via* Catania, to a station situated near the centre of the island, called Valguarnera. The Gallizzi mines, situated about twelve miles from this station, in the province of Caltanisetta, were noted for the superior quality of sulphur produced in them.

Sicilian sulphur, which formerly was employed in large quantities in the chemical works of England, in the manufacture of sulphuric acid, has for many years been superseded for this purpose by iron-pyrites, which is a cheaper source of sulphur. Enormous quantities of pyrites containing a small percentage of copper, are imported from Huelva in Spain. After the sulphur has been extracted by burning the pyrites, and condensing the vapours into sulphuric acid, the copper contained in the residual ore, after undergoing further treatment in the copper works, is an additional source of profit.

At present, the main use of Sicilian sulphur, after being ground into a fine powder, is for the purpose of sulphuring the vines in the vineyards of the island itself, and in those of other Mediterranean countries. Its employment is very extensive for the purpose of preventing the ravages of insects, and for promoting the growth of the vines.

Like everyone who visits sulphur mining centres for the first time, I was struck with the primitive and wasteful systems in vogue for winning and smelting the ore. On descending one of the mines, which was done simply by walking down a very rough incline, there being no shafts for drawing up the ore, or the water, I found the heat insufferable, and what was still worse, the atmosphere was very painful to breathe, being loaded with sulphurous fumes. The pickmen were working in a state of nudity, each man hewing apparently wherever he thought fit, without any system of plotting out the mine; rough pillars of stone being left to support the roof, but no other props. The ore was carried out on the backs of small boys, also quite naked, who toiled up the rough incline, groaning, and often crying under their loads, which bruised their shoulders. The smelting was done on the areas outside, in large kilns, called "calcaroni," the ore being set on fire and simply left to burn out by itself, the sulphur running out in a thin, bright yellow stream into wooden moulds, placed below the exit. Thus a large proportion of the sulphur was thrown off into the air, in the shape of sulphurous acid, poisoning the vegetation around.

The whole thing appeared so utterly primitive and wasteful, that on the face of it nothing seemed plainer than that by introducing a little machinery, and more economical systems of smelting, there was every prospect of effecting great economies, and at the same time giving immense relief, both to the pickers and to the wretched little carrier-boys. Under the management of a competent French engineer, who had had considerable Sicilian experience, we began by introducing steam power for unwatering the mines. But beyond this improvement, such changes as we ultimately effected were the slow work of years of patient perseverance, in order to overcome the prejudices and opposition of the ignorant Sicilian workmen. We never did succeed in entirely dispensing with the labour of boy-carriers, whose earnings went into the pockets of their employers, the pickmen. No coal being found in Sicily, it had to be imported from England, and after paying railway carriage, it was too costly as fuel for any system of improved smelting furnaces.

SICILIAN SCENERY.

During my connection with Sicily, extending over more than twenty years, I visited many of the chief centres of interest in this historically famous island.

On my first approach to Palermo, in a French steamer, on a bright sunny morning, I was struck with the beauty of the city, with its environment of magnificent mountain ranges, much finer, as they appeared to me, than any hills surrounding the Bay of Naples, which is generally considered more beautiful.

In course of time I became familiar with the sights of Palermo and the neighbouring localities: its grand cathedral of Moorish architecture, with all its exquisite and elaborate details, the Royal chapel with its celebrated mosaics, also the still more wonderful mosaics of the great cathedral of Monreale, five miles from Palermo.

As a general remark, I may say that all along the *coasts* of the island, and for a few miles inland, the scenery is strikingly beautiful. The east coast around the lofty town of Taormina is admittedly among the most exquisite scenery of Europe, commanding as it does an extensive panorama of the blue Mediterranean, with the background of the rugged mountains of Calabria on one side, and on the other the massive bulk of Etna in the foreground, giving forth volcanic smoke from its snow-crowned crest. The depth and fertility of the soil near the coast, which is mainly composed of disintegrated lava, renders its vineyards, its lemon and orange gardens, and fruit orchards generally, unsurpassed for richness and fertility. Much of the interior, however, is rocky, mountainous, and barren. This barrenness is largely owing to the fact of the mountains having been denuded long ago of their timber, thus depriving the country of the moisture which is needed for fertilizing the plains below. It is well known that in the time of the Roman Empire, Sicily was the granary of the Imperial City.

BRIGANDAGE.

Amid the sulphur mining centres the country is far from beautiful, but owing to the enforced close season for smelting, there is less actual damage to crops than might be anticipated. The poverty and want among the labouring classes in the interior are often very severe, and tend to foster the spirit of brigandage, which is the curse of the island. Militarism, again, with the heavy taxation inseparable from it, is another main cause of the poverty and ignorance of the people. Merchants in Palermo have assured me that since the establishment of the Kingdom of Italy, with its lavish war budgets, the weight of taxation imposed in Sicily has been *four times* heavier than was formerly the case under the worst of the Bourbons, who was familiarly called King "Bomba."

During our occupancy of the Gallizzi mines, the state of public security in the island often left much to be desired. The residence of our engineer and employés at the mines was threatened, but never actually attacked. When travelling to or from the interior, I have personally passed through districts haunted by brigands, but have never actually been waylaid by them, though, on one occasion, when proceeding from the mines to the station, in company with one of our employés, we had to cross a bridge where, some time before, a band of brigands had been concealed under the arch, and, on the approach of the cashier of mines adjoining ours, they rushed out, shot his horse, and robbed him of all the money he was bringing for the pay day of the mines. In confirmation of the story my companion and I saw the skeleton of the horse on the roadside, with a suggestive bullet hole through its skull, so that our safety lay in a speedy retreat from this infested district. Putting spurs to our horses, after a gallop of a few miles, "*ventre-à-terre*," we pulled up on reaching safe ground near the railway station.

Capture of Mr. Rose.

Possibly the ardour of the brigands in our district was somewhat damped by the fact that the Italian Government maintained a company of soldiers, sometimes at the station, at other times at the mines, in order to guard employés or visitors passing up and down.

A most interesting brigand incident, with which I had but slight connection, was that of Mr. Rose, junior, a merchant of Palermo, who afterwards sent a full account of the whole affair to the London *Times*. Calling on one occasion at the offices of the firm in Palermo, I mentioned that I was going next day across the country to Gallizzi; whereupon I was duly warned that the diligence passed through the country of "Leone," a notorious brigand chief, and that very likely I might be captured and held for ransom. "The next thing will be that we shall have one of your ears sent down, with a polite letter to say that if the ransom is not sent up within so many days the other ear will follow." This was jocosely said to me in Mr. Rose's office.

Of course I kept my own counsel about the time of my departure, and proceeded from the railway station at Palermo by a very early train, as far as Rocca Palumba, where the diligence started for the interior. I travelled for several hours in the diligence without any molestation whatever, and arrived safely at my destination.

Not long after this, Mr. Rose, junior, following the same course into the country, and taking with him a bag containing a large sum of money for the pay day of the sulphur mines, with which he was connected, was himself captured by the very men against whom I had been warned.

Mr. Rose's exceedingly interesting narrative I read in the *Times* some time after my return home. Writing from memory only, I regret that I cannot do full justice to his story. In his narrative he stated that some time after leaving Rocca Palumba in the diligence, there appeared on the scene a single individual with a Winchester rifle, or "sixteen shooter," on his arm. This was no other than the redoubtable Leone, who peremptorily ordered the driver to stop. Then, coming to the door of the diligence, he called to Mr. Rose, "I want you, sir, and you must bring the bag of money with you," thus giving a clear proof that, through some act of collusion, Leone had been forewarned of Mr. Rose's coming. Not one of his Sicilian fellow passengers, of whom there were about a dozen, dared lift a finger in defence of Mr. Rose, the fact being that the people are either terrorised by, or in collusion with, the brigands. Mr. Rose was then placed on horseback and escorted by Leone's whole gang of about thirty men. Not content with getting the money bag, they carried away Mr. Rose himself, with the evident intention of holding him for ransom. After proceeding thus guarded some miles further, Mr. Rose noticed that his guards became careless, and he seized a favourable chance, in a very hilly district, to slip off his horse and make a rush for life, down a steep slope towards the river. Those acquainted with the interior of Sicily will know the characteristic formation of its limestone rocks, which often protrude in pinnacle form from the surface of the ground. By dodging behind these pinnacles, he managed to escape the bullets whistling past his head, and then ran along the bank of the stream which flowed in the direction of the road which the brigands had passed over, until, to his intense delight, he saw the diligence again, slowly toiling up the hill. He at once made for its shelter, congratulating himself, and being congratulated by his fellow travellers, on his marvellous escape.

Rose's rejoicings were, however, soon cut short. Leone, who had coolly watched the whole proceeding, promptly re-appeared alone on the scene, with a more swaggering air than ever, and ordering Mr. Rose to come out, told him emphatically, "I will take better care of you this time, Signor."

The second capture proved effectual. Mr. Rose was taken up into the mountainous district, and kept in one of the caves, with which the limestone rocks abound, and was well guarded night and day, a ransom of no less than £4,000 being demanded for his release.

Meantime, the Government sent scouts and gendarmes in various directions, in search of him. He could see them sometimes in the valley far below, and even hear their talk, but had to keep strict silence on pain of death. Ultimately, after the payment of a considerable ransom, Mr. Rose obtained his freedom.

On my next visit to Palermo, probably the year following, I was struck with a singular looking photograph in a shop window, of a very unkempt looking human head. On making inquiries, I was told it was the head of Leone, the brigand chief, and the explanation given was, that he had been murdered, out of jealousy, by one of his own lieutenants. His head, on which the Government had offered a premium of £1,000, was sent down to the Prefect of Palermo, with a message that if he would send men up to a village named they would find in a certain field the body corresponding to that head. This was done, and the body of Leone was recovered.

Before I left the island, I heard that his whole gang of twenty-nine men had been captured, and that a singular incident occurred which could probably not have taken place in any other country than Sicily. It was stated that the whole of these brigands were being conveyed in a prison van, between the court of justice and the gaol, and that, doubtless by collusion, the van was purposely driven across a trench opened in the street, and there upset, and that in the confusion which ensued, the prisoners managed to overpower the two guards in charge of the van, to obtain the keys, and undo their handcuffs, and thus all effected their escape into safe hiding in the back slums of Palermo.

In a few years time the new leader of the gang, who was a well-known man, had the audacity to return from America, and although disguised, was soon recognised in the streets of Palermo. His capture this time was effectual, and he was tried and sentenced to be hung.

These incidents induced me, on my homeward journey, to make some stay in Rome, to endeavour to see the authorities upon the question of public security in the island of Sicily. Through the courtesy of our then ambassador, Sir A. Paget, I obtained an interview with the Minister of the Interior, Count Corti, and also with the Minister of "Grace and Justice." In my interview with these gentlemen I mentioned the difficulties in the way of Englishmen proceeding into the interior of Sicily to look after their property, and stated that not another sixpence of British capital would, in my belief, be invested in the island until brigandage was suppressed.

"*Que voulez-vous, Monsieur?*" said the Count, shrugging his shoulders, "We keep 40,000 soldiers in that island, and we *cannot* put it down." This seemed to me so humiliating a confession, that my thoughts turned immediately to one of my countrymen at home, who, I thought, would probably be willing to take the job *on contract*, and soon clear the island of its brigands. Sir Samuel Baker, of Central African fame, was the man I had then in view.

The Count went on to say, in explanation of his remarks, that the brigandage in Sicily was an affair of the blood. He was evidently of the same mind as an acquaintance of mine in the island, who knew the people well, and who had occasionally pointed out to me in the streets of Palermo, men of Moorish or African descent, and had told me that brigandage was *in the blood.* "If," continued the Count, "you go into the three

Eastern provinces of Syracuse, Catania and Messina, you will find the labouring population to be mainly descended from the ancient Greek colonists. They are peaceable and law-abiding people, without any tendency to brigandage. If, on the other hand, you go to the western end of the island, in the provinces of Girgenti, Trapani and Palermo, you will find a very large proportion of the descendants of the ancient Carthaginians, who occupied this end of the island for many years. In these you will find that treacherous blood or disposition which the old Romans stigmatised as '*Punica fides*,' and it is from this race that the brigands of the island are generally recruited."

The Pellagra.

Sicily presented, and still presents, a striking object lesson of the evils resulting from lavish expenditure. The very life blood is drained from the people by the crushing taxation and oppressive system of conscription. The fearful disease known by the name of the "*Pellagra*," though not so prevalent in Sicily as it is in Calabria, and in Northern Italy, is known to be the specific disease caused by a starvation diet, bad and unwholesome food, and damp, insanitary dwellings. It produces a peculiar roughness and blackness of the skin, (French "*Peau aigre*," Italian "*Pellagra*"). It seizes on the spinal marrow, travelling upwards to the brain, where it finally ends in insanity and death.

Some years later, as the result of twenty years

acquaintance with Italy, a brief pamphlet of mine was published, entitled "Italy and Militarism." In this, after describing the "*Pellagra*" as one of the deplorable results of the unwise expenditure in Italy on the Army and Navy, I remarked that "Italy has the ambition to be reckoned a Great Power, and is bent upon being a strong nation. With a view to being strong, she so arranges her affairs as to consign thousands of the flower of her population, for generation after generation, to the madhouse, and to despairing agonies which result in wholesale suicide. She knows full well that the supplies voted for her absurdly bloated armaments are raised by taxation, which is not only crushing the nation into an increasing poverty, but is rapidly destroying the physique of the race, and cutting at the roots and hopes of future progress and prosperity."

A leading article in an Italian newspaper recently said: "Had Italy, during the past ten years, devoted one quarter of the energy expended on sustaining the rôle of a Great Power, to the amelioration of her material condition, our hills might have been re-wooded and our waste lands reclaimed; whereas now the financial riches of the State have been amassed at the expense of the communes, some of which, even the most prosperous in former times, viz., Florence, Turin and Naples, are forced to appeal to Government for pecuniary assistance."

It may well be asked, how it is that the working men, who are the victims of this military oppression, do not combine to protest against it, and insist upon disarmament. It used to be said, "War is a game which were their subjects wise, kings would not play at"; but in Italy, under a free, constitutional Government, *the subjects* are, nominally at least, ruling, and exhausting themselves in preparations for this very game. The suffrage, if not universal, is on a wide enough basis. The new Electoral Law confers votes on every male of twenty-one who can read and write and pay twenty francs of direct taxes. The greatest apathy, however, prevails among the electoral body, and not one half of them ever trouble to record their votes. This apathy and ignorance are not to be wondered at, when we consider the long centuries of darkness and misgovernment through which the population of the Peninsula have passed; but light is beginning to dawn, and if ever the eyes of the working men are so opened, that they see clearly their own interest and power, there will be a speedy end to the military system and to the costly institutions which it supports.

On my homeward journey from Sicily, I did not re-visit France as intended, knowing that our relief work was proceeding in the capable hands of a number of volunteers, who had followed us in order to superintend the seed corn distribution throughout the extensive district requiring such relief. Among them was my late friend, James Long, M.A., who though not himself a Quaker, appears later in my narrative, as the Friends' Commissioner, after the massacres of 1876, in Bulgaria. James Long having resided both in France and Spain, proved an efficient and active helper. There being a dearth of milch cows in France, he made a long expedition to Andalusia, in the south of Spain, where he purchased a number of bulls and cows of the beautiful Andalusian breed, the race which is specially in demand for the purpose of bull-fights in Spain. By the French peasants these handsome animals were much appreciated, and they were assigned on loan to various communes, where their milk was a great boon to young children.

As a precaution, to prevent their being requisitioned, or otherwise disposed of, the cows were branded round each horn with the word "*Quakres.*" Ultimately, these Andalusian cattle were left in the country, as a highly-prized gift to the distressed peasantry, by whom they were valued as the introduction of a new and superior stock.

CHAPTER XIV.

BULGARIA—STATE OF COUNTRY, AND ATROCITIES—MY MISSION TO CONSTANTINOPLE—THE SULTAN'S FIRMAN AND TRANSLATION—TATAR BAZARJIK—ZAPTIEHS—RIVER MARITZA: BRIDGE—MR. LONG'S HEALTH—CLIMATE: FROZEN BOTTLE—ARCHIMANDRITE'S KITCHEN—EXCITING DRIVE WITH ARCHIMANDRITE.

IN the early summer of 1876, dark rumours reached this country of horrible cruelties committed upon the peaceable inhabitants of Central Turkey. In the month of June these rumours assumed more definite shape, in the letters of Mr. Pears, the able resident correspondent of the *Daily News* in Constantinople, in which details were given of a large number of villages in Bulgaria that were reported to have been destroyed; also of the slaughter of men, and of barbarous outrages committed upon women and girls.

Inquiries in official quarters at home elicited no information. Nothing had been heard on the subject from Sir Henry Elliott, our Ambassador at Constantinople. In fact, Mr. Disraeli, the leader of the House of Commons, treated the matter with scornful levity, declaring that these "idle rumours were mere coffee-house babble."

In the meantime, the proprietors of the *Daily News* dispatched a special Commissioner, Mr. J. A. McGahan, to institute inquiries into these terrible allegations on the spot. He reached Philippopolis, the centre of the disturbed districts, on the 23rd July, and at once commenced his investigations, in conjunction with Mr. Eugene Schuyler, American Consul-General for Turkey.

When Mr. McGahan's first letters were published, revealing a tale of horror, of sixty or seventy villages that had been burned, and that some 15,000 persons had been slaughtered, of whom a large part were women and children, the English Government could no longer resist the pressure that was brought to bear on them, and they dispatched Mr. Baring as their Commissioner, to report upon the whole matter. Mr. Baring, after investigation, officially reported that in the districts round Tatar Bajarjik alone, according to the lowest estimate, fifty villages had been burnt, without counting those that had been only pillaged, and that nearly 15,000 people had been killed.

It was denied by the Turkish authorities that any acts had been committed beyond what were absolutely needful in order to suppress a serious insurrection in Bulgaria. Mr. Baring found no confirmatory evidence in regard to any rising among the people, and Mr. Schuyler, in his official report, flatly denied that there had been any insurrection in Bulgaria, worthy of the name.

Mr. McGahan's graphic, vivid recitals, which appeared in the columns of the *Daily News*, of the revolting details which accompanied the butchery, startled all civilised Europe, and stirred the moral sense of this country to its centre. Urgent demands were made upon our Government to protest against these atrocities, and to insist upon the condign punishment of the perpetrators of them. All in vain, however, because these men had simply carried out the wishes and intentions of the Turkish Government, if not the positive orders of the Sultan himself! They did their behest, and were rewarded accordingly!

The "Turkish Atrocities" in Bulgaria, as they were termed, have in recent times been so far surpassed by the wholesale massacres perpetrated by Turks and Kurds upon the Christian population of Armenia, that they have in comparison sunk almost into insignificance. It should not, however, be forgotten that the bloodshed and wanton cruelties of twenty-three years ago, committed on the unprotected Christians of Bulgaria, not only aroused the passionate indignation of this country, but led to a war of fearful retaliation, undertaken by Russia against Turkey.

By the unwise diplomatic intervention of England after the Russo-Turkish war, Turkey was saved from dismemberment; and through England's mischievous influence in the Treaty of Berlin, the Government of the Sultan was so far rehabilitated, that it has been enabled to continue on its evil career of misgovernment and tyranny over its Christian subjects for a further lease of twenty-three years.

Mr. Eugene Schuyler, a thoroughly impartial witness, who, at the instance of the American Government, had proceeded to Bulgaria about three months after the occurrence of the massacres in 1876, in order to investigate the facts, stated, in his cautiously worded report, that "these atrocities were clearly unnecessary for the suppression of the insurrection; for it was an insignificant rebellion at the best; and the villages generally surrendered at the first summons. Nor can they be justified by a state of panic, which was over before the troops set out on the commission. An attempt is, however, made—and not by Turks alone—to defend and palliate them on the ground of the previous atrocities which it is alleged were committed by the Bulgarians. I have carefully investigated this point, and am unable to find that the Bulgarians committed *any* outrages, or atrocities, or any acts which deserved that name. . . No Turkish women or children were killed in cold blood; no Moslem women were violated; no Mussulmans were tortured; no purely Turkish village was attacked or burned; no Mussulman house was pillaged; no Mosque was desecrated or destroyed. The report of the special Turkish Commissioner, Edib Effendi, contains statements on this point, as on every other, which are *utterly unfounded* in fact; and the whole report may be characterised as a tissue of falsehoods."

The bitter cry of the suffering people appealed, like the cry of the victims of the Franco-German War, to England, and met again with a noble response. Several relief expeditions were organised, one of the best known of which was that under the care of Lady Strangford. The Society of Friends also raised a considerable fund, which was administered under the care of their own Commissioner, the late James Long, who had served them so well in France. Mr. Long proceeded to Tatar Bazarjik, which was situated in the centre of the disturbed districts, accompanied by a staff of carpenters from Alsace, his object being to erect, as quickly as possible, on the site of the destroyed villages, a number of wooden huts, or barracks, in order to shelter the homeless people.

Mr. Long having obtained permission from Baron Hirsch to cut all the timber he required for this purpose from the Baron's own forest of Bellova, set up a steam saw mill there, and thus provided a large supply of planks. These were allotted to the districts according to their need ; and on the villagers themselves was laid the task of fetching the timber from the railway station at Tatar Bazarjik to their various homes, after which the carpenters were sent to put up the houses. By this means all the destroyed villages, within a radius of twenty-five miles around Tatar Bazarjik, were rapidly supplied with wooden houses, sufficient to shelter about ten thousand homeless people, before the inclement winter of 1876-7, in all its severity, was upon them.

Mr. Long, however, who was in delicate health, having fallen seriously ill, it became absolutely necessary for some one to go from England to his succour, and to take charge of the work. The Committee first applied to Thomas Whitwell, as the best man for the object in view; then failing him, I was pressed to undertake this service, which was known to be one of no little difficulty, and even of danger.

At Constantinople.

Accordingly, again leaving my home and business, I landed from a French steamer in Constantinople, in the month of November, 1876. There I learned that it was impossible to proceed into the interior, the railway line being completely blocked with deep snow, and the traffic at a standstill.

Remaining for about two weeks in Constantinople, I received much assistance from Mr. Pears, the able correspondent of the *Daily News*, who was also a Judge in the Consular Court. The intervening time, before the line was re-opened for traffic, was employed in obtaining, through the British Embassy, the Sultan's Firman.

I was advised, that before proceeding into the interior of Turkey, especially in war-time, it was needful to have the authorization of the Porte. On the application of the British Ambassador, I was accordingly supplied with a "Sultan's Firman," a strange looking document measuring 33 by 22 inches, the Turkish characters being written on ordinary paper, from left to right upwards, finishing with the Sultan's "*Paraphe*," or signature, at the top. Parchment would have been more serviceable, as the document had often to be shown; but, although a fee of one pound sterling was charged, parchment was far too costly to be afforded by the poor Turkish Government!

I append a translation of this document, as a specimen of the inflated and hyperbolic language that is employed in State documents in Eastern Europe, and in Asia. My translation is from the French rendering of it, by my Turkish Dragoman "Victor." The document, it will be seen, is addressed to Assim Pacha, Governor of the province of Adrianople.

"Most glorious Councillor, Director of the World, Regulator of the institutions of the peoples, he who directs public affairs by thoughts full of penetration, who conducts to a good end the important transactions of nations by a right judgment, who confirms the happiness and strengthens the pillars of prosperity and of magnificence, who is crowned with divine and terrestrial favours, my illustrious Vizier, Assim Pacha, Governor General of Adrianople, etc., is invited to the reception of the present Firman, delivered at the request of the English Ambassador, to the English Citizen, Mr. William Jones, to grant him every facility of transport and of sustenance, during his travels in the interior of the Vilayet of Adrianople, on condition, however, that the said Mr. Jones submits to all the conditions required by the laws of the Empire.

"Given at Constantinople, the 14th day of Moharrem, 1293" (A.D. 1876).

Before leaving Constantinople I also made it my business to collect information about the state of Bulgaria. One of the most interesting visits then made by me was to the "Robert College" on the Bosporus, where young men, chiefly of Bulgarian nationality, are educated and trained as missionaries.

Tatar Bazarjik.

At length I was able to quit Constantinople, and passing through Adrianople and Philippopolis, arrived at the end of the second day's railway journey at Tatar Bazarjik, which was at that time the terminus of the railway. It was also our headquarters, Mr. Long having hired a house for himself and assistants in the town. Great was my astonishment, on arriving at night at the outer gate, to find myself confronted by a Turkish soldier with fixed bayonet. "You are a worthy representative of the Society of Friends," I remarked to my friend Long, "to have a soldier on sentry at your door to receive your friends, with bayonet fixed." "Oh," said he, "I can soon pacify your conscience about that matter. I have always a considerable sum of money in the house, as we have no bank nearer than Constantinople, two days journey by rail. Well, I first employed a 'zaptieh' (armed policeman) to guard the house, but as I am generally awake at night, I soon found that my guardian was doing his level best to rob me. I dismissed him and got another, who proved to be no better, and so, one by one, I went through all the zaptiehs in the town, and found them untrustworthy, every one. On complaining of this to the Turkish Commandant, he said, 'Yes, these zaptiehs are all thieves. Their pay is always in arrear, and the poor fellows must live; but I will put a man at your door whom you can trust—a common Turkish soldier.' Since then," said Mr. Long, "I have no care at all about thieves."

Mr. Long and party had been confined to the house for some weeks, owing to the deep snow rendering travelling impossible. It was resolved that we should now make an attempt to visit some of the villages which required relief. Accordingly, the horses were brought out next morning, and my first experience of Turkish travel was a pretty rough one. The horses, having stood idle in the stables for some weeks, were so frisky on starting in the snow, that it was no easy matter to keep a firm seat in the saddle. On crossing the river Maritza, which is very wide at Tatar Bazarjik, by a long wooden bridge, the flooring of which was in an unsafe condition, my spirited Turkish horse pranced and curvetted so vigorously, that one of the loose planks rose up on end, so as to nearly strike him. This made him bound with startling suddenness to one side, almost against the frail wooden parapet, and for a moment a catastrophe seemed imminent. Having thus narrowly escaped being precipitated into the river, I was thankful that my mount now sobered down and kept pace quietly with his companions. He proved to be an excellent and wiry animal, but our forty miles or more of travel in that rough country took all the lightheartedness out of him, and we came home at night, both man and horse, almost exhausted by fatigue and hunger.

Owing to confirmed insomnia it was Mr. Long's habit every night to sit up after the others had gone to bed, writing up reports and accounts, until four or five o'clock in the morning. He would then lie down and sleep for two or three hours, and be ready to join the party on horseback after an early breakfast.

This practice he kept up the whole time I was with him, and the amount of work he got through on so small an allowance of sleep was a constant marvel to me. Yet even he occasionally succumbed to the irresistible demands of nature. When traversing the country together in the daytime, I have seen him asleep on horseback, and continue so for some time even when the horse was trotting, until awakened by some sudden jerk or stoppage.

BULGARIAN WINTER.

The severity of the climate in Bulgaria during the months of December and January greatly astonished me, bearing in mind that the latitude of the country was about the same as that of the middle of Spain. It recalled forcibly to mind what Lord John Russell, speaking in the House of Commons, had termed "the horrible and heart-rending" sufferings of our soldiers in the wintry weather of the Crimea, during the war of 1854-5. Anyone that knows what winter in the Balkans is like, will appreciate what we endured on these lofty storm-swept plateaux. On leaving England, I had been somewhat reluctant to encumber myself with a warm fur-lined coat; my Balkan winter experiences, however, soon convinced me that without warm furs the very conditions of existence would have been wanting for a constitution like mine. As we could carry no thermometer on horseback, we kept no record of the actual temperature. A special instance may be given as an illustration of the extreme cold.

Occasionally it became necessary for us to pass the night in villages which were situated high up on the Balkan mountains, too distant for us to return home before darkness rendered travelling unsafe. On one such occasion, passing the night on the floor of one of the wooden barracks erected for the Bulgarians, the keen air finding its way in through innumerable crevices, I found sleep impossible, owing to the deadly cold. My companion, who suffered from internal pain, had placed at his side an indiarubber bottle filled with boiling water, and after a lapse of three or four hours I took

ARCHIMANDRITE OF THE BULGARIAN CHURCH,
AT TATAR BAZARJIK.

it up with a view to replenish it, when to my surprise I found it frozen solid. Not a drop of water would run out on unscrewing the stopper. It had frozen, in spite of the warmth of its position.

My frequent companion on these rough cross-country rides was a French engineer, who had been employed in making the railway, and was now one of Mr. Long's assistants. His pertinacity in watching my nose against frost-bite often amused me. "Now dismount," he would say, "and run a mile, or you will lose your feet.' His experience of the climate had taught him the necessity of this care, and no doubt his watchfulness often saved me from much suffering. There were, strictly speaking, no formed roads, only mere tracks, and these of the roughest description in the hilly part of the country.

Occasionally it was necessary to take with us the Archimandrite, or Chief Priest of the Bulgarian Church of Tatar Bazarjik, to the opening ceremonies of the newly erected village homes.

It was my practice during my stay at Tatar Bazarjik occasionally to call upon the Archimandrite in the evening, in order to gain information about the state of the country; and also to satisfy his very intelligent inquiries about English politicians, especially about Mr. Gladstone, whose name was then held in great reverence throughout all Bulgaria.

On these occasions I was always accompanied by my interpreter, Mr. Slavcho-Taptchileshtoff. This youth had been educated by the American missionaries at the Robert College, on the Bosporus, and spoke English and French, besides Bulgarian and some Turkish. He was very intelligent and well instructed, and after we had left the country he was promoted to the position of private secretary to Prince Alexander of Battenburg, the first Governor of emancipated Bulgaria. Proud of the promotion, he wrote to me in England to announce his good fortune.

The Archimandrite seemed to have unbounded confidence in the Society of Friends, who had shown their practical benevolence by sending two representatives to help Bulgaria in its hour of distress. He was very urgent that I should bring home with me to England his son, a youth of sixteen, to be educated by the Society of Friends. Mr. Long and I, however, came to the conclusion that it would not be a wise step to take the youth from his evil surroundings, and to accustom him for some years to the freedom of political and social life in England, as it would make it an impossibility for him in the future to reconcile himself to a life under the cruel despotism of the Turks. I therefore recommended the Archimandrite to send his boy to the Robert College, on the Bosporus.

On one of these social occasions at the Archimandrite's house, he asked, "Would you like to see that which cometh upon me daily, besides the care of all my churches?" I asked him to what he referred. He invited me to accompany him to his kitchen. There I found a company of Bulgarians of both sexes, gathered from various parts of his jurisdiction, who had come to lay before him complaints of their treatment by the Turks. One man unwound a shawl from his head and showed a deep gash from a Turkish sabre; another had a terrible story of outrage to members of his family; a third had had his bullocks stolen; another had suffered a severe beating for no offence, but simply because he was unable to pay his taxes; and so it went on all round the room. When we had completed the investigation, I turned to the Archimandrite and said, "Do you mean really to say that this comes upon you *daily?*" He replied, "Yes, more or less every day of my life." I then said, "This state of things would drive me mad. Why don't you complain to the Turkish authorities?" He shrugged his shoulders, and said, "My dear Sir, you don't know the Turkish authorities as I do. When I first came here, I went often to the 'Konak,' or Government House, to complain to the Commandant of the treatment of my people, but the Turks took no notice of my complaints, and at last, wearied with my importunities, threatened to kick me out of the Konak. No, Sir," he added impressively, "we have no redress, but we look up to God."

Mountain Drives.

The Archimandrite being no horseman (though the horse is almost the sole means of locomotion in these mountainous regions), when accompanied by him we hired a conveyance and drove along as best we could, over wretched tracks which were little better than goat paths, on the foot hills of the Balkans.

The roads were unspeakably bad, with the sole exception of the old Roman road which runs the entire length of the country from Constantinople to Belgrade, and, under the Roman power, connected the two capitals of the Empire, Rome and Constantinople.

The object of taking the Archimandrite with us was, that he might pronounce his blessing upon the temporary wooden houses which we had built in lieu of the burnt villages, the blessing thus pronounced by him being, among the Bulgarians at least, equivalent to a policy of insurance upon those erections. In these fearful excursions into the hills, our little carriage was often placed in very critical circumstances. The driver was an old Turk, a perfect fatalist, who had lost one hand whilst an artilleryman, and he drove three spirited Bulgarian ponies abreast, with his one hand and a hook. The carriage sometimes approached so near the edge of an abyss, that Mr. Long, who was a man of strong nerve, when sitting on the outer side—the Archimandrite being between us—could look over the wheel down into the depth below, and tell us with composure, "We are within an inch of the verge." On more than one occasion I had to shout to the driver to stop, telling Mr. Long that flesh and blood could endure this no longer, but that I must be out and trust to my own limbs.

I remember one drive of special difficulty, on account of the snow and frost in that extremely hard winter. It taxed the skill of our Turkish driver, who had all the courage of his fatalism, and would face difficulties which no English driver would dream of attempting in a wheeled vehicle. On the occasion alluded to, the conveyance, with four of us in it, was sliding down the frozen face of a slope, pushing along the three ponies down the incline towards the precipice at the bottom, the driver meantime pulling them back almost upon their haunches. Before reaching the abyss, the Turk, with marvellous skill, gave his three ponies such a sharp slew round, that he succeeded in landing them safely on the wooden bridge crossing the adjoining ravine at a sharp angle, and which had no parapets or side rails to it. The centrifugal force of this action flung the outer pony over the edge of the bridge, and left him dangling in his rope harness above the boiling torrent which roared far below. We three sat still, wondering what course the old Turk would now take. He deliberately dismounted, searched under his seat for a large knife, which he stuck between his teeth, stood over the spot where the pony was swinging in the air, and after taking a careful survey of the situation, deliberately cut the ropes, and let the animal fall into the torrent below. I saw the rapid current roll the poor brute over and over, showing the shining plates on his hoofs now and then in the air. Ponies in Bulgaria are usually shod with a flat plate, in the same way as bullocks, a most unsafe plan during frost and snow. After cutting loose the pony thus suspended over the torrent, the Turk now returned to his seat and drove the other two ponies across the bridge. Here he stopped, and we all four sat in perfect silence. After a while, to my utter amazement, thinking, of course, that the pony was either drowned or dashed to pieces among the rocks, we heard a faint whinnying sound at a considerable distance down the stream. Our remaining ponies immediately pricked up their ears, and gave an answering whinny. In a little while the marvellous little creature, looking like a drowned rat, came trotting towards us, apparently no worse for the rough usage he had undergone, and delighted to rejoin his fellows. Our driver was ready for him with a new set of ropes, yoked him up and drove on. Strange to say, we were all so absorbed in our driver's proceedings, that not a word was spoken by any of us, the whole procedure being conducted with the silence and decorum of a "Friends' Meeting." This will give some idea of the amenities of a driving tour in midwinter through the mountainous regions of Turkey.

CHAPTER XV.

BULGARIA CONTINUED—THE HORRORS OF BATAK—BULGARIAN FAMILY LIFE—BRIGANDAGE—A CIRCASSIAN WARRIOR—STATE OF THE COUNTRY—BASHI-BAZOUKS ON THE WAR PATH—FLIGHT OF RURAL POPULATIONS.

THE special place—which was regarded as typical of the Turkish massacres—I resolved if possible to visit, before leaving the country. This was the village of Batak, a place of eight or nine thousand inhabitants, situated some forty miles south-west of Tatar Bazarjik, beyond the district in the relief of which we were engaged. Having no carriage road to it, and being accessible only by steep mountain tracks across the lofty spurs of the Balkans, it was no easy matter to reach it in winter.

Accompanied by our Turkish dragoman, "Victor," and one zaptieh, I set off very early one morning in a carriage, as far as the small town of Pestera, where the road terminated. The rest of the distance—fifteen miles or more—had to be accomplished on mountain ponies. The Mudir, or Turkish Governor of Pestera, did his utmost to delay our starting, by various devices and pretences, as the Turks threw every obstacle possible in the way of Europeans visiting Batak. Finally, after showing him my Sultan's Firman, and threatening to report him to the Vali, or Governor, of the province, he was cowed, and gave orders at once for horses to be brought. Thus, after some hours of precious daylight had been wasted, we started on the most toilsome and dangerous part of the journey, over the mountain tracks. The scenery was everywhere striking, and in some places even grand, covered, as the rocky peaks. the forests, and the valleys were, with a deep mantle of snow. But, as on the unbeaten tracks over which our guide took us we had frequently to dismount, in order to help our ponies to flounder through the snow, the labour became so severe and exhausting, that I was in no mood to appreciate scenery. By and by it became an anxious question whether I could possibly hold out to the end of the journey, so utterly exhausting was the hard work of pushing on, mile after mile, through snow, which was in places about three feet in depth. Late in the evening, when we were all completely worn out, Victor suddenly exclaimed, "*Voilà Batak*," as we perceived a faint light in the valley, deep down below us, where Batak was, lying in the hollow of a basin, surrounded by lofty hills.

Near as it looked, it took fully two hours of further toilsome tramp to reach the village, where I was most thankful to find shelter and rest for the night at a small wooden hospital, that had been built there by Lady Strangford.

Recruited by our hospitable reception in this Home of Benevolence, Victor and I set out next morning, after an early breakfast, on a tour of investigation through the village, taking with us as guide a delicate looking youth, himself a patient in the hospital, who spoke a little English. His father, who had been the schoolmaster of the village, had been treated by the Turks, he told us, with peculiar cruelty, the wretched man having been slowly hacked to pieces, joint by joint, for no crime but that of being the schoolmaster.

Schoolmasters and priests were singled out in every place, and made the victims of specially cruel treatment by the Turks.

The first thing that struck our notice, on going out of doors, was the utterly ruined appearance of the whole place. Every house had been burned, the effect of the whole reminding one of the streets of Pompeii. Batak had been a well-built village, with solid stone houses, and inhabited by a peaceable, industrious, law-abiding population, who had a thriving trade in sawn timber, there being a large number of little sawmills on the mountain rivulet which ran through the valley.

We looked into the church, a low building with a roof supported by heavy arches and looking as strong as a casemate. Into this church many hundreds of the inhabitants had fled for refuge from the murderous Bashi-Bazouks, thinking they would be safe in such a sanctuary. They were soon miserably undeceived; no Christian sanctuary is sacred from fanatical Moslems. The church was surrounded by armed men who fired through the windows with their rifles, into the dense crowd; then, weary of this slow work, they unroofed part of the church, and flung down among the shrieking mass of women and children a large quantity of combustibles, saturated with petroleum, and thus set all on fire. This fearful work continued, until the silence of death told a tale of horror.

Our guide from the hospital showed us a mark on one of the thick pillars inside the church, about shoulder high, that indicated the depth of the hideous mass of burnt and charred bodies, which were actually *seen* by Mr. Schuyler and Mr. McGahan, when they visited the spot. They also noticed a festering mass of about three thousand bodies of murdered Bulgarians lying in a heap in the adjoining churchyard. During the five months which had elapsed since their visit, the Turkish Government impelled, not so much by shame as by fear, in consequence of the prodigious stir throughout Europe which these savage barbarities had caused, ordered this putrifying mass of corruption to be buried, and quicklime scattered thickly over the spot. All this, however, did not remove the sickening charnel-house odour in the church itself, from which Victor and I were glad to escape, as out of a pest-house.

Being anxious to see the place where the terrible tragedy of the massacre, in cold blood, of the young women of Batak had taken place, of which

Mr. McGahan had sent so vivid and powerful a description to the *Daily News*, we proceeded up the road for a short distance, where the fatal plateau was pointed out by our guide, and by a Batak notable, who followed us from the village. No words of mine can so well describe the tragic scene which took place on this spot, as a few sentences from McGahan's description. "We asked," he writes, "about the skulls and bones we had seen up on the hill, upon first arriving in the village, where the dogs had barked at us. These, we were told, were the bones of about two hundred young girls who had first been captured, and particularly reserved for a worse fate than death. They had been kept till the last. They had been in the hands of their captors for several days—for the burning and the pillaging had not all been accomplished in a single day—and during this time they had suffered all that it was possible that poor, weak, trembling girls could suffer, at the hands of brutal savages. Then, when the town had been pillaged and burnt, when all their friends had been slaughtered, these poor young things, whose very wrongs should have ensured them safety whose very outrages should have ensured them protection, were taken, in the broad light of day, beneath the smiling canopy of Heaven, coolly beheaded, then thrown in a heap there, and left to rot. Mr. Disraeli was right, when he wittily remarked in the House of Commons that the Turks usually terminated their connection with people who fell into their hands, in a more expeditious manner than by imprisoning them. And so they do. At the time he made that light-hearted remark, these young girls had been lying there many days."

The associations connected with this scene of blood, which nature had now kindly covered up with a mantle of snow, were really too terrible to dwell upon. Our guide and the old man were both in tears, probably because they had lost relatives there on that fatal day. They told us that the cries and shrieks of the young girls, when they realised their doom, and saw the gleaming sabres of the fierce-eyed ruffians drawn to murder them, were heartrending. They fell at Achmet Aga, the leader's feet, pleading piteously for mercy; for bare life! Appeal! Alas! They might as well have appealed to the howling wilderness. There is no pity, no compassion, no bowels of mercy in bestial savages like Achmet Aga and his fanatical horde. In a few minutes the whole company of these innocent victims, comprising the flower and beauty of Batak, was reduced to a mass of bleeding headless corpses. This was the heap of skulls, intermingled with putrid human bodies, human hair, and clothing, that was actually seen and described by the two reliable witnesses, Schuyler and McGahan.

Could anything be said in justification of the severities inflicted on Batak? Absolutely nothing. Not even the wildest alarmist could pretend to accuse these innocent girls of conspiring against the Turkish Government. There was no conceivable excuse for their murder. It was unmitigated, wanton cruelty, out of sheer delight in bloodshed. In spite of all the efforts of our then Foreign Secretary, Lord Derby, to have the guilty leader, Achmet Aga, brought to justice, this low ignorant brute, who could neither read nor write, was decorated and advanced by the Government to the dignity of Pasha, as a reward for his "noble deeds"! Such are the creatures this Sultan, Abdul Hamid, "delighteth to honour." Nothing even in the recent terrible record of this "Crowned Assassin" in Armenia, exceeds in brutal savagery the treatment of the young and innocent women of Batak, and it remains to this day to be the *blackest* of all the black deeds of the infamous reign of Sultan Abdul Hamid.

Bulgarian Homes.

On our way back to Tatar Bazarjik, night overtook us when we reached the village of Raddovo, and as a blinding snow storm had come on, and we were still a long way from our destination, we stopped at a Bulgarian house to refresh ourselves and our horses. We were hospitably offered shelter for the night. This induced me to begin to take stock of the situation. Bulgarian families are often large, consisting of the grandparents, parents and children, to the number sometimes of fifteen persons, or more. Looking around, I saw three or four cows on one side of the common room, in which the family lived. There were also calves, goats, and a number of fowls; so that, with our two selves, it might fairly be classed as a "populous place," and probably, very populous indeed in minuter life! The prospect of lying all night, huddled on the floor of this crowded den, between two Bulgars who had not been washed for fifty years, was not inviting, so turning to Victor, I said, "Let us go!" I could face the horrors of the storm better than I could stand Bulgarian village hospitality, with all its concomitant charms. Out into the stormy dark night we went accordingly, and in due time, thanks to the mettle of our good horses, made our way through tempest and darkness to Tatar Bazarjik. Every time we crossed the shaky long wooden bridge over the Maritza, after dark, we took the precaution to dismount, and lead our horses carefully over the flooring of the bridge, so dangerous was the condition of this, the main entrance to the town, there being holes in the rotten planking large enough to let a man fall through into the dark, swift current below.

Batak furnished another instance of the utter neglect of the Turkish Government to supply proper means of communication throughout the country. It was a place of considerable trade in sawn timber, the mountains surrounding it still having, like Bosnia, some of the primeval forest remaining. After the timber was felled and sawn up into planks, it had to be carried on the backs of ponies, over the rough tracks across the spurs of the Balkans, for nearly forty miles to the railway station of Tatar Bazarjik. Here it was forwarded by rail to the port of Dede-a-gatch on the Black Sea, to be shipped to Smyrna, and there utilised for making the "Eléme" fig boxes, so well known in this country. And yet Batak, in spite of the taxes it had paid for centuries past, was left without a decent road, or any bridges over the numerous streams on the way to it. In short, it may be asked, "What does the Government of the Porte do for its subjects, Moslem or Christian?" It taxes them to the very verge of endurance, and gives them *nothing* in return, not even protection for life and property.

The Circassians.

Brigandage was rife throughout the country. It was a confused, lawless, cut-throat period in the history of Bulgaria, and although at Tatar Bazarjik we were not molested, probably owing to the constant passage of soldiers to and from the Servian and Russian Wars, yet a few miles away the rural districts were infested by bands of roving Circassians on horseback, or by armed Albanian and other brigands. My companion and I passed on one occasion such a band of marauders, but happily without molestation. Mr. Long, on seeing a troop of these "Tcherkess" (as the Circassians were called) approaching us, armed to the teeth, said aside to me, "Our lives are not worth five minutes purchase." It certainly looked very serious, for these relentless marauders "neither feared God nor regarded man." It occurred to me that to meet them with a smiling face, throwing up one's hands, to show that we were *unarmed*, might conciliate them, and induce them to let us pass unmolested. They eyed us hard as they rode past, but, to our wonder, made no attempt to attack us.

It may be thought that this was owing to our having a zaptieh with us, whom they might look upon as a symbol of authority. Such, however, was not my own thought. Far otherwise, my confidence rested on that Higher Power in whose hands alone was the safe keeping of our lives.

I often felt a desire to interview one of these redoubtable "Tcherkess" warriors, and on one occasion had my desire amply gratified. It happened thus: Bonifay, the French engineer, and I, were riding together on the road to Sofia. In the distance, in front of us, we noticed a solitary Circassian horseman, who pulled up at the roadside "Khan" or Inn. We hitched our horses at the door and followed him in. He glared at us scowlingly as we entered, but Bonifay spoke a few words in Turkish and offered him a "Baksheesh" of tobacco. This at once promoted friendly relations, and now I could take stock of him at leisure. He was a really handsome fellow, of about thirty years of age, lithe, active, wiry-looking, with an oval face and good features, a very small hand, and high instep, in fact a typical Circassian. I counted sixteen weapons in his shawl-belt, and taking out one of them, a Damascus blade, the handle of which I found to be too small for my hand, I handed it back to him with a smile. He took it and began to display for my special benefit his expertness as a swordsman. With a marvellous suppleness of wrist, he flourished the glittering blade before my eyes, and round my head, with a speed and a dash, that made me tremble for the safety of my nose. Now it was gleaming in front, and now at the back of my head, thus fixing me, as it were, in a vice, so that I feared to stir an inch back or forward. There was no alternative but to "grin and bear it" until he grew tired of his playful game, when I began to breathe freely once more, saying to myself, "A little of this sort of thing goes a long way! No more interviews with playful Tcherkess for me!" Happily the fellow was perfectly good-natured, though grave as a judge during the performance; he smiled complacently at the close of the feat, as though lost in admiration of his own skill. My own smile, however, was not altogether one of disinterested admiration of his really clever performance.

There were said to be more than 50,000 of these Moslem refugees from Circassia, after the occupation of their country by the Russians, who had been quartered upon the Christian villages of Bulgaria; and as large bands of them continually raided the country in all directions, stealing horses and everything they could lay their hands on, murdering and marauding at large, to the terror of the inhabitants and of travellers, their conduct grew at last so intolerable, even to the Turkish Government, by whose special invitation they had crossed the Black Sea into Bulgaria, that shortly after the war, the bulk of them were shipped back into Asia Minor.

TERRIBLE CONDITION OF COUNTRY.

This brings me to a consideration of the state of the country. As regards its physical aspects, the examples I have mentioned of the roadless and bridgeless regions around Bazarjik and Batak may be taken as a sample of the whole. In Macedonia things were even in a worse state. Roads there were of a kind, but so utterly out of repair, that their dangerous condition went far to prove that not a single stone had been laid on them since Philip of Macedon marched his celebrated phalanx over them. The only really good carriage road then existing was, as before mentioned, that which traversed the country from north to south, formed by the old Roman Power as a means of communication between Rome and Constantinople; and even this road, close to the important town of Philippopolis, had been so damaged by floods when we were there, from the overflowing of adjoining rice fields, that a mail coach might have been engulfed in one of the holes, through which vehicles of every description, entering or leaving the town, had to flounder as best they could. The main line of railway, made by Baron Hirsch, being entirely under the management of Austrian officials, was maintained in fairly good order, and this, of course, relieved the highways of much traffic.

The condition of the people, both Mohammedan and Christian, during the Russo-Turkish War, was deplorable in the extreme. Often as we entered the villages on horseback, being compelled always to take a zaptieh with us, I noticed the terror depicted on the countenances of the villagers. The women used to approach us and ask, with faces white with fear, whether the enemy, *i.e.*, the Turks, were coming. On our trying to calm their fears, they would ask piteously, "What must we do, must we flee to the mountains?" Alas! there was little we could say to comfort them. Never before had I realised how awful it must be to live under an ever-present dread of impending massacre!

Later on in the progress of the war, when the Russians had overcome their difficulties at Plevna, and had fought their way through the Shipka Pass in the Balkan Range, and were advancing directly south towards Constantinople, the Moslem population everywhere fled in panic before them. Just in the same way, the Christian populations of

Bulgaria fled in terror before the Turkish armies, marching northwards to encounter the Russians. Too well did these Christian populations know what the advance of Bashi-Bazouks meant for them—burnt villages, pillaging, murder and every outrage, marked the progress of these Moslem hordes, who left in their track ruin, death, and despair. Many thousands of these helpless, terror-stricken rustics left their homes and took to the roads, having packed their few household goods upon their small bullock wagons. They wandered aimlessly about the country, some fleeing northwards, some to the south, literally "not knowing whither they went." The roads everywhere were encumbered with their bullock wagons, extending in some places for the distance of twelve miles or more. Eventually, they were caught up in inextricable confusion between the two great advancing armies, Russian and Turkish, as between the jaws of an enormous vice. Numbers of them succeeded in making their escape westwards, as far as the Rhodope Mountains.

In this desolate region, freed at last from their fears of pursuit by their dreaded enemies, they soon encountered still more deadly foes, in the shape of hunger and cold. Ill-provided with food and clothing, they perished by thousands from sheer famine and exposure to the severity of the climate. The Rhodope Range, on its snow-covered slopes, was thickly dotted over with the sick, the aged, and the dying. The untold sufferings and enormous loss of life among these, the non-combatant part of the population, both Mohammedan and Christian, were, according to competent observers, on so vast a scale, as almost, if not altogether, to be unprecedented in the annals of warfare.

Many thousands who had fled south as far as Constantinople, utterly destitute, were suffered to die of famine, in spite of the charities that were doled out to them in that city. One considerable section of these miserable refugees directed their flight towards Tatar Bazarjik, which was then the northern terminus of the railway. The panic-stricken mob stampeded in terror through the town, down to the railway station, where they took possession of a train of empty carriages. When the officials came to start the train for Constantinople, the wretched, worn-out creatures stolidly refused to be dislodged, their fears urging them to flee to Constantinople, *or anywhere*, from the presence of enemies, by whom they believed themselves to be pursued. The train was at last compelled to start, with every carriage crammed with men, women, and children. Many clambered upon the roofs of the carriages, while others stood on the steps clinging to the handles. In this condition the train actually proceeded on its two days journey towards Constantinople. My friend Mr. Long, who accompanied it, to see what became of the wretched fugitives, told me afterwards that from his place in the last van he could see, by the tail lights of the train, the frequent dropping of *frozen corpses* from the roofs of the carriages into the snow upon the railway line, the effect at night being weird and ghastly in the extreme.

The commission of foreign consuls, sent to investigate these calamitous results of the war, reported that more than 150,000 homeless and starving refugees were wandering about the villages of this inhospitable region, with no resources of food or clothing for the impending wintry season. It was stated to be within the limit of fact, that more than half a million of Mohammedans had abandoned their homes, when finally the Russian advance surged forward without interruption to the gates of Constantinople. A large proportion of these fugitives eventually perished. In addition to these, about 300,000 Bulgarians fled from their villages. The sufferings of all these destitute wanderers can never be told, much less appreciated. To myself it threw an entirely new light upon the saying of our Lord to His disciples, "Pray ye that your flight be not in the winter."

In the preceding paragraphs, describing the state of the country, I have availed myself of some of my friend Mr. Long's experiences, in addition to my own. We were in constant communication with each other after my return to England, and as he remained in Bulgaria throughout the whole of the Russo-Turkish War, and was for a considerable time afterwards engaged in doing what he could to relieve the distress occasioned by it, his accounts, as an eye-witness of its horrors, I could accept as perfectly reliable.

How much has the Sultan profited by the object lesson of these calamitous sufferings of his subjects, Moslem and Christian alike? The answer is not far to seek. The woes of Armenia, which have sent a thrill of horror throughout the civilised world, are a sufficient answer to the question. The magnitude of those wrongs, and the cool cynicism of their guilty contriver, have never been surpassed! In war-time the thought has often been present with me, of all the sorrow which befalls humanity, how small a part falls upon the *specially guilty*.

In our occasional rides across the country situated between Tatar Bazarjik and Philippopolis, over extensive plains once noted for their richness and fertility, but now in many parts gone out of cultivation and become mere prairie waste, we were impressed with the lack of signs of human habitation. We passed by many old cemeteries in the most neglected, forlorn condition. In a few of these the crosses at the head of the graves indicated Christian burial, but in most of them the carved turban, on short stone pillars, evidenced Moslem sepulture. But where were the villages? No village, no house, no sign of human inhabitants for mile after mile, could be recognised over this silent, solitary wilderness; it was the very "abomination of desolation."

How impossible to resist the conviction, that was

continually forced upon the mind when riding across these desolate wastes, that these people (the Ottoman Turks) are slowly, but surely, *dying out!* That the Ottoman Empire is doomed has long been accepted as a settled fact in Europe. The Czar Nicholas believed it when he propounded his views in 1853, as to the division of the "Sick Man's" estates. Richard Cobden and many others believed, in their day, that the end of Turkish misrule was almost in sight. It evidently is not safe to prophesy *when* its death-knell will sound. When asked, on my return from Bulgaria in 1877, how long the Turkish power would still endure, I thought that ten years would about see the end of it. It has lasted more than twenty years since then, and after the recent fiasco called the "Concert of Europe," the ability, and the diplomatic astuteness of the wily Abdul Hamid, have so completely outshone that of any other crowned head, or European minister—if not indeed that of the whole of them put together—that the Turkish power to-day is not only rehabilitated, but is actually stronger than it has been at any previous time in the century!

It is instructive to glance at the past history of the Empire of the Ottoman Turks. The tree is known by its fruits. In our own times we have seen in Scio, in Bulgaria, in Armenia, in Crete, what these fruits have been. Scenes of violence, of rapine, of blood and of relentless oppression, have invariably marked every chapter of Turkish history. It has been one long tale of the might and ruthless ferocity of a conquering race, ruling over the peace-loving populations of Western Asia and Eastern Europe. Even the worst barbarities of slavery pale before the frightful crimes and atrocities, which have been for nearly a thousand years the every-day history of the unhappy Eastern peoples.

The Ottoman Turk has always asserted, and to this day asserts, his divine right to oppress; and the richest rewards of his sensual paradise are to be the happy lot of those who have distinguished themselves by the amount of "Giaour," or "Infidel," (*i.e.*, Christian) blood they have shed.

"What is the meaning of the conflict that has been waged in the East for so many centuries?" asks a modern writer. "Is it not that of barbarism against civilization, of brute force and the sword against moral power, law, and the arts of peace? Wherever the standard of the Prophet has been planted, there civilization, arts, sciences, and law have died away, and provinces which were once rich and fertile have returned to nearly the desolation of the desert."

How long the sink of corruption and of effete barbarism called the "Ottoman Porte" may yet continue, no man may venture to predict, but as surely as there is a just God who rules in the kingdoms of men, so certain do I feel that the day of retribution, for a thousand years of ruthless oppression and wrong, is inevitable.

Turkish misgovernment and oppression *must*, and *will* perish, *because* the Omnipotent reigns! "That men may know that Thou alone, whose name is Jehovah, art the Most High over all the Earth."—Psalm lxxxiii. 18.

As one ponders over these well-established facts of Turkish misrule, which must have been known to every European Statesman, how is it possible, one asks in amazement, that the traditional policy of England has for so long been that of bolstering up, for our own purposes, such a desolating and loathsome oppression as the Government of Constantinople? Let us hope for better things, however, in future, since a Foreign Minister (Lord Salisbury) has publicly recanted in the House of Lords his own personal share in the past. His language, though savouring of the turf, was unmistakable in its meaning, when he declared that—"we have been putting our money on the wrong horse."

The great transformation that has been effected by Austria in Bosnia, which came under her rule after the Berlin Treaty of 1878, proves conclusively what twenty years of good government can do in the marvellous improvement both of the Mohammedan and Christian populations, and demonstrates that with just and fair treatment, the whole standard of civilization and progress can be materially raised among these Eastern peoples.

Pity it is that, owing to the jealousy of the Powers, the like benefits have not been extended to Macedonia and other provinces which are still groaning under Turkish misgovernment.

Bulgarian Characteristics.

Little has been said about the people of the country. It will be evident that the shortness of my residence among them precludes any sweeping generalisations about the national characteristics and habits of the Bulgarians. A few peculiarities of interest may, however, be worth noting. Physically, the Bulgarian is strong, healthy, and sturdily built, whilst his whole equipment, bodily and mental, is slow and stolid, forming in this respect a marked contrast to the active, vivacious Circassian. My remarks have no reference to the citizens or cultured classes, with whom my intercourse was very slight, but apply exclusively to the village populations. Their reverence towards the ceremonials of their religion was remarkable. Upon the occasions of the blessing of the new habitations by the Archimandrite, nearly the whole population of the village—men, women, and children—were present.

One singular trait, that I noticed repeatedly, was the entire absence of any expressions of gratitude for benefits received. Presents of warm clothing, etc., would be accepted at our hands with a stolid stare of indifference, and without a word of thanks. The only occasion on which such expression was given in my presence was from a poor leper, whom we found sitting by the roadside on a heap of stable manure, in order to obtain some little warmth for his shivering limbs, his clothing being thin and ragged. In his case, thanks in return for warm garments were profuse and sincere. So unaccustomed for generations past has the Bulgarian peasant evidently been to receive any kindness or charity, that the very sentiment of gratitude appears to have died away in him.

Another feature in their character was the timidity they showed whenever we entered a village on horseback. The men would gather into a distant corner, and watch with jealous eyes every movement of the one or more zaptiehs by whom we were escorted, reminding one of the way in which a flock of sheep in a field huddle together, eyeing the movements of the butcher's dog. "*C'est une population de moutons, Monsieur*," was the remark of one of our Frenchmen. It made one naturally query whether this cringing, timid population could possibly be the descendants of the barbarous Bulgar race, whose fierce, impetuous onslaughts, in the sixth century, filled the Byzantine Empire with panic. The martial genius and skill of the ablest General of the Empire, Belisarius, were taxed to the utmost before he succeeded in repelling the incursions of these formidable barbarians.

Does it not, however, appear as one of the notable object lessons of our own times, that within a short period after their emancipation from Turkish tyranny, and the attainment of self-government in 1878, this very down-trodden people showed something of the energy and courage of their distant ancestors ?

They won the respect of Europe, according to the late W. E. Forster, M.P., by the wise and capable administration of their country, and by their educational zeal and commercial enterprise. More striking still was the result of a few years' training of their newly-formed Militia, by their first Governor, Prince Alexander of Battenberg, himself an officer in the German army. These raw battalions withstood, firm as a rock, the onslaughts of the Servian army, which had attacked them in anticipation of an easy victory, greatly to its loss and discomfiture.

Since 1878, Bulgaria has proved herself, notwithstanding her former disadvantages, to be one of the most progressive of the States of Eastern Europe. Primary and secondary schools and colleges have been established, roads and bridges have been constructed, and railways extended. Agriculture and the improvement of the breeds of horses and cattle have been encouraged, and as the result, the condition of the peasants generally has been vastly ameliorated.

CHAPTER XVI.

FAMILY RELATIONSHIPS—PROMOTION OF ARBITRATION TREATY—VOYAGE TO AMERICA—INTERVIEWS WITH PRESIDENT CLEVELAND AND MRS. CLEVELAND—ANECDOTES OF JOHN BRIGHT, M.P.—LORD STRATFORD DE REDCLIFFE—RICHMOND CONFERENCE.

SOON after the marriage of our daughter in January, 1883, my wife and I, no longer having the society of our young people—our two sons being widely separated from us—reluctantly left our much appreciated home, "Undercliffe," at Great Ayton, Yorkshire. A new sphere of work had opened before me as Secretary of the Peace Society. We therefore removed to London as the centre for my future operations. For several years these included much organising work, and the delivery of addresses and lectures in all parts of the United Kingdom.

Whilst actively engaged in the prosecution of this work, the greatest sorrow of my life befell me in the illness and death of my beloved wife.

The severance of a most happy union, of thirty-four years' duration, was indeed a heavy blow, leaving an ever-present sorrow in my lonesome life. It was on the Queen's Jubilee day, the 21st of June, 1887, that the earthly life of the loving, devoted wife and mother was closed, in the presence of two of our children and myself. In company with a few sympathising friends, we followed her mortal remains to their last resting place, in the graveyard attached to the Friends' Meeting House at Stoke Newington.

Arbitration Treaty with America.

A new field of active operations in the Peace cause now opened before me in the United States of America.

The great work of establishing a permanent treaty between England and America, which should stipulate for the submission to arbitration of any differences that might arise between the two nations, has for many years claimed the earnest attention of the friends of peace on both sides of the Atlantic.

Some thirty years ago Dr. Miles came over from the United States to this country in order to confer with the late Henry Richard, M.P., my predecessor in the secretaryship of the Peace Society, and with others who were favourable to the project. For many years Henry Richard laboured earnestly in Parliament, and through the press, the platform, and the pulpit, to create a public opinion in favour of the proposed treaty. He did not live, however, to realise the fruition of his efforts, and others have since entered into his labours.

In our own times we have been privileged to see the great work carried still further, the proposed treaty, in all its details, having been agreed upon and actually signed by the accredited ministers of both nations, although it remains to be ratified by the Senate of the United States. Perhaps of all those who have in recent years contributed to bring about this desired result, there is no one to whom more credit is due than to W. R. Cremer, the Secretary of the Workmen's Peace Association. During the period that he was in Parliament, by persistent efforts he succeeded in getting a memorial in favour of the Treaty signed by upwards of 250 members of the House of Commons. Mr. Cremer further organised and carried into effect the project of a Deputation, consisting of eleven members of Parliament, who, with himself, crossed the Atlantic in October, 1887, in order to present to President Cleveland the memorial in question; also to hold public meetings in favour of the proposed Treaty in the principal cities of America.

About the same time I was appointed one of eight representatives from England to the first Conference of the "Yearly Meetings" of the Society of Friends in America, when various questions of religious doctrine and practice came under consideration. It was held in Richmond, Indiana, a Peace Conference afterwards meeting at the same place, with a view to promote the proposed Treaty of Arbitration between the two countries.

First Visit to United States.

I accordingly left Liverpool in the *Etruria* in August, 1887.

Ere our steamer had reached the wharf at New York, a telegram was handed me from the Secretary of the American Peace Society, urging my attendance at an important meeting to be held at Boston, Mass., on the next morning. Accordingly, I decided to proceed by the first night train to Boston.

The Committee, with their able Secretary, the Rev. Rowland B. Howard (brother of General O. O. Howard), gave me a hearty welcome, as the representative of the English Peace Society. They impressed upon me the importance of seeking an interview with President Cleveland before proceeding to the Peace Conference at Richmond. On September 23rd, 1887, I was granted a private interview with him in the Executive Mansion at Washington.

I presented my letters of introduction and of support of the object in view, furnished to me by the Right Hon. John Bright, M.P., John Greenleaf Whittier (the Quaker poet of New England), and George W. Childs (the proprietor of the *Public Ledger*, Philadelphia). With all of these the President expressed his satisfaction, and stated that every American revered the name of John Bright, for the eminent services which he had rendered to the cause of the North during their great war.

He then inquired, "When is Mr. Bright coming to visit America? He would be received with demonstrations of respect and esteem, surpassing anything hitherto accorded to any of your countrymen." I replied, "I fear you will never see him in America. I know he has a very strong personal objection to such demonstrations. I am inclined to believe that the fear of such an ovation has helped to keep him away from your country." After my return home, later in the year, being invited by Mr. Bright to dine with him at his residence, "One Ash," Rochdale, I related this conversation with the President, and asked him if my answer were correct. He said with a smile, "Quite right, William, and you might have added, 'He doesn't like the sea.'"

I ventured to express to President Cleveland my personal hope that he would show himself no less favourable to the principle of Arbitration, as a substitute for war, than several of his distinguished predecessors in office, including Presidents Grant, Hayes, and Garfield, each of whom had taken a most satisfactory position in relation to this great international question, and copies of whose utterances on it were now laid before Mr. Cleveland. The President, in reply, stated that the subject was one with which he might confess himself to have been hitherto but little acquainted, and further, it was a matter respecting which it behoved him to speak cautiously. But he might acknowledge that he had been impressed by the statement made by General

Sheridan, at the Centennial Banquet of the previous week, that "the tendency of modern warfare is to become less and less a test of skill, strategy, and courage, and more and more a system of *sheer organised murder.*"

The President said that he regarded this tendency, and the collateral growth of public opinion in favour of Arbitration, as two kindred movements converging towards one end, namely, the abolition of war among civilised people, and the establishment, in some form, of a High Court of International Arbitration, as a substitute for the decision of the sword. He added that, as to himself personally, he was, in common with every right-minded man, most averse to war.

The President then entered into some general conversation with me, in the course of which I mentioned some of my own experiences, when distributing relief during the Franco-German War.

I then showed President Cleveland the credentials which I had carried with me in France, bearing the signatures and written expressions of approval of numerous official and private personages. The President was much interested in looking over this document. On my requesting the addition of his autograph, he remarked, "This is higher ground than I can well take." I told him he was quite at liberty to write whatever he might see fit.

He then affixed his own signature, as having perused it with pleasure, though so long after the occasion of its original use, as follows:—

"September 22nd, 1887.

"The labour undertaken by Mr. Jones, under the above Commission, has my hearty approval.

"GROVER CLEVELAND,
"President, U.S.A."

Some inquiries now followed respecting the Memorial signed by more than two hundred members of the English Parliament, that was shortly to be presented to him. After receiving information from me on this subject, and learning that although not a member of the Deputation, I had, as the accredited representative of the English Peace Society, been requested to attend the interview, the President expressed a hope that I would do so, and the interview terminated.

MRS. CLEVELAND.

Having informed the President that I was the bearer of a letter of introduction to Mrs. Cleveland, from her personal friend, Miss Frances E. Willard, President of the National Women's Christian Temperance Union, he kindly invited me to the White House at noon the next day. Accordingly I went, and had a most gratifying reception from Mrs. Cleveland. There was a charm of manner and a perfect simplicity, accompanied by a winning smile, which placed one quite at ease with "the Queen of sixty millions of free people." She spoke of Miss Willard as a dear friend of hers, with whose life-work she was much in sympathy. I told her that at Miss Willard's invitation, it was my intention to address at Nashville, Tennessee, the National Convention of Women, on the subject of "Peace and Goodwill." Mrs. Cleveland assured me of her earnest sympathy with the efforts of the Convention, in the promotion both of Temperance and Peace. She made some brief allusions to her own personal experiences in Europe, instancing the condition to which the peasantry of Italy had been reduced by militarism and war taxation. I mentioned my small pamphlet on "Italy and Militarism," a copy of which she stated she would read with pleasure.

Mrs. Cleveland impressed me as being a woman of noble aspirations, evincing a mind above the mere love of position or display. Her allusions to the South, and to Nashville, showed a heart in sympathy with suffering. "There you will find they know something of war in its reality," she observed, in allusion to the miseries that had been inflicted by the Civil War. In conclusion, I ventured to say, that the position of influence in which she was placed, afforded a vantage-ground for speaking, on occasion, a fitting word in favour of the incalculable blessing of peace to her own people and to the world at large. In taking leave, she intrusted me with a message from herself to the National Convention, shortly to be held at Nashville.

JOHN BRIGHT, M.P.

In connection with this visit to America, the encouragement I received from the late John

Bright, M.P., was most helpful. I had long known something of him, and was ever an ardent admirer of him as a man and an orator, both in the days of the Anti-Corn-law League, and in his subsequent career as a statesman, also as the "Great Tribune of the People"; but it was not until the later years of his life, after I had become the Secretary of the London Peace Society, that I was drawn more frequently into closer relations with him. We generally worshipped side by side in the Friends' Meeting House at Westminster, when I had frequent opportunities of observing the impressive devoutness of his attitude, in the solemn silence of portions of the Friends' mode of worship.

When about to proceed to America, he kindly gave me the following autograph letter, which greatly facilitated my interviews with men of "light and leading" in the United States:—

"London,

"Aug. 9th, 1887.

"Dear Friend William Jones,

"I am glad to hear that you are going to the United States, on what I may term a Peace Mission. You will find many friends of peace on the other side of the Atlantic, more perhaps than you will leave on this side; for our people have seen nothing of war amongst them during this century. They know something of taxes, the result of war, but they have seen nothing of the bloodshed of war. There is talk of a permanent Arbitration Treaty between England and the United States. The project is a reasonable one, and discussion on both sides may bring it about. I think if the government of the States were willing, and were in any way to signify their willingness, to become a party to such a Treaty, there is a force of good men with us to induce our government to consent to it. If this can be done, it will be a grand step forward in the world's march, and would be followed, at some not distant time, by some other nations willing to escape from the sore burden of their military armaments.

"You will doubtless see many intelligent and leading men in the States, and will learn something of their feelings on this matter. They may receive you as a trustworthy representative of the moral and peace-loving people in England, and I hope your interviews may do something in the direction that you and I so greatly desire. I find that nearly two hundred members of the House of Commons are addressing a Memorial to the Government at Washington to suggest an Arbitration Treaty, such as I have described. More, far more, I hope, than this number will be ready to urge the acceptance of such a Treaty upon our Government, if the action at Washington should meet with any favour and success. England and the States will remain two nations; but I would have them regarded by themselves as *one people*. An Arbitration Treaty, honestly made and adhered to, would tend much to this blessed result.

"I wish you a pleasant voyage and some good results to your labours.

"I am, sincerely yours,

"JOHN BRIGHT."

Many reminiscences crowd upon me in connection with John Bright, whose loyalty to the cause of peace and goodwill never wavered. None of these, perhaps, was more striking than this. Calling upon him one morning at his hotel, the "Alexandra," near Hyde Park, I found him engaged in reading the "Memoirs of the Marquis of Bath," which, he said, from his personal recollections of the principal public men and events recorded, he found most interesting. He read me a paragraph to this effect: Lord Bath went up the Dardanelles to Constantinople, before the actual outbreak of the Crimean War, and told our Ambassador, Lord Stratford de Redcliffe, that the British fleet had cast anchor in Besika Bay, near the entrance to the Dardanelles. Lord Stratford received the news with exultation, exclaiming, "That is an act of war! Now I shall be avenged on the Czar!" referring, it is supposed, to the Czar's refusal to accept him as Ambassador at St. Petersburg, he not being a "*persona grata*"; and so the "Great Eltchi," as Kinglake, in his history, styles him, on account of his predominant influence over the Sultan, exulted in the prospect of bloodshed and slaughter between the Russians and English.

I found Mr. Bright had not then seen the recently published biography of Lord Stratford, written by his private secretary, Mr. Skene. I called his attention to a paragraph which I had taken from this book, which had forcibly struck me. It was to the effect that after the war was ended, Lord Stratford proceeded to Sebastopol, accompanied by Mr. Skene. "After landing in the bombarded city," Mr. Skene writes, "it was a scene of complete devastation—walls tottering, doors driven in, windows smashed, and roofs gaping with enormous clefts opened by the bombardment.

"'*John Bright is fully borne out by all this,*' said Lord Stratford, holding up his hands in amazement. '*If this is a sample of the effects of war, who would not be willing to join his Peace party. It is more like the crater of a volcano than a ruined city.*'"

Mr. Skene continues: "Riding through some deserted streets, we left the houses and proceeded to the monastery of St. George, which had acquired an especial interest for Lord Stratford, by its being made use of as a hospital and sanatorium. He said that of all the results of war, wounds and diseases were the least questionable, and therefore the most to be taken into account by those who might ever have it in their power to exercise an influence in making war or peace. Turning sharply round, he caught my eye. 'You understand me?' he added with a note of inexpressible sadness. What I understood, whether accurately or not, was, that having taken a conspicuous part in bringing about the Crimean War, he had fallen into a morbid habit of comparing the reality of its political issues, for which he had so earnestly laboured, with that of the amount of suffering produced by it." *

Surely, one may see something more than "a *morbid habit*" in these moralisings of Lord Stratford. His query, "You understand me?" is significant of much more than this, to my mind. Standing in the midst of this resemblance to the "crater of a volcano," "feeling inexpressibly sad," and there realising something of the enormous waste of human life and property, caused by the disastrous Crimean War, in promoting which he was so conspicuous an actor, to me, his utterances seem more like those of a troubled conscience, to which even these *half confessions* of the fatal and far-reaching error of his life brought a certain sense of relief. Considering the well-known character of the man, his wonderfully self-reliant, proud nature, and his lofty position in the diplomatic world, may not the candid admission recorded by Mr. Skene be regarded as a remarkable proof of the power of an awakened conscience?

Mr. Bright expressed his astonishment that Lord Stratford, of all men, should make such an admission, adding, "When he came to London I sat by his side at a banquet in Willis's Rooms, and he said somewhat reproachfully, 'You have been saying some hard things of me in your speeches, Mr. Bright.' I replied quietly, that if I had said anything that

* Extract from Mr. J. H. Skene's "With Lord Stratford in the Crimean War." London, 1883.

was not absolutely correct, I should be most willing to withdraw such statement. But," Mr. Bright remarked, "he did not point out anything I had said that was incorrect."

A conspicuous trait in Mr. Bright's personal character was his love of animals. A favourite parrot had learnt the elementary truth, which he often repeated, to the delight of visitors, that "John Bright loves Polly!" Again, in the visit which I paid him at Rochdale, he amused himself for an hour after dinner, in playing with a ball, with his two pet Skye terriers. It was great fun to me also to join in the game. These long-haired animals forcibly reminded me of the famous simile with which he had amused the House of Commons, during the Reform debates of 1866, when he compared the famous "Party of Two" (Horsman and Lowe) to a hairy Skye terrier, in which one could hardly tell "which was head and which was tail."

The allusion which told on the House with the most lasting effect, was his apt comparison of the small band of malcontents to the "Cave of Adullam." The reference to Adullam at first puzzled many of his fellow members, who were not so much at home in biblical history as Mr. Bright. It was said, however, to have had the good effect of sending them to the Bible to read up the story of David, when he received into his famous cave "everyone that was in distress, and everyone that was discontented," and became a captain over them. The name of "Adullamites," in its application to small parties of malcontents, long survived in parliamentary life.

John Bright's *last* public speech took place in March, 1887, when he presided at a lecture which I gave on International Arbitration, with illustrations drawn from my personal experiences in war time, in the Friends' Meeting House at Westminster.

It having been advertised that Mr. Bright would take the chair, inhabitants of London, many of whom had never heard him make a speech, flocked to the meeting in crowds, far beyond the capacity of the House to contain them. Seeing this, I remarked to him, "These people have not come to hear *me*, I will make my lecture shorter, in order to give you full opportunity"—as he preferred to speak after me. Accordingly, at the end of the hour I sat down, when Mr. Bright, turning to me, made the surprising remark, "What am I to do? It is so long since I spoke in public, that I feel like beginning over again." I expressed my surprise and said, "What! Does John Bright ever feel like that? You have but to rise to your feet, and all your old power will come back."

He spoke on that occasion with his accustomed power for fully fifty minutes, chiefly on the topic of the war in the Soudan, every word being taken down by reporters from the leading papers of the Metropolis, and a summary of the speech telegraphed to every quarter of the world. At the close of the meeting, a number of Americans who were present, came desiring me to introduce them to Mr. Bright. I told him they only wished to shake hands with him, and then would go home, as they said, "contented, to their friends." Mr. Bright said, "Oh! let them come." He shook hands with them individually, and had a courteous word for every one, and they left the building evidently highly gratified.

Wishing to publish his speech, I sent Mr. Bright a proof, leaving out his statement about the killing of wounded Arabs after the battle of Abu-Klea, which was much controverted in the papers of the day, and seemed to me not to be material to the teaching conveyed in the speech. I pointed out to him how the papers were drawing the attention of the public to this side issue, instead of to the great lessons inculcated in the speech itself. My letter only drew from him, however, this characteristic reply, which in the light of the recent revelations of the still more extensive slaughter of wounded and helpless Dervishes after the battle of Omdurman, in 1898, will be read with interest.

"March 11th, 1887,
"Reform Club, S.W.

"Dear Friend, William Jones,

"I return the speech with some corrections. I see you have left out the paragraph about the killing of wounded Arabs. The story is *quite true*, and I have abundant evidence as to its truth. I should, therefore, prefer that the paragraph should be inserted, only I wish to see the precise words of it before it is published. I cannot consent for you to make it appear that you think Lord Wolseley's word is better than mine. He was a hundred miles from Abu-Klea, and his authority is worth nothing in this case. . . . I have undoubted evidence of many instances of the horrors I describe, therefore I cannot shrink from the statement I made.

"Yours very truly,

"JOHN BRIGHT."

The life of the great statesman came to a close in 1889, after I had left the country on a voyage round the world. The news was received by me in the city of Auckland, New Zealand. The editors of local papers sent their reporters to interview me, and I gave them a few of my reminiscences of Mr. Bright, which circulated afterwards through each of the colonies, and were of great service, in paving the way for my subsequent labours in the Peace cause, in every one of the Australasian colonies.

It may be remembered how the incident of the bombardment of the forts at Alexandria, in 1882, was the means of causing Mr. Bright to resign his position as a member of the Cabinet of Mr. Gladstone.

From frequent conversations with the late Henry Richard, M.P., who was in almost daily intercourse with Mr. Bright, I knew how dissatisfied the latter was with the course of events then taking place in Egypt. I knew that he had protested strongly against our interference in Egyptian affairs by force of arms, or by sending our fleets into Egyptian waters. For a time, however, he was pacified by Lord Granville's assurances that the presence of the fleet was only a "demonstration," and that nothing more would be needed. The temptation, however, to put to the test their new ironclad fleet, and powerful forty-ton guns, proved, as we now know, to be irresistible to our Admiral and his officers. The opportunity was too good to be lost of solving the question of forts versus ironclads, so the bombardment took place.

Thus was that fatal *first step* taken in Egypt, which led to all the subsequent complications with France and other Powers; and no one can yet say what is to be the end of it all. What we do know is, that it led directly to the death of General Gordon, and some thirteen years after that tragic event, our country has again been made to incur the responsibilities of Atbara and Omdurman, with their prodigious slaughter of the brave Arab tribes of the desert.

What John Bright thought of the bombardment of Alexandria may be gathered from a conversation I had with him some time afterwards. He said: "I saw Lord Granville on the afternoon previous to the bombardment, and was assured by him that all was going on well in Egypt. Next morning appeared the telegram announcing the destruction of the forts. The news fell like a bomb-shell in the Cabinet. Every one was taken completely by surprise at this unexpected turn of affairs, and I resolved that I could no longer remain a member of the Cabinet."

Mr. Bright incurred much obloquy at the time, for taking a step which would inevitably embarrass the Government, but the subsequent verdict of his countrymen, on the whole, has been, that he acted nobly in obeying the dictates of his conscience.

What is difficult for plain people like myself to understand, in connection with serious affairs like the bombardment of Alexandria is, why peerages and pensions should be thought to be the appropriate rewards of responsible officers who thus 'take the bit in their teeth," and bombard cities, or forts, not only without express orders from their Government, but to their utter surprise and astonishment.

Richmond Conference.

From Washington I proceeded direct to Richmond, Indiana, where the conference of delegates from all the "Yearly Meetings" of the Society of Friends was to be held. In addition to the delegates from Great Britain, and nearly all the Yearly Meetings of the United States, a large concourse of members of the Society was assembled, evidencing a very widespread interest in the objects of the Conference. The large meeting-house, seating some 2,000 persons, was filled to its utmost capacity, and on certain days, when *special* religious services were announced, extra trains were run from various quarters; people gathered in large groups, and addresses were given in the open air. The hundreds of "buggies," and vehicles of other sorts, standing in the extensive yard, on the occasion of a religious gathering, constituted a novel sight to an English stranger.

The principal outcome of the discussions of the Conference was the adoption of a "Declaration of Faith," which was mainly a re-affirmation, on ample lines, of the views of religious truth which had always been held by the Society of Friends.

Two days after the Conference the document appeared at full length in a Chicago daily paper, thus conveying its contents to half a million of readers.

By invitation I attended, immediately after the Richmond Conference, the weekly gathering of all the Methodist Ministers of Chicago and neighbourhood, numbering over two hundred. At the close of my brief address I was interviewed by several ministers. One of them told me he had that day read the whole of the "Declaration of Faith" in the paper, adding, "I was delighted to learn, for the first time, what were the views of religious truth held by your Society." On my asking him what he thought of it, he promptly rejoined, "Oh! It is grand, it is Scriptural!"

A Peace Conference was also held at Richmond, under the presidency of Augustine Jones, of Providence, R.I.

At one of its sittings I was invited to lay before the Conference the subject which formed my special mission to America, that is, the proposition to establish "A Permanent Treaty of Arbitration between the Governments of Great Britain and the United States, binding them beforehand to refer all differences, which cannot be settled by diplomacy, to the decision of a Court of Arbitration."

The subject took deep hold of the meeting. After much discussion the Conference decided upon the following course of action:—

Firstly. It adopted an address to the American Legislature, and to the President, in favour of the Treaty.

Secondly. A deputation of three influential men was appointed to present these addresses at Washington.

Thirdly. An address to the various Yearly Meetings of "Friends" in America was adopted, recommending the appointment of local committees in aid of the work.

Fourthly. The Conference appointed a number of "Friends" in each "Yearly Meeting" to bring the Peace question, and the proposed Treaty especially, before the various Conventions of other Christian Churches.

CHAPTER XVII.

THE POET WHITTIER—PRESIDENT CLEVELAND AND THE ENGLISH DEPUTATION OF MEMBERS OF PARLIAMENT—NASHVILLE: W.C.T.U.—METHODIST BISHOP—MISS WILLARD—LADY HENRY SOMERSET—LECTURES IN U.S.A.—DR. OLIVER WENDELL HOLMES.

THE genial American Quaker poet, Whittier, on whom I called at Danvers, U.S.A., in 1887, where he was paying his customary autumnal visit to his relatives, appended his signature to my certificate, with these words, "I am glad to add my name to this testimonial, J. G. Whittier." As he appeared somewhat feeble and delicate, I decided not to make my visit burdensome to him, though I greatly enjoyed the old man's bright and genial conversation. John Bright's letter, which I showed him, led him to remark that Mr. Bright was an esteemed correspondent of his, and that he much appreciated his letters. He expressed his entire approval of my Peace mission to America, adding that Friends of all shades of thought, whether "Hicksite" or "Orthodox," would gladly receive me and help on my work. They were all lovers of Peace alike. He gave expression to the thought that a mission like mine, in which all could freely unite, might have a reconciling tendency upon the separate sections of the Society of Friends in America. He said, "It will help to break down the present stand-off attitude towards each other, and by causing them to work together shoulder to shoulder, they will learn to appreciate and love the good that is in all."

He told me that many young men, members of the Society of Friends, carried away by their anti-slavery and patriotic feelings, had fought during the War in the Northern army. He could not, however, commend their laying aside, even for a time, the paramount duty of loyalty to Christ, the Prince of Peace. He said I should find some congregations of Friends in the West whose modes of worship differed widely from those of the good "Quaker of the olden time," but that, notwithstanding these departures from what he termed the root principle of the Society, namely, the "Divine Immanence," our principles remained unchanged.

His whole manner was so sympathetic and kind, that I felt drawn in spirit towards the loving, gentle old poet, whose stirring ballads and eminently spiritual verses had been to me "household words" for many years, and I left his presence feeling that I was the better for this interview, and departed with the sense of a good man's blessing resting upon me.

SECOND VISIT TO THE PRESIDENT.

The 1st of November having been appointed for the reception of the English Deputation of Members of Parliament at the White House, I returned to Washington in order to accompany it. The Deputation consisted of one member of the House of Lords (Lord Kinnaird), and ten members of the House of Commons, including Sir Lyon Playfair, Sir George Campbell, and Mr. William R. Cremer.

The Deputation was accompanied by two or three other gentlemen, and by the Rev. R. B. Howard, the Secretary of the American Peace Society, and by myself, on behalf of the English Peace Society. Mr. Andrew Carnegie introduced the Deputation to the President, with a few introductory observations. He was followed by Sir Lyon Playfair, Mr. Cremer, and others.

President Cleveland expressed his entire sympathy with the noble object of the Deputation, and said that to him there was nothing more touching, or persuasive, than the part which the labouring men of England had taken in this movement. He could not but think those were object lessons for the working men of America, which would readily awaken their sympathy with the desire for a condition of International understanding, which should alleviate the death and distress that war brings to their households.

After the more formal part of the proceedings, Mr. Cleveland, when shaking hands with each delegate in turn, referred, when taking leave of me, to our former interview. This afforded me an opportunity of telling the President how helpful that interview had been in my Peace campaign in the United States, and that the seed sown appeared to have fallen into good ground, the American people being even more prepared than my own countrymen to adopt the principles of International Arbitration.

W.C.T.U. Convention.

Two days journey by rail from Washington, took me to the city of Nashville, Tennessee. I found it a much larger and more prosperous-looking place than I had anticipated, containing many fine public buildings and large churches. Here, by the special invitation of Miss Willard, the President of the Women's Christian Temperance Union, I attended the convention, consisting of between four and five hundred women delegates, from nearly all the States and Territories of the Union. It was an object lesson to me, to see how admirably these earnest and capable women managed their Convention, on strict Parliamentary rules, under the able and tactful presidency of Miss Willard.

Nothing could exceed in interest an interlude, in which the whole assemblage united to present Miss Willard with her portrait in oils, as a mark of their esteem and affection, to commemorate her fiftieth birthday. The whole company was profoundly moved, when some Southern ladies spoke through their tears of this, as the first *real union* of the South with the North—a union of hearts—since the great war of more than twenty years before.

In the opportunity that was made for me to

address the meeting, their sympathies were won by my conveying to them the gracious message with which I was entrusted by Mrs. Cleveland. Addressing this representative gathering of the womanhood of a great nation, and urging the unspeakable importance of permanent peaceful relations between the two great branches of our Anglo-Saxon race, I reminded them that what the *women* of a Christian country say to-day, the *men* will say to-morrow.

In the result, a resolution was unanimously passed, adopting the subject of Peace as one of the "planks" in their "platform." A Peace department was formed with a superintendent, Mrs. Hannah J. Bailey, a member of the Society of Friends, by whose successful efforts the principles of Peace have been adopted by most of the World's Women's Christian Temperance Union organizations in America, and also in other parts of the world.

Through the kind arrangement of Miss Willard, it was my good fortune to be entertained in one of the principal mansions of Nashville, that of Colonel E. W. Cole. The rooms here were on such a scale, that they easily accommodated, at a reception given to the Convention, an assemblage of about 800 people, including many of the rank and fashion of Nashville. Placed as an honoured guest at the right hand of the stately hostess, I was introduced to the whole company, the aggregate hand-shakings with whom, in and out of the house, amounted to over 1,600 in all! My reminiscences of the hostess herself still picture her to me as a dignified representative of the refined and courteous "Southern Chivalry"—to which this was my first introduction.

The butler of the household, a tall, stately negro, with a wide expanse of white shirt front, under a face of polished ebony, was to me a new study in human nature. He escorted me to my room with a grace that betokened his self-conscious connection with an aristocratic family. "You shet you doh, and you is at home here, Sah!" he remarked, with a graceful bow. "Miss Cole (Mrs. Cole) like her guests feel at home, Sah!" he continued, with another low bow. His pompous manner broke down next day, however, when, having occasion to go to my room, I found him in his working costume and a child of three years running after him. I coaxed her to me, and taking her up in my arms, looked upon the comical little ebony face, the whites of her eyes, as they rolled, forming a curious contrast to the surrounding blackness.

On my giving the child a kiss, the trifling act went straight to the father's heart. After this, there was no limit to his devoted attentions to me. Finding me to be a willing listener, he delighted in relating stories of the war—how he and other coloured men had fought, and could not be restrained by their officers, especially in the bloody battle of Franklin. "Of course you fought for your Master, John," I said. "No Sah" (emphatically), "I fought for de Norf, libbahty is sweet, Sah!"

John saw me off at the railway station on leaving Nashville, with a smile on his shiny black face, and with a deference which, had I been the Prince of Wales himself, could not have been more profound, nor, as I believe, more sincere.

Quite the most interesting local personage I met with in Col. Cole's house, Nashville, was the able Methodist Episcopal Bishop of the district. His denomination being the most numerous religious body in the South, much activity was going on in extending its borders, and the Bishop informed me that Methodist Churches were being built at the rate of two a day! Doubtless many of these would be temporary wooden structures.

In a free conversation, the Bishop asked me whether I had read the report published by a "Friend" named Hubbard, who was in charge of an Indian Settlement, on the work of civilizing the wild Indians. The Bishop continued, "Your Friend Hubbard may be only a plain farmer, but judging from his report, I look upon him as a man of remarkable intelligence, and very fertile in resource in the adaptation of means to end. Many of his statements would bear much pondering over, but he passes on, in his quiet way, without enlarging on them. Here is one that I have thought over a hundred times, 'When I want to settle and civilize a young Indian buck, I make him a present of a heifer calf.' He merely mentions the fact, and passes on, but the more I have dwelt on it the more I have admired his practical wisdom.

You observe it is not a calf of the other sex! No, that would soon become beef, and would find its way down his throat. Neither is it a horse, for that he would soon want to mount, and to scour the plains as a wild hunter. No, it is just a harmless, helpless animal—a heifer calf. But just think what it involves. Think of the responsibility it puts upon that young Indian savage. There is a helpless young creature, entirely dependent upon his care and watchfulness for food and warmth, and for its very existence. He is being trained to habits of method and punctuality every day of his life; then, granting he fulfils these conditions, in the course of two or three years there is promise of ample riches for him, in the possession of a valuable cow. I can conceive of no method so likely to be efficacious in civilizing a young Indian, and of gradually inducting him into a life of order and usefulness. Oh! I assure you, I hold your plain Quaker farmer to be a philanthropist and a philosopher of no mean order. Get his report, read it, and think it out, as I have done, and you will be convinced of this, too."

The foregoing is a mere sketch from memory of the sentiments of this "old man eloquent." I wish I could do more justice to the elevation of his thought and language, which impressed me much at the time.

In about two years after this interesting conversation with the Bishop, I had the pleasure of meeting with the "Friend" in question, Jeremiah

Hubbard, at the "Yearly Meeting" of Friends at Lawrence, Kansas. In our conversation I mentioned the Bishop's opinion of his excellent work among the Indians, at which the good man appeared to be considerably astonished.

Miss Willard.

It was during my first visit to America, in 1887, that I became acquainted with the late Frances E. Willard. We met at a private house in the City of Baltimore, when she extended the invitation to me to address the Nashville Convention of the W.C.T.U.

On the same evening, I attended a public meeting, at which some 1,500 persons were present, many of them students of the University. It was my first opportunity of observing the marvellous power with which Miss Willard held, as it were spell-bound, for upwards of an hour, a large audience, consisting, in great part, of men of culture and intelligence. After the first sentence or two, with a few humorous touches, she placed herself thoroughly *en rapport* with her audience. The whole address was on a plane very much above the usual level of temperance speeches. Her eloquence, the melodious tones of her voice, her splendid command of language, her vocabulary, both rich and rare, together with her perfect mastery of her subject, all combined to make this great speech a most memorable one.

Two years later, my wife and I proceeded, by invitation, from Lawrence, Kansas, to Chicago, to meet Miss Willard, but on arriving at the offices of the Women's Christian Temperance Union, we were disappointed to learn that she had left that very day, and could not be seen, as she had gone into "retreat," in order to prepare her presidential address for the coming National Convention. On learning the circumstances, however, her confidential officials arranged a visit for us to her temporary abode, with a letter of explanation.

Miss Willard gave us a characteristically cordial reception. She kindly promised us a copy of her autobiography, which was just published, under the title of "Glimpses of Fifty Years," which, she humorously remarked, was far too long, but she had not time to write a shorter memoir. The book duly followed us to England, containing her autograph and brief dedication—prized more than ever now that we shall see her face no more.

Within a month of her death, I received my last communication, dictated from what proved, alas! to be her death-bed, in which, in a few characteristic lines, she alludes to a subject that was engrossing much mutual thought and anxiety.

I esteem it one of the privileges of my life to have been counted among Miss Willard's personal friends. Few women ever scored a deeper mark on their times, and their nation, than this gifted daughter of the Western World. To none has it been given more cordially to be accepted, as a great organiser and leader, by the almost universal consent of the women of both hemispheres. Tributes to her memory have continued to flow in from every part of the habitable globe, her favourite maxim, "For God, and Home, and every Land," having obtained a place in women's hearts throughout the civilized world.

Lady Henry Somerset.

Reference may here be appropriately made to Miss Willard's most intimate friend and fellow-labourer, Lady Henry Somerset, whose signature, "Isabel Somerset," was placed a few years ago upon my credentials. Lady Henry Somerset is so widely known and beloved by multitudes the world over, that any notice of her from my pen need be but brief. Her signature on my document is significant of her being in sympathy with every cause, tending, to use her own expression, to the "uplift of humanity."

The most impressive personal incident that has occurred in my connection with this truly noble and gifted woman, was the account which she gave in public, at the time when she was our guest in Sunderland, of her own conversion. I had accompanied her to a public meeting for prayer, over which she was to preside, and sat by her side on the platform. After a hymn and a prayer it was expected that she would address the meeting, but a secret wrestling of spirit was evidently going on in her mind, and she asked that prayer might be continued.

Presently she seemed quite calm, rose to her feet, and in her well-known sweet tone and refined language, proceeded to say that she had intended to address the meeting on a subject altogether different from that which she was now called to speak upon, and which she felt she must not put aside. She then quoted a text from Acts xxii. 9—"They saw the light, but heard not the voice of Him that spake,"—and went on to say how needful it was that we should be patient with those who had not the same advantages as ourselves. Certain people among those who were called by some "the upper classes," who were well educated in all things bearing upon their happiness in this life, knew nothing about the things of eternity. "They may have seen the light, but have not heard the voice of God speaking to them." And then she added, in a very touching manner, "I was one of those, and when the trials and realities of life came upon me, I was unprepared for them." She proceeded to say, that on one bright June day, six years previously, she was seated in her garden at home, and thinking over these things in much perplexity of mind, on account of the trials and sorrows of life. She knew there was a way of good and a way of evil, but did not understand their operation. As she pondered over these matters, there came a voice to her ear, sounding as clearly as her own voice to that audience, "Act as though God were, and thou shalt *know* that He is." She immediately rose, crossed the garden, and went upstairs into her own room. She took down the Bible, the book that had rarely or never been opened, unless for the purpose of verifying or refuting such authors as Strauss or Renan. In the quietude of her closet she read through the Gospel of John, knelt in fervent prayer, and surrendered her heart, thus calmed and solemnised, wholly to God, and prayed Him to use her for the "uplift of humanity."

The effect upon the audience of this remarkable address, delivered without excitement, with the utmost calmness and deliberation, in an exquisite voice and appropriate language, was so impressive that there was scarcely a dry eye in the room.

Further American Travel.

After completing my engagements at Washington, Richmond (Indiana), and Nashville, I was anxious to return to home duties. Invitation upon invitation poured in upon me, however, from many of the principal cities of the United States, in which it was urged that public interest had been aroused on the "Treaty Question," and that at no previous time had there been such an open door for the reception of Peace principles. I therefore decided not to neglect this golden opportunity, but to continue to lecture in several important centres before returning to England.

Among these places may be mentioned Cincinnati, Baltimore, Chicago, New York, Philadelphia, Boston, Lynn, and other cities, besides numerous important educational establishments, such as Haverford College, Bryn Mawr College for Ladies, Swarthmore College, West Town School, etc.

As a rule I found American audiences undemonstrative and hard to move. They listened, however, with earnest attention to details of the effect of militarism in Europe, and to my personal experiences during the Franco-German War. It was only when some *home* allusions were made, such, for example, as to the profound sorrow which the assassination of their revered President Garfield had evoked throughout England, that something like enthusiasm showed itself among these highly decorous assemblies. Their conclusions, however, were always right, and resolutions in favour of the Treaty with England, which were usually proposed by some leading citizen, were generally cordially adopted. The fondness of Americans for titles often amused me. When the notices announcing my Peace meetings were being prepared I was sometimes asked, "Have you no letters to your name? Ain't you a F.R.S. or something?" "Haven't you even a middle letter to your name?" To which my plain answer of "No!" seemed to create surprise.

Whether it was anything more than a mere printer's error I was unable to make out, when in the large city of Cincinnati it was gravely announced on a card that a Peace lecture would be delivered by the "Hon. Colonel William Jones!"

Some members of the English Deputation of M.P's. also held public meetings in favour of the Arbitration Treaty, but as my movements were arranged entirely independent of theirs, I had no opportunity of uniting in their labours. I was, however, much interested in finding at Boston that a grand banquet to welcome the Deputation had been given, at which the eloquent Senator Hoar, Dr. Oliver W. Holmes, and others, had spoken cordially on behalf of the object in view. Dr. Holmes also read from one of his own poems the following stanza, giving expression to his love for England :

"Land of our Fathers, Ocean makes us two;
But heart to heart is true.
Proud is your towering daughter in the West,
Yet in her burning life-blood reign confest
Her Mother's pulses beating in her breast,
This holy fount whose rills from heaven descend,
It's gracious drops shall lend,
Both foreheads bathed in that baptismal dew,
And love makes *one*, the old home and the new!"

On December 3rd I bade adieu to the American shores and to the many kind friends who accompanied us to the s.s. "*Servia*," bound for Liverpool, where we landed on December 12th, 1887.

CHAPTER XVIII.

SECOND MARRIAGE — RESIDENCE IN SUNDERLAND — TRAVELS: VESUVIUS, POMPEII—VOYAGE TO AUSTRALIA —RED SEA—DR. MACLAREN OUR FELLOW-PASSENGER—YOUNG DIVERS AT ADEN—CEYLON—WEST AUSTRALIA—VICTORIA, MELBOURNE—ITS GROWTH AND PROSPERITY —THE AUSTRALIAN BUSH—THE LOFTIEST TREES IN THE WORLD — SOUTH AUSTRALIA, ADELAIDE — VICTORIA, BALLARAT—TASMANIA—COLOSSAL BASALTIC ROCKS—FRUIT FARM—JOSEPH B. MATHER—SIR ROBERT HAMILTON—MOUNT WELLINGTON—SCENE OF THE CONVICT SYSTEM.

THE year 1888 is memorable in the annals of my life. In the month of September of that year I was united in marriage to my second wife, Katherine, daughter of the late Alderman Joshua Wilson, of Sunderland. Local circumstances gave me the opportunity of becoming acquainted with her Christian character, and bright, cheerful disposition. Our union has brought into my own life much blessing and lasting thankfulness.

The pleasant northern seaport of Sunderland now became my home, and here I have found congenial society, as well as the advantages of a good Friends' Meeting.

Having been appointed delegate from "London Yearly Meeting of Friends," to the first Intercolonial Conference of "Friends" in Australasia, which was proposed to be held in Melbourne, November, 1888, it was needful for my wife and self to start promptly after our marriage. Crossing the Continent of Europe, we proceeded to join the P. and O. steamer at Brindisi, in which our passages for Australia had been taken.

We spent a few days *en route* in viewing the well-known antiquities of Rome, and in seeing the marvels of art rescued from the buried cities of Herculaneum and Pompeii, now deposited in the museum at Naples.

We also ascended Vesuvius, part of the way by carriage, and the rest by the Funicular Railway, which we found at that time to be by no means in a safe condition. From the summit the panorama was magnificent. Our attention was in degree absorbed, however, in reiterated efforts to avoid the suffocating fumes which veered about with the wind. Here a number of men who had followed the party busied themselves in escorting the visitors to the mouth of the crater, "*La bocca del Inferno*" (the mouth of the Lower Regions), as they called it. When my wife had accomplished this feat, and had been brought safely back, it was my turn to be seized and rushed off to the threatening looking "Bocca." Just as I reached it a tremendous explosion took place, huge masses of red-hot lava being projected to a great height in the air. My wife, in her account of this incident in a letter home, says, . . . "These two men looked so utterly helpless before these fearful forces of nature. The huge, shapeless masses of red-hot lava, instead of mostly falling back into the fire, came over to where they stood, and fell all around them. The guide wanted to fly back at once, but William, seeing it was too late, stood watching a huge mass that was falling over their heads, which they managed to avoid, and then flew back to where I was standing. It was an awful moment. You can imagine the relief I felt in seeing my husband safely back again."

There was, in fact, little real danger to anyone cool enough to look up, and avoid rushing amidst the falling lava, whilst carefully watching his chance of getting clear of the descending masses. Happily no accident occurred, and we returned to Naples much gratified with our excursion to the crater of Vesuvius.

Suez and the Red Sea.

In a few days we entered the Suez Canal at Port Said. The passage through was accomplished in twenty-one hours. The centre only of the canal being deep enough for vessels of the tonnage of the *Britannia*, she had to be tied several times to the bank in the "sidings" to allow other vessels to pass her, so that our speed did not average more than four miles per hour.

The strong electric lights reflected from the bows of the ship at night had the effect of an optical delusion, as we appeared to be sailing between lofty banks of snow, instead of mere desert sands. Emerging at Suez into the Red Sea, what struck us as remarkable was the extraordinary blueness of the water, rivalling that of the Mediterranean. The whole region around abounded with Scriptural associations. The peak of Sinai itself, we were informed, is not visible from the Red Sea, but as we sailed down the Gulf, the rose-tinted Sinaitic Range came impressively into view, rugged and bare through the haze of the intervening desert. As the temperature at no time exceeded 92 degrees, we much enjoyed sitting on deck whilst sailing by these shores, so replete with historic interest.

Among our fellow-passengers was the eminent Baptist Minister, Dr. Maclaren, of Manchester, who, with his two daughters, was taking a six months' holiday journey to Australia. His racy and instructive conversation remains one of the pleasantest reminiscences of the voyage. A public reception was accorded to him by his numerous friends, soon after our landing in Melbourne, and it was gratifying to see the demonstrations of affectionate regard and esteem in which he was held in the southern hemisphere. At Aden we parted with a contingent of Indian passengers, who were transferred into a steamer bound for Bombay. It was a pleasant exchange for us to have for the rest of the voyage, a roomy, airy cabin, instead of the cramped and close "rabbit-hutch" in which we had passed through the Red

Sea. As we did not care to land at this dreary, desolate looking spot, where not a blade of grass or any green thing was visible, we amused ourselves by watching from the deck a number of Somali Arab boys, who spent many hours in deep water around the ship, uttering unintelligible cries, which at length we understood to be, "Have a dive, oh!" "Have a dive, oh!" It was only their way of earning an honest penny by diving for coins thrown by passengers into the water. No sooner did a coin reach the water than down went thirty or forty heads, whilst double the number of bare legs and feet were upheaved into the air, and after a scramble of some seconds under water the coin was secured, and they all returned to the surface, and joined once more in the monotonous cry of "Have a dive, oh!"

The amphibious habits of these urchins, and the extraordinary length and thinness of their legs and arms, gave rise to some semi-serious discussion on the deck, as to whether they were really human beings at all, or some strange evolution from tadpoles or monkeys. By and by an amusing incident helped to settle the question. One of the urchins climbed on board in his "birthday suit," his object being to exchange twelve pence in copper, which he found it inconvenient to carry in his only pocket, *i.e.*, his mouth, for a silver shilling. A passenger held out a shilling, which the boy seized and carefully examined, then satisfied apparently that it was good, popped it into his mouth. Counting his coppers, the young Somali deposited a pile on the top rail of the ship's bulwark. Just as the gentleman was reaching out his hand for it, the crafty rogue, with the quickness and dexterity of a conjuror, snapped up the copper, stuffed it also into his mouth, and disappeared like lightning, head foremost over the ship's side, and after a long dive came up among a crowd of others, all so exactly alike, that he was undistinguishable, and, of course, remained in the safe possession of his ill-gotten treasure. Recovering from his astonishment, the amiable passenger, evidently lost in admiration of the smartness and daring of the boy, exclaimed, "Well, that is the cleanest swindle I ever saw!"

After the laughter of the party had subsided, it was generally agreed that no "monkey" could count twelve pennyworth of copper, or so artfully secure both the coin and the change, and when I put the question, "Now, what is your verdict, a monkey, or a 'man and a brother'?"

"Shockingly *human* altogether!" was the prompt response.

The business-like way in which the transaction was put through, made one wonder how often this sort of "clean swindle" had been successfully practised upon unsuspecting passengers at Aden.

Clearly, Somali morality greatly needs raising to a higher standard!

CEYLON.

As the *Britannia* now turned her head towards

the Port of Colombo, where she was to spend some hours in taking in coal, we eagerly looked forward to passing a few hours in the beautiful island of Ceylon. On reaching the Port, after a few days pleasant sail, we gladly joined Dr. Maclaren's party in driving through the crowded streets of Colombo to Mount Lavinia, at a distance of five or six miles. Here we breakfasted at the hotel, situated amidst the beautiful scenery of this part of the coast. The glimpse we obtained in this drive of the interior of Ceylon, impressed us much with its luxuriant vegetation, its splendid groves of cocoa-nut palms, and wealth of flowers. Many of the cottages of the natives were completely covered to the tops of the roofs with masses of the rich floral colouring of bougainvilleas, hibiscus, both scarlet and yellow, and other flowers familiar to us in conservatories at home.

On our return, we drove to the cinnamon gardens, the perfume from which we had perceived when yet half a mile out at sea, reminding us of the hackneyed lines about the "spicy breezes" in Heber's well-known hymn. After spending some time in the interesting museum we returned to the ship, delighted and refreshed with our excursion.

We quitted Ceylon with regret that our time-limit did not admit of our staying until the departure of the next steamer for Australia, in a fortnight's time. The grand mountain ranges visible from Colombo offer many attractions to the tourist, in addition to those of the ancient capital of Kandy, and all the historic antiquities of the island.

Again the anchor was hoisted, and we were making for George's Sound, in West Australia. The Port of Albany, then a small town of 1,500 inhabitants, appeared to be a place of little importance, but of great expectations, in connection with the railway then in progress from Adelaide to Perth, in West Australia.

On landing, in the latter part of October, 1888, we were amazed at the wealth of wild flowers growing on the hills, and in the immediate vicinity of the town. In two or three hours our party had collected about fifty specimens that were entirely new to us as wild flowers. The handsome "Waratah," with its large red brush-like flower, and the "Arum," so common in our greenhouses, flourished abundantly. Leaving West Australia, which had not then become a gold-producing colony, the *Britannia* proceeded on her voyage, and on October 23rd we cast anchor in Hobson's Bay, Melbourne.

One of the Melbourne "Friends," J. H. Horsfall, kindly met us on board, and conducted us to his own home, in South Yarra, a suburb of Melbourne. Here we were hospitably entertained during our stay in that city. To be at rest again, and sojourning among friends on shore, after the weary shaking and tossing of the ocean, was indeed a welcome experience.

Melbourne.

In the course of a few days the first Intercolonial Conference of Friends took place, at which there were representatives from every meeting in the Southern Hemisphere. Visitors came from Queensland, a distance of about 1,400 miles, and others a like distance from New Zealand, with a still larger attendance from Tasmania, New South Wales, and from South Australia.

The meetings were characterised by harmony and mutual good feeling, and many of the visitors, hitherto known only to one another by correspondence, now warmly greeted each other face to face.

The magnificent appearance of the city of Melbourne, with its beautiful suburbs extending many miles along the bay, greatly exceeded our anticipations. A complete system of cable cars, which run swiftly along the remarkably wide thoroughfares, render the suburbs easily accessible. As an indication of the rapid advance in prosperity of this wealthy southern capital, a corner lot was pointed out to me by my brother Henry, which he had known some forty years previously as a grass field with a small outhouse upon it, and which was then purchased by a Methodist congregation for forty pounds, with a view to erect a chapel thereon, but which has been in recent years acquired by a banking company for the sum of forty thousand pounds!

On inquiry about this, of a person familiar with the value of property in the city, he ventured the remark that as the bank and adjoining premises now stand in the most valuable part of the main street, you may, in estimating its present value, almost add another nought, to the forty thousand pounds which were paid for this "corner lot."

A striking peculiarity of this population of about 400,000 is their love of holidays, of racing, and outdoor sports of various kinds. No such holiday-loving people has come under my notice in any other part of the world, and one almost wondered how the business of the city was carried on amid the numerous picnics and jaunts to which the population was addicted. Royal birthdays and other such events were availed of as excuses for holidays, and never in our experience were the strains of the National Anthem so often heard as in and around Melbourne. Doubtless the fineness of the climate was one great incitement to this out-door life, the weather being warm and settled for weeks together, the temperature at times rising to three figures Fahrenheit in the shade, in the streets of Melbourne. On the morning of December 26th—corresponding to our midsummer—a hot wind, known as a "brickfielder," was blowing from the north, *i.e.*, from the hot interior deserts of Australia, causing intolerable heat, necessitating our keeping all windows closed; but so sudden and violent are the contrasts of heat and cold, that in the afternoon of the same day, as we were proceeding out of Hobson's Bay towards Tasmania, the wind had veered round to the south, and was blowing from the Antarctic ice-regions, causing a fall of no less than fifty-two degrees in the thermometer within a few hours, compelling us to avail ourselves of all the winter wraps we could find to hand.

THE "BUSH."

Before leaving the Colony of Victoria, we arranged to visit Fernshaw, in order to obtain a glimpse of the Australian "Bush." The following extract from one of my letters, written on the spot, conveys some idea of the natural scenery and luxuriant vegetation abounding in the interior of Australia.

"*Narbethong*—(In the bush, fifty-five miles from Melbourne) December 18th, 1888.

"Over a ridge of the Black Spur Range, we have come here, in one of Cobb's four-in-hand coaches, to see one of 'Nature's Ferneries.'

"Fernshaw is the usual centre of attraction, but crossing the Spur, we have taken quarters for the night in a wayside inn, in the Bush, there being only two other houses in the township. Yes! 'Nature's fernery' on a grand scale! Looking down into the depths of the gorge, we see a bewildering tangle of greenery, with the graceful coronals and magnificent fronds of tree-ferns by the hundred, converting the gorge into a sub-tropical garden, or rather wilderness of verdure, where these graceful ferns range from one foot to forty, or even in rare cases, to seventy feet high!

"Above, below, and on every hand, tower aloft the smooth white stems of gum trees (eucalyptus).

Of trees 200 feet high there are forests; while trees of 300 to 350 feet are not uncommon. Some have been measured even up to 400 feet high. The prodigious height of some of these trees is accounted for by the fact of their growing crowded together in the bottom of the valleys, and in deep soil. In consequence of this overcrowding, there is a struggle for air and light, and individual trees are sometimes known to shoot up to the height of 200 feet, without putting out a single branch. The struggle continuing in the daylight, the ultimate height of the competitors is determined by the 'survival of the fittest.'

"Watching the gorge, one sees flocks of four or five Rosella parrots flit across with joyful screech, their crimson and blue plumage glittering in the sun. Smaller birds of a species unknown to us dart about the foreground, but we miss the brisk little 'mannikin,' whose note we heard nightly at Mount Barker, S.A., absurdly ordering us to 'send Bridget to Egypt!' In its place, however, the whole wood for miles, now resounds with the weird, hollow, mocking cries of the 'laughing jackass' as if parodying 'the hoarse, loud laugh, that speaks the vacant mind.' Custom not having yet 'staled our ears,' we listen with interest, as the sound is caught up and returned from distant 'jackass' throats, until it dies out faintly over the woods in the far distance. It is not safe for strangers to wander many yards from the path, or they may be lost in the dense scrub.

"Another sound now strikes our ears:—a sudden crash and roar in the midst of a death-like silence, when 'not a leaf hath leave to stir.' The last fibres which upheld some big tree on the slope of the hill, suddenly give way—no uncommon event —and the giant form is prostrated with a crash, never more to rear his head into the skies.

"Even round the house, in the cool of the evening may be seen 'wallabies'—a small species of kangaroo—the pest of the farmer, whilst opossums and bears frequent the woods around. None of these have we seen alive, but in the gloaming, not over 100 yards from the house, we had the pleasure of listening to the growling of two 'bears,'—these animals are in reality a species of harmless sloth.

"The returning coach ride through these grand woods and over the ridge, was through scenery finer than any we had previously seen in Australia. Hills are around us, crowned to the summit with timber, and in the distance are many mountain peaks. It is not to be wondered that the Melbourne people think highly of Fernshaw.

"An intelligent photographer whose acquaintance we made, had got photographs of trees much larger than any seen by us, taken by himself in the Bush, where he has several times been lost. In a monograph upon these, he states his belief that some of these Australian trees are 450 feet high. If this be so, they must be the loftiest, though not the thickest trees in the world! That distinction still belongs to the Mariposa grove of Sequoias in California."

SOUTH AUSTRALIA.

South Australia was the next Colony we visited. The city of Adelaide is about 500 miles north-west of Melbourne, and the railway to it crosses Australia's greatest river, the Murray, also the "Ninety-mile Scrub," a desert chiefly covered with the Wattle, a small species of Acacia. At Adelaide, in a temperature ranging from 98° to 105° in the shade, we found that a good programme of work had been arranged for us. I was kept fully occupied in addressing meetings during the twelve days of our stay. We visited in this interval Mount Barker, a cooler and more elevated spot, and much enjoyed a picnic on Mount Lofty, a magnificent elevation, from which we looked down on Adelaide in its wooded environment, which reminded us of the Scriptural description of the "City which lieth four square." It was a time of grievous drought in the Colony, no rain having fallen for months; the wheat crops were almost a total failure, and the sheep were perishing of famine and thirst. We heard of flocks of five and ten thousand being offered at sixpence per head, and no buyers!

We have the pleasantest reminiscences of Adelaide, and of the kind hospitality which we enjoyed there from many attached friends. The very house-flies (and they were "legion") were the most closely *attached* of their species! Nothing short of physical force could sever the connection between them and our perspiring countenances. I was courteously received by the Governor of South Australia, Sir William Robinson, and by Chief Justice Way, with whom I breakfasted, and who afterwards showed us his beautiful garden and aviary of Australian birds, the parrots especially being the pets of the Chief Justice.

Much pressure was put upon us to prolong our stay in Adelaide. Ministers of religion and others urged that public attention had been aroused on the Peace question, and that in order to impress it still more, Sunday addresses were needed to the various congregations.

Here it may be well to observe that for brevity's sake further details of lectures connected with Peace and Arbitration, delivered by me throughout the whole of the Colonies, are largely omitted. These lectures were based upon my own experiences in war-time, some of which have been already related in this book, as well as upon the oppressive militarism prevailing in Europe. As the actual observations of an eye-witness, these narratives were listened to with the profound interest which is evoked by revelations that are wholly new to the audience. Reluctantly we left our kind Adelaide hosts, and retraced our journey over the "Ninety-mile Desert" to Melbourne.

At Ballarat, where I addressed a large company, several gentlemen spoke pleasantly to me of their recollections of my late brother, the Hon. Joseph

Jones, who was Member for the borough, and also for a time Minister for Railways, under the Free-trader, Macculloch's premiership.

TASMANIA.

Our work in Victoria being now accomplished, we took steamer on 26th December for Hobart, in Tasmania. The voyage proved to be very rough, and in face of a bitter wind blowing straight from the Antarctic ice-fields, as already mentioned.

Near the entrance of the estuary of the Derwent leading up to Hobart, Cape Raoul, with its colossal basaltic rocks, towering to the height of about 300 feet, presents a strikingly magnificent spectacle. Before this grand columnar structure, the "organ-pipes" of Staffa and of the Giant's Causeway, in the British Isles, sink into utter insignificance, and it is questionable whether any other basaltic columns in the world will compare with those of Cape Raoul.

A few miles up the river, Hobart comes into view, nestling under the mass of Mount Wellington, whose commanding height of 4,300 feet seemed to dominate the landscape, and was all visible at a glance from the actual sea-level.

We were met at the steamer by our kind host, William Benson, who drove us to his house, situated about two miles from Hobart. The view from the front of the house reminded us of the English Lake District. On one side was a broad reach of the Derwent river, corresponding in appearance to the lake at Keswick, and on the other, Mount Wellington, with its beautifully wooded slopes. English fruits in abundance were ripening in the eight acres of garden ground : apples, pears, plums, apricots, of the finest quality, and excellent grapes, fully ripe. The climate and soil of Tasmania are well adapted for fruit growing.

Soon after we arrived we accompanied a party of friends on a visit to the noted fruit farms of the Shoobridge family. This was termed a "surprise" party. The Premier of the Colony, Mr. Fysh, and his wife joined us at luncheon. We examined with interest the 260 acres devoted to apple trees, the produce of which was destined for the English market. The trees were all pruned on scientific principles, being arranged like the ribs of an umbrella turned upwards, thus giving to every apple the same amount of light and air, securing uniformity of size and appearance in the fruit.

There was also a large area devoted to hop growing, the luxuriant plants climbing up poles thirty to forty feet high. The plantation was sheltered from strong winds by a hawthorn hedge which had quickly grown to about forty feet in height. Cheaper labour, Mr. Shoobridge informed me, was their great want, and he wondered why we in England did not send out a number of pauper children from our workhouses, to this land of plenty, where all would easily find employment.

For want of cheap labour there were on this farm alone, acres of prime fruit, such as apricots and raspberries, which it did not pay to gather, and which, therefore, were left to rot upon the ground.

The "Friends' Meeting" in Hobart is, I believe, the oldest in Australasia, having been established as the result of the religious labours of two English Friends, James Backhouse and George Washington Walker, who paid a long visit to this colony, then a penal settlement, about the year 1832.

Our visit was kindly welcomed by the "Friends," and especially by the late Joseph Benson Mather, the patriarch of the Meeting, and a man universally respected, being then one of the oldest colonists.

He appeared to know the antecedents of almost everyone in Tasmania, but was exceedingly cautious never to make use of the word "Convict," or to give any information in response to inquiries from anyone, as to "who was who" in the Colony.

Through his efficient aid I was soon again in the full swing of lectures and addresses, which kept me employed during the two weeks we stayed in Hobart. The most important meeting was held in the Town Hall, when the Governor, Sir Robert C. Hamilton, and Lady Hamilton were present, as also the Prime Minister, Mr. Fysh.

My wife and I accepted the invitation of the Governor and his Lady to dine at Government House, where we met some of the principal people of the town. The Governor invited me to call next morning, when we had a free talk about politics and home affairs generally.

It will be remembered that he was the Permanent Under Secretary for Ireland in Mr. Gladstone's ministry, and is said to have given Mr. Gladstone much assistance in drawing up his Home Rule Bill. He was relieved of office by the Tory Government, and sent into "splendid exile," to the well-remunerated post of Governor of Tasmania. The domain around Government House is very extensive and beautiful, being well wooded and containing several fine sheets of water.

I accompanied our host, Mr. Benson, several times to the premises which had been recently acquired for the "Friends' School" in Hobart, which is now a flourishing institution. As a boarding school for boys and girls, as well as a superior day school for Hobart children, it has earned in a few years a reputation both for the high class education given, and for its excellent moral tone.

As regards the children of the Society of Friends, some of whom come from colonies distant about 1,500 miles, the school is to them much what Ackworth School is to "Friends'" children in England.

Our Hobart friends were unwearying in their efforts to make our time there pass pleasantly. One day they organized a large picnic for us, up the side of Mount Wellington. We found the climb up the fern-tree valley rather severe, the path being frequently blocked by fallen trees, and as some of these were giants of five to seven feet in diameter, it was no light matter, especially for ladies, to scramble over them. The ferns and other vegetation were truly magnificent. After some hours climbing we emerged at last at an old hut near the top; here we rested and enjoyed our meal, tea being made in regular Colonial fashion in a "billy," or large can, in which the water was boiled. Everyone was in the best of spirits and thoroughly disposed to enjoy both the refreshing meal and the glorious views far below our feet, stretching "from inland regions to the distant main." From our point of vantage we could look down upon the Tasman peninsula, where in former days were located the penal convict settlements, separated by a narrow neck from the mainland. This isthmus was then closely guarded and fortified, rendering escape almost impossible.

Here also a number of formidable bloodhounds were kept, in order to pursue and track down any wretched convicts who might succeed in effecting their escape in the darkness. The terrible associations connected with the transportation days during their worst condition, gave one almost a shudder to recall, as one beheld the scenes of the baneful convict-system, now happily abolished, spread out like a map before us.

CHAPTER XIX.

NEW ZEALAND: SOUTH ISLAND—THE SOUNDS TRIP—OTIRA GORGE—CROSSING RIVER IN FLOOD—THE SOUTHERN ALPS—NEW ZEALAND: NORTH ISLAND—TAITA—WONDERFUL GARDENS—MAORI STORIES—TIKITERA BOILING LAKE—MUD BATHS.

FINDING that lecturing night after night in these southern climates was very enervating work, and feeling that a change and rest were indispensable, we were glad to leave Hobart for Dunedin, in New Zealand, in the s.s. *Rotomahana* on the 18th of January, 1889. We had met with such unbounded kindness from friends in Hobart, many of whom, including our host, W. Benson, came to see us off in the steamer, that the leave-taking on board, viewed in the light of a final farewell, was somewhat sad and affecting. In the retrospect, however, the times of social enjoyment in the company of Hobart friends are among our brightest reminiscences.

In about four days of a rough and tumble voyage, so common on these coasts, we arrived at Port Chalmers. The city of Dunedin, which is situated about nine miles inland, impressed us with the beauty of its environment of lofty hills, and with its handsome buildings and wide streets; also with the life and stir of its busy population, who are mostly of Scotch origin.

Here we arranged to join one of the "Western Sounds trips," which were organized every summer from Dunedin, to an uninhabited region on the west coast of the South Island, which, for the magnificence of its scenery, has attained a world-wide fame. We joined on board the s.s. *Tarawera* a party of nearly a hundred persons, most of them from England, and the courtesy which distinguished the whole company enhanced the pleasure of our ten days' excursion.

Facing the mighty South Pacific Ocean, the whole region is subject to frequent rains, and the downpour might sometimes be described as terrific. Our steamer put into each of the eight or nine fiords in succession, usually casting anchor for the night. The scenery is hardly so grand and wild as that of the Norwegian fiords, but it is much more varied and often strikingly beautiful. The landscape abounds nearly everywhere with the characteristic New Zealand vegetation, consisting of tree ferns, etc., down to the water's edge. The last place we anchored at was at the head of Milford Sound, twelve or fourteen miles from the sea. Near us, on the right, were the Bowen Falls, 500 feet high, one of the loveliest waterfalls in the world, the lower portion spreading out into feathery wreaths of spray, glowing in the sunlight with all the colours of the rainbow. Beyond is Pembroke Peak, 6,700 feet high, from which descends, to within two thousand feet of the sea, a resplendent glacier, whose lower edge terminates abruptly, seeming to be about 250 feet thick. On the opposite side of the Sound is Mitre Peak, 5,600 feet high, which, rising directly from the sea level, shows its entire height, and is almost as impressive as the Swiss Matterhorn. In the far distance is a very lofty range of snow-covered peaks, being part of the New Zealand Alps, glowing in the sunshine, and at times assuming a lovely roseate tint. In a word, Milford is at once the grandest and the most beautiful of the Sounds, and is alone worth the voyage to see.

This part of New Zealand is the paradise of fern-hunters, for the Bush abounds with rare ferns in great variety. My wife's enthusiasm in the pursuit of ferns led us sometimes pretty deep into the Bush, the density of which, unless entered with every precaution, renders it an easy matter for visitors to be lost in its mazes.

About twelve miles inland were the far-famed Sutherland Falls, 1,904 feet high, being among the highest known falls in the world. We wished much to visit them, but as it involved ten hours tramp through the Bush each way, and as the track had been partially destroyed by a land-slip, we found it impossible. We had also to take into account the fact that the steamer which left the next day was the last for the season.

The plague of life in the woods of Southern New Zealand is the swarms of sand-flies. In spite of veils or anointings, these tiny tormentors penetrate through all, and their poisoned proboscces cause great irritation for a week or more. In its lasting effect, the sting of this insignificant foe is worse than that of the mosquito, which also abounds in these woods. It was a great relief, when out at sea once more, to escape these insect pests.

On our return to Dunedin we found that the introductions brought from England proved of great service. Through them I obtained the efficient help of the proprietor of the principal newspaper, and through his friendly aid, public interest was so aroused in the question of International Arbitration, that one of my addresses was delivered to a crowded meeting in the largest Presbyterian Church in the city. The lessons sought to be enforced in the lecture were taken up and obtained a wide circulation in the local press.

Our next destination was Christchurch, which we found to be a much less stirring and "go-ahead" place than Dunedin. Under the auspices of the Young Men's Christian Association we succeeded in getting up more than one good meeting, and as at Dunedin, a Local Peace Association was formed.

Here the evidences of a recent earthquake were still visible. The spire of the Church had lost some of its upper tiers of stone-work, about twelve tons in weight, and several loose stones hung in a dangerous way in iron bands from the top for some time afterwards.

No visitor who is interested in Natural History should omit to pay a visit to the museum at Christchurch, which contains, among many other objects of interest, a unique group of skeletons of the gigantic extinct bird the "Moa," together with specimens of its enormous eggs.

The Otira Gorge.

Christchurch being the best centre from which to cross the island to the west coast, and the drive through the Otira Gorge being reputed to be "the finest coach drive in the world," we concluded to make the trip, at least so far as to the end of the Gorge. It is only after the coach reaches the mountain range, which traverses the island from north to south, that the picturesque portion of the journey begins. Once upon the range a constant succession of grand mountains and valleys keeps one's attention on the stretch. A night has to be spent on the road at an elevated spot called "Bealey's," where accommodation of a limited and somewhat rough character is provided. From this point the scenery grows grander and wilder. The road becomes often a mere shelf, high up on the hill-side, whilst deep down below are a wide valley and a large river, the Waimakariri. In some of the abrupt angles of the road, the coach swings dangerously near the edge of the precipice. It was on this route that Archibald Forbes, the *Daily News* war correspondent, is said to have confessed that he felt more nervous than he had ever done under the hottest fire in war-time. Perched up, as my wife and I were, on the roof, just behind the coachman, we enjoyed the most panoramic of views. At one specially sharp angle of the road, observing that the outer horse of our three leaders was trotting upon the very verge of the precipice, I ventured to call the driver's attention to the fact. His prompt reply, meant to allay our fears, conveyed but cold comfort, "Bless you, sir, that horse no more wants to go over the edge than you do!" True! methought; and it set me reflecting that these five horses were not a mere "scratch pack," got together anyhow, but virtually, with the driver and the coach, were one compact machine, which regularly traversed these risky spots. Evidently the best thing to do was to derive whatever comfort we could from these reflections, and turn our thoughts towards the magnificent prospects before us! In crossing the river in the valley below, we counted upwards of twenty different channels or streams, occupying the entire width of the valley, which was thus denuded of its surface soil, beyond all hope of restoration for agricultural purposes, by the devastations of the river when in flood.

Further on, the Otira Gorge became resplendent with the crimson flower of the "Rata" tree. This tree, which begins as a parasite, depending for its existence upon some other tree, soon waxes strong enough to stifle and destroy its supporter in its firm, tenacious grip, and becomes an independent tree, whose tough red wood is much valued. To see a whole mountain-side covered with the glowing crimson blossoms of the "Rata," in full bloom, is indeed a never-to-be-forgotten sight.

We left the coach after crossing the river at the foot of the Gorge, and stayed the night at a wayside inn named "Jackson's." On the lofty hill behind the house miners were at work, prospecting for gold. Some of these men kindly brought us down some specimens of the New Zealand "Edelweiss," which closely resembles its European congener; but the leaves of the plant are somewhat shorter.

Early in the morning, as we were dressing, we heard a loud rumbling sound, and simultaneously the floor of the bedroom shook violently, and the timbers of the house, fortunately a wooden one, creaked and groaned ominously. These earth-tremors, so alarming to strangers, are so frequent in certain parts of New Zealand, that the inhabitants hardly take any notice of them.

On the return of the coach we took our places for Christchurch in a downpour of rain, and when driving towards the river, the driver expressed some doubts as to its being fordable, the water having come down during the night "in spate,"—as they say in Scotland. On approaching the bank, seeing the flood, he put the ominous question aside to me, "Can your wife ride on horseback?" Presently a man on horseback appeared on the opposite bank, who urged his horse into the ford, and cautiously rode, as though feeling his way towards the middle of the stream, where the water, though deep, was still fordable; he then turned abruptly round, and slowly worked his way back to the bank from which he came. This move was evidently for the purpose of "giving a lead" to our horses, who, seeing their companion walking safely through, unhesitatingly followed. Once or twice in mid-stream we felt the coach lift a little, the pressure on one side causing the water to stand several inches higher than on the other, and we seemed to be almost on the point of being swept away by the powerful current, so that we were right thankful to effect at last a safe landing. We found at the hotel a party of gentlemen, whose acquaintance we had made on the "Sounds trip"; they had followed us in a phaeton, which being so much lower than the stage coach, had been detained several days at the hotel, being unable to cross the flooded river. Such are the uncertainties of New Zealand driving tours, owing to the vagaries of the unbridged rivers in these mountainous regions. Frequently they carve out for themselves new channels, leaving the old ones high and dry. Occasionally we observed an expensive bridge left uselessly standing over a dry river bed.

As we continued our journey eastward we came again into full view of the lofty snow-covered Alps, in the background of the Otira Gorge. Among this range is Mount Cook, the highest peak in New Zealand, being nearly 13,000 feet high. The sublime appearance of these glorious peaks, glinting and glistening in the morning sun, was enhanced by that of a magnificent glacier, whose dazzling whiteness, tinged here and there with opalescent hues, presented throughout the entire mass a wonderfully crystalline effect. Neither in Switzerland nor among the Rocky Mountains of America, have I ever witnessed Alpine scenery which surpassed in beauty and splendour these Southern Alps of New Zealand.

TAITA, NEAR WELLINGTON.

The North Island soon became our destination. Crossing "Cook's Straits" by steamer from Port Lyttelton, the port of Christchurch, we landed at Wellington, the capital of the islands, and proceeded at once to the home of our kind friends Mr. and Mrs. T. Mason, at Taita, in the valley of the Hutt River, twelve miles from Wellington.

Our host and hostess had emigrated from Yorkshire about forty years before, and settled at Taita, a hamlet situated about three miles above the point where the Hutt enters Wellington Bay.

The fame of their garden, extending over eleven acres around the house, had reached us months before in Australia. Nowhere indeed, at home or abroad, can I recall having seen any private garden so rich in floral and arboreal beauty. The influence of climate and soil, combined with the fostering skill of the owner, whose special hobby it is, have caused trees and plants to flourish in a way that a northern Englishman could hardly conceive of beforehand.

To us it was difficult to realise, in the midst of this exuberance and beauty, that less than forty years ago, primeval bush and scrub held undisturbed sway over the spot. Magnificent conifers from California, the Himalayas, China and Japan, flourish there in vigorous life, and noble cedars of Asiatic, African and American species adorn the lawn. Yes, a real smooth-cropped *lawn*, a piece of green, well-kept turf, a treat which our eyes had not beheld since quitting England. Nothing could better illustrate the accommodating geniality of the New Zealand climate, than the magnificent collection of plants that Mr. Mason has culled from almost every latitude and longitude. Besides native trees and tree ferns, there are fine single specimens of abies, picea, and araucaria, some of them very rare in the Colony, the cork tree of Europe, and the maiden-hair tree of Japan, orange, lemon, loquat, and fig trees. We found, also, growing side by side with the sweet-smelling favourites of British gardens, roses, lilies, stocks, an abundance of our greenhouse ornaments, such as lapagerias, begonias, amaryllises, ericas, hydrangeas, plumbago, and many others which space fails me to enumerate.

During the rhododendron season, we were informed, some three hundred varieties of that plant may be seen there blooming in profusion;

also about eighty varieties of camellia! Nothing could convey a better idea of the *embarras ae richesses* to be found in these gardens than these two examples.

No wonder that Mr. Mason, who for years was a respected member of the Legislature, has many friends who, from the Governor downwards, come to revel in this scene of beauty, natural and cultivated. None go away empty handed, but often laden, like the spies of old, with the choicest fruits and flowers of the land. Nor are the hospitals overlooked by the bountiful owner; twice during our visit, two young lady nurses in Wellington Hospital paid us visits, returning each time laden with basket-loads of what we should call in England splendid greenhouse flowers, to feast the eyes and gladden the hearts of their charges in the hospital.

Mr. Mason was then above seventy years of age, but "the dew of his youth was yet upon him." He possessed an amount of "go" that few younger men could boast of, as I found sometimes to my cost when taking long walks with him. Constant out-door occupation in an ozone-laden atmosphere like this cannot fail to invigorate. A few months or years residence in the life-giving air and sunshine of these islands would be the best of restoratives to many a sickly, consumptive patient at home.

The early reminiscences of our host and hostess were a constant fund of interest to us. Coming out to New Zealand in 1841, they found both lowlands and hillsides around Port Nicholson, as Wellington was then called, covered with dense bush down to the water's edge. Their first night was spent in a canvas tent pitched on the side of the hill, their blankets and goods, brought out for trading with the natives, being all stored in the tent. Night brought a deluge of rain, which, pouring through the canvas, soaked the bed, themselves, and their goods, and they passed some miserable hours till daylight under shelter of an umbrella.

They afterwards removed into the Hutt Valley, and purchased the land they still occupy, and built near the banks of the river a "wharé," *i.e.*, a hut made of wattle and mud, as their first family abode.

In this solitude, surrounded by dense bush, with no white neighbours near, they lived for some years, and here several of their children were born. Every article of food, except what the land produced, also clothing and implements, had to be fetched from Wellington, at no small cost of time and trouble. The goods were brought in a rowboat up the bay from town, to the mouth of the river, and thence were carried on men's backs through miles of rough bush track.

Starting from home at 2 a.m., and finding their way through the forest by lighted torches of Totara pine, the return journey from Wellington was not usually accomplished until 9 or 10 p.m., long after darkness had set in. Mrs. Mason's piercing "coo-ey," and her husband's equally vigorous response, could be distinctly heard re-echoing through the sombre, silent forest for fully one hour and a half before he gained the river bank opposite the wharé, where the canoe stood ready to ferry his goods and himself across the river. Many a lonely hour she thus spent with her young family, with savages often prowling around the wharé, when her husband was absent on these long tramps to the city.

The Maories at first were well disposed; some of them would fetch water and do other little services for Mr. and Mrs. Mason. In order to keep up friendly relations, Mrs. Mason sometimes boiled for them a large pot of rice. This dish, well sweetened with sugar, quite won their affections, and the quantities they could eat seemed hardly to know a limit. By way of testing their capabilities, she rewarded a friendly native for some little service with a large potful of boiled rice. She watched him lay himself down beside it with demonstrations of satisfaction, evidently intent on gorging the whole contents. There are limits, however, even to a Maori's capacity; so, after a long struggle, she was amused to see him retire towards the bush, rubbing himself with both hands, casting meanwhile a "longing, lingering look behind" on the tantalizing luxury; when lo! presently he returned to the charge, and succeeded this time in devouring the last spoonful!

The more knowing among the natives eventually became troublesome, insisting on being paid in "money-gold," as they termed it, for the land. Large purchases of land had been made *en bloc* from the natives by Colonel Wakefield, the agent of the "New Zealand Company," and had mostly been paid for in goods, blankets, muskets, and food. When the food was consumed, the natives, especially those from the interior, declared that they had been robbed of their birthright, and were loud in their demands for "money-gold," the value of which they had learnt to know.

Wishful to satisfy them, Mr. Mason would fain have given them blankets and goods; but being enjoined, for the sake of other settlers, not to make a precedent, heedless of their threatening attitudes, he boldly refused their demands. On one occasion a noted warrior menacingly demanded "money-gold," saying that the "goods were all eaten." There being no protection to the wharé, door and windows being simply closed with calico, Mr. Mason, who, though not tall, was strong and wiry, stood in the doorway to preven the entrance of the huge Maori, who was determined to force his way in.

The big savage threw his arms around him, and was carrying him off like a child, when his wife bravely rushed to the rescue. She gave the warrior a vigorous slap in the face; the astounded savage immediately dropped his burden, and there ensued a *tableau vivant*, worthy of being commemorated in colours:—the enraged Maori, holding his tomahawk menacingly close to Mrs. Mason's forehead, whilst she, never flinching in the least, stood staring him full in the face! "You have done it now, Jane," said her husband disconsolately, fearing the consequence of her rash bravery. But the chivalrous Maori, astonished no doubt at the white woman's courage, at a word from his chief, slowly lowered the weapon and withdrew.

Curiously enough, this very warrior became for years afterwards one of Mrs. Mason's best friends. He would wait for hours by the river for her return from town; and then, with evident pleasure, would place himself in position, and, in spite of her remonstrances, would insist on her mounting on his broad shoulders, and would carry her safely across the stream.

At the outbreak of the first Maori War, she often watched at grey dawn from the windows of the wharé, hundreds of warriors dancing and gesticulating threateningly on the opposite side of the river, yelling, and violently slapping their thighs in their excitement. These unsophisticated savages, however, were lovers of truth, and, finding by experience that Mr. and Mrs. Mason always told them the *exact truth*, and kept their word, "yes," or "no," conceived such a regard for them, that they not only left them unmolested, but also, for their sakes showed similar respect to some of their neighbours.

In short, Mrs. Mason never felt, even during the war scare, so much fear among the Maories, as she experienced when residing later on, temporarily in Tasmania, in the midst of the white "Convict" element of Hobart. Two of these criminals, with crape over their faces, once forced their way into their abode in Hobart, and knowing that the men were out of the way, created terror and dismay among the women, and retired at their leisure laden with plunder.

The Maories.

Numbers of civilised Maories now reside in the neighbourhood of Taita, in neat wooden houses, each with its well-cultivated plot of land attached. One flourishing vegetable garden was pointed out to us as being rented by an industrious Chinaman, who thus became, so to speak, servant to the proud Maori. Some of the latter have grown comparatively wealthy, especially such of the chiefs as claim the lion's share of the "reserved" lands, which the Government, for their protection against "land-grabbers," no longer allows them to *sell*. The revenue derived by some from these lands is considerable, large areas being much in request for sheep-runs and farms. One chief, who was a member of the Legislature, was said to possess an income of £30,000 a year from land.

At the time of our visit two or three educated natives sat in the Upper House, and four in the Lower, interpreters being provided for those who could not (or would not) address the House in English.

This unearned increment from the land, however, has proved a not altogether unmixed blessing to the Maori of to-day. Without occupation, and with ample means, more than a few of them have degenerated into tobacco-smoking, beer-drinking, gambling, loafers about town, inferior in physique, and even in *morale*, to their cannibal ancestors!

It was interesting to watch groups of natives engaged in lively discussion in their soft mellifluous tongue, every syllable of which ends in a vowel. Their gesticulations surpass even those of Southern Italians. The great mobility of their eyelids and of the muscles of the face gives an uncanny expression to their dark countenances when agitated or excited. These scenes helped one to understand the wild terror which dark tatooed faces and rolling eyes, accompanied by fiendish yells and brandishing of weapons, were wont to create in former days, when these warlike savages swooped down on the homes of the colonists.

The entire Maori population of the islands exceeded 120,000, it is believed, when Captain Cook landed on them upwards of 100 years ago. In the North Island they number now less than 38,000, and in the South Island, which is larger, but colder, only about 2,000.

In spite of education and the paternal care bestowed on them of late years by the Government, this manly, intelligent people, like other native races, seems destined to dwindle away and disappear before the strong liquors and the imported diseases of the whites. One source of loss, strange to say, is the very security of life which they enjoy among their white neighbours. No longer living in constant fear of each other, they have ceased to dwell in the healthy, hilly regions, where they formerly constructed their hill-forts or "pahs" for defence; the natives now build their wharés upon their cultivated patches on the plains, or sometimes on swamps, where their surroundings are conducive to fevers and other fatal complaints. The children also are now sufficiently clothed and sent to school, but as their mothers are too ignorant to change their wet garments in rainy weather, they are apt to contract lung diseases, and many die from this cause in early life.

The North Island had about the time of our visit passed through a terrible scare, on account of Te Kooti, a fierce old warrior, who about sixteen years before had raised a rebellion and caused the colonists much alarm and trouble. Unmindful of his past defeats he advanced with a considerable native following upon Gisborne, with the intent, it was supposed, again to revive "Hau-hau-ism" among the natives. The Maori is intensely superstitious, and under the influence of "Hau-hau-ism," which is a sort of wild religious fanaticism, throws off his thin veneer of civilisation, and, reckless of consequences, while the paroxysm lasts, becomes once more a marauding, murderous savage. Happily, the contingency which thus makes him a most undesirable neighbour does not often occur, and his habits have in modern times usually been quiet and peaceable enough.

On this occasion the Premier in hot haste collected a strong possé of armed police and soldiers to put down the redoubtable Te Kooti. No violence or bloodshed, however, was called for; the old chief, demoralised by his love of "fire-water," was captured in a state of helpless intoxication, and imprisoned; but as soon as all was quiet, being deemed no longer formidable, Te Kooti was set at liberty.

Even in the untravelled fastnesses of the "King Country" in the North Island, which is nominally independent and subject only to a native King, there is not cohesion or unity enough among the natives to attempt another rising, well knowing as they do that the colonists have grown stronger and more numerous with each advancing year.

The conditions of life among many of the Northern Maories are not calculated to develop a manly or independent spirit. In the hot-lake region we saw numbers of them sitting idly for hours up to the neck in the pools of warm water which abound. Others sit, or lie, through the live-long day smoking, eating, or sleeping upon the hot stones, between the crevices of which steam issues from the regions below. Often one sees a wooden box, perforated at the bottom, in which their provisions are cooked *gratis*, and without trouble, by steam; thus, with no cooking and no housekeeping to do, the lazy native gives full scope to his loafing propensities.

There was something strangely fascinating to me in the immense cauldrons or lakes of boiling mud which we visited in these regions, specially the one at Tikitera, where I long stood intently watching the black, smooth, oleaginous mess, writhing, tumbling and jumping up into weird fantastic shapes, while volumes of sulphurous vapour were emitted from unknown depths below. So penetrating were these fumes of sulphur that silver articles, and even the coins in our purses, were turned black in a few moments. But whilst gazing, lost in reverie, deaf alike to calls and warning cries, as I stood on the crumbling, treacherous edge of the black "Maëlstrom," a tug at my coat laps from the hand of my watchful wife, aroused me to the risk I ran of suddenly disappearing overhead into that vortex of unspeakable slime.

Turning our faces away from this "abomination of desolation," where not a tree, nor green blade was visible, we adjourned for lunch into a neat wharé, where a Scotchman was living with his Maori wife, who had personal or tribal rights over the property. Here he had constructed some mud baths, which could be filled from the inexhaustible cauldron at a higher level, for the accommodation of such patients as could overcome their disgust whilst wallowing in the black mud, reeking with the rotten-egg odour of sulphureted hydrogen!

Here, on reflection, one could well realise the marvellous power of adaptation in the human frame, in every land and clime, to the curiously manifold phases of its environment.

CHAPTER XX.

NEW ZEALAND: NORTH ISLAND (CONTINUED)—TE MATA ESTATE—FORTY THOUSAND SHEEP—AUCKLAND—SIR GEORGE GREY.—SYDNEY: BOTANICAL GARDENS—COLLISION AT SEA.—BRISBANE: TROPICAL FRUITS.—TO CHINA FROM AUSTRALIA: THE GREAT BARRIER REEF—THURSDAY ISLAND.—SOUTH AUSTRALIA: NORTHERN PART—PORT DARWIN—ABORIGINES.

THE main object of our visit to the Colonies was not overlooked at Wellington. Several Peace meetings were held, over the most important of which the Governor, Sir William Jervoise, kindly consented to preside, when he ably advocated the cause of Arbitration, taking the ground that in no case should the sword be drawn until Arbitration had been tried and had failed to settle the differences. Such impartial views from a military officer of his rank were greatly appreciated. Here, as in other New Zealand towns, we had the advantage of a kindly-disposed local Press. Excellent reports of the addresses were published in the leading journals, together with favourable editorials.

We now travelled northward to Palmerston by rail, and thence by coach through an interesting district, styled the "Forty Mile Bush," to Hastings, where our friend John Chambers met us, and drove us about four miles to his home at Te Mata. His estate of Te Mata consisted of about twenty-five square miles of picturesque hill and arable land, containing a run for about 40,000 sheep, but at the time of our visit the property was divided into separate farms for three of his sons. The general condition of the agricultural labourer here struck me as being the best I had met with in any part of the world. The best hands at Te Mata had each a horse kept for his own riding, a cow, a good house and garden, and twenty-five shillings a week wages. Of course it is only the skilled and steady men who command these high wages. Inferior or unsteady hands are as little esteemed in New Zealand as at home. One Saturday, as we were driving back from Hastings, we passed on the road four of Mr. Chambers's men on their own horses. This led Mr. Chambers to remark, "They are going to do their marketing; they can buy in Hastings market four pounds of the finest mutton chops for one shilling."

During our stay at Te Mata, we watched with much interest the process of separating a flock of about 5,000 sheep, which had been collected from the hills, into the various sorts known as "wethers," "hoggets," and three and four year old sheep. This was not accomplished without much vociferation of men and barking of dogs. When the flocks of sheep were brought into something like order, they were driven between parallel palings towards some pens, where the head shepherd was stationed. Within his reach were three or four swing gates, just large enough to admit one sheep at a time, each gate leading into a separate pen. As the sheep were driven rapidly down the narrow gangway towards the head shepherd, he decided at a glance into which of the pens every animal ought to go. The skill and precision with which this was done, in the case of every individual out of a large herd, reminded one forcibly of that saying of our Lord, "I know My sheep and am known of Mine."

Our friend's home is situated in a pleasant district of the Province of "Hawke's Bay," and we could fully realise here that New Zealand, differing widely from Australia in general, is truly "a land of rivers and springs of water," which accounts for its greater fertility, and its adaptability for rearing sheep and cattle.

Some pleasant excursions which our friends had kindly arranged for us had to be omitted, as it was time to push on across the country to Auckland, formerly the capital of the colony.

Auckland.

We were delighted with the picturesque situation of this beautiful city, near the foot of Mount Eden, and occupying part of an isthmus between two sheltered and capacious bays. From the summit of Mount Eden itself the panoramic views of sea and land, embracing islands with lofty rugged outlines, are very extensive. The hill is an extinct volcano, and has a distinctly marked crater. Below are masses of lava and scoria, and we found the house of a friend on whom we called, actually built upon scoria. Fruits, vegetables, and flowers throve wonderfully upon this fertile volcanic soil in his garden.

To the north is the peninsula, which is pre-eminently the country of the valuable Kauri pine, which grows here to the greatest perfection. Large quantities also of the amber-like Kauri gum are exported from the North Island. The regular gum-hunters, from long practice, become skilful in finding it, lying as it often does at a considerable depth in the soil of the forest. They plunge long steel rods into the ground, and when they strike a piece they dig for it. Lumps many pounds in weight are sometimes found, and are considered quite a prize.

SIR GEORGE GREY.

The most eminent personage then resident in Auckland was Sir George Grey, statesman, engineer, explorer, ex-governor of Cape Colony and of South Australia, and twice Governor of New Zealand. Sir George was at once the most interesting and the most respected of New Zealand colonists. Having, after the expiry of his term of Governorship, come to England, and failing to obtain a seat in Parliament, he returned to live in the colony he loved so well. During his term of office he had been the constant friend and protector of the Maori race. To this day they speak affectionately of him as their "Father," for his invaluable aid, in the face of much opposition, in maintaining their territorial rights to the soil, thus enabling them to live in independence and comfort, instead of being mere disinherited paupers, dependent upon their white masters.

The Government being anxious to do justice to the Maories with regard to their land, a Land Court is held from time to time to decide doubtful cases. The Judge is a European, but there are two Maori assessors. Sometimes a Maori claims certain land because one of his ancestors had *eaten* the former owner, and so having swallowed the owner he maintains that he has thereby assimilated the right of succession to the property. This claim, strange as it may appear to us, is duly taken into account when judging the case, as it is considered consistent with Maori law.

Sir George received me most courteously, and entered freely into the object of my mission, with which he expressed full sympathy. In the course of an hour's conversation, I learnt much from him about the island upon which we were, its inhabitants, resources, and places worth visiting. He also told me about his former home in the beautiful Island of Kawau, which he had bought of the Government, and which is situated in the bay about thirty miles from Auckland. In addition to its native products, Sir George had enriched it with a variety of foreign timber trees, shrubs, and plants, and had imported several varieties of deer and other ornamental animals, which roamed at large quite unmolested. I quite longed to visit this enchanting isle, but, there being no regular means of communication, time failed me.

Among other benefactions, Sir George had presented to the city of Auckland his valuable collection of MSS. and books, which he had amassed at a great cost of time and money, and which are now treasured in their public library.

It was an unlooked-for privilege to have Sir G. Grey presiding over my public meeting, and the attendance of Sir William Fox and Professor Aldis, amongst other leading citizens, testified to the interest that was felt in the cause advocated.

Since that date, this great Englishman, wise administrator, and most successful of Colonial Governors, has passed away at the venerable age of eighty-six, and his remains have been honoured by a public funeral, and by interment in the great national fane of St. Paul's, London.

In every place where the beneficent sway of Sir George Grey has been known, his memory will long be cherished, not only as an able ruler, one not afraid of incurring responsibility, and where needful of taking the initiative, but still more for his unfailing courtesy and tact in dealing with native races, and for the unflinching courage with which he maintained their rights, and thus secured their grateful loyalty to the British Crown.

Having found many kind friends in Auckland, and being much interested in the small community of the Society of Friends there, we quitted it with feelings of regret. The climate may be too warm for some constitutions, but for myself I found it almost perfect, and were I obliged to choose a residence abroad for health's sake, I know of hardly any place where I could enjoy more of the pleasures of life, and of congenial society, than in Auckland, New Zealand.

SYDNEY.

We left Auckland on April 9th, in the steamer *Waihora*, and after a voyage of four or five days arrived at Sydney in the evening, too late, unfortunately, to see the beauty of its celebrated harbour.

Sydney presented the appearance of a longer-established city, than any we had yet seen in the southern hemisphere. Being the seat of Government, it possesses many fine public buildings, and the bustle and life of its streets betoken an important centre of business. Communication with all parts of the suburbs is rendered easy by its extensive system of street-railways, along which the cars, which are usually two-storied, are drawn by locomotives. At first I felt doubtful as to how far this busy population would care to hear anything about the progress of International Arbitration; but on calling on the Premier, Sir Henry Parkes, I was much encouraged by the hearty way in which he entered into the question, and agreed to preside over a public meeting. This was soon arranged to take place in the largest Congregational Church in the city, on which occasion Sir H. Parkes's statesman-like address was eagerly listened to by an audience of over 2,000 people, and was widely circulated in the New South Wales journals.

This important meeting led to many other engagements in various quarters of the city. The largest of these was held in the new and handsome Town Hall, and was presided over by another member of the Government. As in the other colonies, a local Peace Association was then formed.

There is to a stranger an amusing rivalry, amounting to jealousy, between the two capitals, Sydney and Melbourne, as to their respective claims to priority, and to the general admiration of strangers. One question invariably asked by every Sydneyite is, "What do you think of our Botanical Gardens?" Not that there is any difficulty as to the answer, as one can, without straining the truth, say, "For beauty of situation, adjoining, as it does, the celebrated harbour, and for the variety and extent of its floral and arboreal equipment, your public gardens are among the finest in the world."

As the season for monsoons and heavy rains, which would interfere with our further work in China and Japan, was rapidly advancing, we left Sydney and embarked on May 8th in the steamer *Eurimbla* for Brisbane. Punctuality is not a strong point of coasting steamers, and instead of starting at five p.m. as advertised, night was falling before we left the quay, again disappointing us of a view of the whole harbour. Little did we think as a group of our Sydney friends clustered around to see us off, some of them loading us with flowers and fruit from their own gardens, of the accident which was about to occur before we had steamed many miles away.

Collision at Sea.

Quoting from a letter written on board immediately after the occurrence, my record proceeds thus :

"Presently the moon shone out with brightness, as we sped away down the long harbour towards the 'Heads' and the open sea. In an hour's time, as the vessel approached the 'Heads,' my wife and I were standing together on the upper deck, enjoying the moonlit landscape, and calm glittering water. We observed two steamers, one some distance behind the other, both taking a course nearly at right angles to our track. We passed the stern of the first all right, according to the 'rule of the road.' Our vessel then continued on her straight course towards the 'Heads,' regardless of the second steamer, which soon appeared to be bearing down upon us, our captain having apparently made up his mind that the other captain would port his helm, and pass under our stern. This was just what he would *not* do, even when a collision became a certainty. Having the 'rule of the road' on his side, he stuck to his course, regardless apparently of consequences! It was an exciting moment. Three or four minutes beforehand I told my wife he was running straight into us. A collision was inevitable! I only hoped he might not strike us amidships and thus sink our vessel! 'Stop her,' roared out our captain to the engineer, when it was too late. 'Full speed astern,' but the 'way' on the ship was too great to be suddenly checked, and on we went, though with greatly reduced speed. At this moment the stranger struck our starboard bows with a terrific momentum, that resounded over the ship and sent everything reeling. Fortunately the shock gave her such a recoil, that she did not strike us again. Moreover, our reversed screw now drew us out of further harm's way. The cries and screams of passengers on the foredeck, the yells and shouts of the two captains to each other, were something frightful.

"Presently, as the stranger sheered off, the men became calmer. 'What ship is that?' asked our captain. 'The *Kurrara*.' 'Got any damage?' 'Yes, a hole in my bows, what ship is that?' 'The *Eurimbla*.' And so, after giving each other a staggering blow, we parted friends!

"Our captain now turned his vessel back towards the lightship which we had passed an hour or two before, to give an opportunity for ascertaining the damage, and to see whether she was making any water. The boat was lowered, and the captain and chief engineer proceeded to the bows, and found that we had received the blow exactly on the stem, the very strongest part of the ship!

"Strong as it was, and composed of many plates of iron, it was bent much out of the perpendicular, and a metal plate on the deck above, two inches thick, was broken in two. Had the blow been even two or three feet further aft, or had it been amidships, it was enough to have cut us down to the water's edge. To a landsman, it seemed passing strange, that two steamers in full sight of each other for fifteen or twenty minutes, on a bright moonlight evening, in perfectly calm water, and with no wind, should come into collision at all!

"With several other passengers, I begged the captain to put back to port if there was the slightest risk in proceeding. He assured us there was no real damage done, no plates started, and no water coming in. So we resumed our voyage, and arrived at Brisbane a few hours late, feeling thankful that we had passed the night in safety."

From the foregoing narrative, it will be seen how, from the recklessness and obstinacy of some sea-captains, the lives of the human freight on board are exposed to danger. Both these commanders were surely to blame. He who had the "rule of the road" in his favour unquestionably did wrong to persevere in a course that he must have seen could not possibly end otherwise than in a collision. Such instances of recklessness, it is to be hoped, are very rare. In the many other voyages, longer or shorter, which I have performed, the watchfulness and care of the captains to avoid such catastrophes have been conspicuous.

The sequel of this incident was curious. The owners went to law, and the Court decided in favour of our vessel, the *Eurimbla*, on the ground that as the captain was steering for the "Heads," he was within his rights, though transgressing the "rule of the road!" A paper that had been drawn up on board and signed by many of the passengers may perhaps have helped our captain in gaining the verdict. I declined to sign the paper, giving as my reason that I, a mere landsman, had seen the danger in ample time for the collision to have been prevented, and that the captain had neglected his duty towards his passengers in not stopping his ship sooner.

BRISBANE.

Owing to extensive shoals our steamer had to go nearly fifty miles round by the north of Moreton Island before entering Moreton Bay. We then steamed some miles up the beautiful winding Brisbane River, which is larger than the Thames at London, before arriving in the heart of the city, which occupies both its banks, these being connected by a long iron bridge. Brisbane, the capital of the extensive Colony of Queensland, we found to be a well-built and enterprising city, numbering then some 80,000 souls, within three miles of the Post Office. We received a warm welcome from several "Friends" who met the steamer, and we were hospitably entertained at the house of one of them. One indication of the prosperous state of things in Brisbane, is that the cost of frontage sites in the main streets was quite as high as in many of our large provincial towns in England. Possibly the "land boom," which was then at its height, might have something to do with these high prices.

Our time was fully occupied, as in the other colonies, and my wife found numerous engagements in connection with the Women's Christian Temperance Union, which was very flourishing here.

The most popular statesman in the colony, Sir Samuel Griffith, presided over a meeting addressed by me in the largest Assembly Hall.

In the gardens of our friends, some of which are beautifully situated on Kangaroo Point, overlooking the river, we found many tropical fruits growing, such as jack-fruit, as large as pumpkins, pomelows, monsteras, with fruit which takes eighteen months to ripen, guavas, oranges, lemons, Japanese date-plums, mangoes, and custard-apples. The houses are principally built of wood, and the colonials live very simply, tea being the usual beverage at every meal. The semi-oily, bilious-looking article known here as butter, is sold in the shops in glass jars.

The country up the Brisbane River, to the west, is well wooded and beautiful. From the top of "One-tree Hill," a drive of seven miles from the city, we obtained a grand view of this fine valley, extending beyond the town of Ipswich to the distant mountains on the horizon.

On leaving Brisbane a party of friends accompanied us on the river steamer which took us down to the bay, where the s.s. *Chingtu*, which was to take us to Hong Kong, lay at anchor. Here, as the final leave-taking took place, we sadly felt that these were the last farewells to the many dear friends we were leaving behind in Australasia, whose constant kindness and pleasant social intercourse will never be obliterated from our memories.

THE GREAT BARRIER REEF.

Our course now lay northwards, in the *Chingtu*, one of the fleet of steamers belonging to a company of Chinese merchants of Shanghai. It is only due to that company to say, that this boat was the cleanest and best-appointed, with the most perfect cooking and service, of any vessel, not even excepting the P. and O. steamers, in which we had previously taken passage. The captain, doctor, mate, and one or two under-officers were English; the whole of the crew and stewards were Chinese. The captain told us that he much preferred Chinese to English sailors, as they never got drunk, and always implicitly obeyed orders. The stewards waited at table in delicately clean attire, and flitted about as silently as ghosts, the plates and dishes being changed as if by magic.

Passing Rockhampton, we were soon within the "Great Barrier Reef," that wonderful rampart of coral rock, forming a natural breakwater against the swell of the mighty Pacific, which, with the accumulated momentum of 6,000 miles of tempestuous ocean, dashes upon the impregnable barrier in a "league-long roller, thundering on the reef." Our course, for the distance of about 1,500 miles, as far as Cape York, was as smooth as a river, the only danger being from sunken rocks, to avoid which, our watchful captain sometimes stopped the vessel for the night.

It was tantalizing to be so near to this magnificent coral reef and yet to be unable to examine it. It is known to be a perfect treasure-house of shells, corallines and sponges, while sea-anemones of almost every shape and hue everywhere abound.

It was interesting to contrast our smooth progress in a modern steamer, with the difficulties experienced by Captain Cook in his voyage of discovery, within this great reef, just 119 years previously. Reading near the spot, on passing Cooktown, since founded and named in honour of the great navigator, in a condensed history of his voyages, how his ship the *Endeavour* encountered many dangers from cross-currents, sunken rocks, and shoals, and how she was ultimately driven on to a lee shore, and with enormous difficulty repaired and floated again, one was enabled to realise the prodigious advance which the introduction of steam has made since his day, in the safety and comfort of navigation.

On Thursday Island we landed for a few hours, which gave us an opportunity of inspecting the many specimens of conical ant-hills there, some of which were upwards of twelve feet high. Pearl-fishing, and the collecting of "Bèche-de-Mer," were also being industriously carried on, this article, a species of sea-slug, being in great demand in China for making soup.

Our last call in Australia, after passing through Torres Straits, and leaving New Guinea to our right, was at Port Darwin, west of the Gulf of Carpentaria, and in the northern district of the Colony of South Australia. The spot is interesting from the fact of the electric cable being landed here, connecting the Australian Colonies with Java and the whole civilised world. Port Darwin contains a large Chinese colony; here also we saw parties of Australian aborigines, poor, emaciated-looking creatures, eagerly searching for shell-fish or any edible refuse to be found on the seashore, to satisfy their hunger.

In complexion, these natives are dark maroon, almost sooty, but their features are less coarse than those of many African tribes. One curious practice among the women, is that of cutting deep wales longitudinally in the flesh of the upper arm; earth is then rubbed in, which causes the flesh to swell, leaving large unpleasant-looking cicatrices upon the arm.

The men have their own idea of ornamenting their persons. This consists of a stick of bamboo six or eight inches long, stuck through the gristly part of the nose, just above the mouth, the effect of which was peculiarly odd.

To a naturalist the whole district round Port Darwin appears to be specially attractive. During our short stay we came upon a magnificent climbing-fern, with a considerable stem, more than twenty feet high. Butterflies in great variety and of dazzling beauty abound. There are also leaf insects and other strange varieties, to interest the entomologist.

Leaving Port Darwin, our steamer was headed towards the north, and passing by the large islands of Borneo and Celebes, we were soon among the interesting group of the Philippines, which have since risen into such unhappy prominence, through the Spanish-American War.

Whilst passing through these various groups of spice-growing islands, our attention was kept continually on the alert, by the splendid views of tropical forests and lofty mountains which some of them contained. It was tantalising to pass without landing upon these enchanted isles, as they had appeared to one's imagination in school-days. Our disenchantment, however, was complete, when the captain prosaically informed us, that some of them were inhabited by cannibal races, thus rendering it unsafe to land. There was one of their environments, however, to which we were not left merely to imagination. I refer to the terrific thunderstorms, through several of which we passed before reaching Hong Kong. Lightning so vivid, crashes of thunder so appalling, rains so torrential, we had never before experienced in any part of the world; vivid flashes of forked lightning were to be seen darting around three-fourths of the horizon.

CHAPTER XXI.

CHINA—HONG KONG IN FLOOD—HONG KONG GAOL: OPIUM SOTS.—SHANGHAI: OPIUM PALACE—HONESTY OF CHINESE MERCHANTS.—TIENTSIN: ATHLETIC CHINAMEN—MR. AND MRS. LEES, OF THE L.M.S.—INTERVIEW WITH LI HUNG CHANG—SIR CHIH-CHEN LO-FENG-LUH, K.C.V.O.

THE rainy season had now set in; what this meant in its full sense, we understood better on landing at Hong Kong. The main street was almost blocked up with huge mounds of earth, and even uprooted trees, which had been washed down by the deluge from the hill above the town—the result of a rainfall, as we were told, of twenty-four inches in twenty-four hours! Certainly, the encumbered condition of the main street, and its burst sewers, and the flooded basements of the houses, went far to corroborate the statement. The funicular railway being torn up by the rains, we did not attempt to climb the hill, upon which are situated the residences of the principal foreign citizens; in fact, the close, sultry atmosphere, and dampness pervading everything, made us anxious to get away from Hong Kong as soon as we could. The linen we wore, the pillows we slept on, felt not merely uncomfortably damp, but actually wet. The boots we put outside our bedroom door, were covered with green mould in the morning; kid gloves and every article of leather, were ruined with mildew; stearine candles hung down their heads; furniture came to pieces through the glue melting, and rain in torrents fell almost every day.

Apart from the rainy season, Hong Kong is not an unpleasant place to live in, especially to residents in the more genial atmosphere of the lofty hill. Its financial and commercial importance are well known throughout the East, and its magnificent harbour is frequented by the vessels of every civilized nation.

One of the most interesting visits we paid, before leaving the port, was to the gaol, where a large number of Chinese criminals, many of them refugees from justice from Canton, were detained. The Governor himself kindly escorted my wife and self round. In passing through the open yards, where prisoners were engaged in chopping fire-wood, and were armed with hatchets, it was curious to watch the motions of the hawk-eyed Sikh soldier, who shadowed the Governor everywhere, revolver in hand, his eyes watchfully scanning the faces of every prisoner, while his fingers played nervously upon the trigger of his weapon. Six of the worst opium sots, imprisoned for smuggling, were brought out at my request for our inspection. They had been deprived of their drug for five or six days, and were consequently at the very acme of their sufferings. Poor wretches! they made the most pitiful grimaces, and seemed too limp almost to stand on their feet. The doctor stripped one man's shoulder, and asked me to feel it. It was simply bone covered with loose skin, the muscle having all wasted away. He was just a living skeleton! I said, "He surely cannot live." "Yes," the doctor replied, "he will begin to eat in a day or two, and then he will gradually come round." "Do you not break them *by degrees* from the opium habit?" I inquired. "No," was the reply, "we cut it off at once, and absolutely. We find this plan to answer well, however much they may suffer in the process." There was evidently much to learn from the curious phases of human nature in Hong Kong gaol, as well as from the conversation of its courteous governor and doctor.

Chinese Mercantile Integrity.

High testimony was borne, at the time of our visit to Hong Kong, to the reliability in commercial affairs of Chinese merchants generally, on the occasion of a public banquet, which was given on his retirement from his position, to the General Manager of the greatest financial undertaking of the East, "The Hong Kong and Shanghai Banking Corporation." The striking statement which was made by the General Manager, was, that during the twenty-five years in which he had personally been connected with the bank, an extensive business, amounting to many millions of dollars annually, had been done in granting advances to Chinese merchants, upon their personal security only ; "and," he added, impressively, "during all those years the bank has never lost a single dollar by these transactions."

These customers of the bank carried on extensive business with Singapore, and the East India Islands, and invariably met their engagements to the bank when due.

On my remarking somewhat later to the manager of a branch bank in Japan, "If this account be true, I know of no other country in which such an unqualified statement could be made ; no bank manager in England or America that I ever heard of, would habitually advance large amounts upon the mere promissory notes of their customers. Would you do so in Japan ?" "Certainly not," was his reply, "no banker would consider it safe to do business on these lines with the *Japanese*. What can be done with perfect safety in China cannot be done here. The Chinaman attaches so much importance to the value of his credit, that he will borrow or beg of all his friends, or sell everything he has if needful, in order to meet his pecuniary obligations."

These testimonials are all the more remarkable, in view of the common ideas in regard to Chinese morality, which find expression in the proverbial phrases about "Ways that are dark, and tricks that are vain."

It cannot, however, be denied that the merchant class have, as a rule, in their pecuniary transactions, realised the truth that "Honesty is the best policy."

Hong Kong being the greatest emporium of commerce in the East, vessels of all nations make it their port of call, and we noticed on starting for Shanghai, in the French mail steamer, *The Djumna*, thirty or forty large steamers, lying at anchor in the magnificent harbour. We were rowed to our vessel more than a mile out in the bay, in a Chinese "Sampan," in which the whole family, consisting of father, mother, and several children, lived entirely, as is the custom with many Chinese here. Thirty thousand of them are said to pass their whole lives in boats. It is a truly risky life for young children, of whom no doubt many are drowned by falling overboard, but coroner's inquests are not considered a necessity in China.

In two or three days we landed at Shanghai, and were not a little surprised with the noble frontage to the river of the "Bund," consisting of the public gardens and promenade, with the fine houses of the European merchants in the background.

We were welcomed by many excellent friends and helpers, both among the members of the London Missionary Society and of the China Inland Mission, also by several American Missionaries. Through these friends many opportunities for useful work were found for me, during our stay in Shanghai.

There was much of interest to see in Shanghai, but one of the most curious sights was the grand opium-palace, three stories high, situated in the main street, and accommodating a thousand smokers. We were conducted over this at night, by an active American Missionary, and were surprised at the luxurious fittings and accommodation for smokers, including electric lighting, provided throughout the establishment. A considerable number were already enjoying, or were preparing, their opium pipes, at so early an hour as nine o'clock; but few cases, however, of confirmed smokers were visible. In this palatial establishment none of the poorer class of opium sots had the means to enter. As a rule, those who can afford to buy good food, and do not smoke to excess, do not appear at first to suffer much from the practice. It is the very poor, who cannot buy both food and opium, upon whom the vice tells with the greatest force, as in the case already related of the individuals we saw in Hong Kong gaol. Our conductor gravely informed us that we were now in the "wickedest street in the world," though something like this may be heard of certain streets in Sydney, also in San Francisco! Later on, still worse opium dens, where vice in every form flourishes, were pointed out to us in the back streets and slums of Shanghai.

It was the fashion here among the Europeans who mix very little with the Chinese, to say that no Chinese adults were converted through the

Missionaries to Christianity, or that the few who made a profession of the Christian religion were worthless characters, contemptuously described as "Rice-Christians." Very different, however, were the reports of the Missionaries themselves, who spend their lives in intimate contact with the people. The meetings which we had the privilege of attending, both among China Inland Missionaries and others, convinced us that, notwithstanding the acknowledged difficulties connected with the conversion of the Chinese, a great and good work was going on at many of the mission centres throughout the Empire. The fact of my having personally addressed, through an interpreter, a congregation of *adults*, of whom about 400 were attached to one American Mission in Shanghai, may be mentioned in further proof of the conversion of adults.

Within the walls of this native city, with its million of inhabitants, we were in contact with the ever-varying aspects of Chinese life. The barber, the cook, the shoemaker, and many other craftsmen, were busily plying their trades, in the narrow unsavoury streets, crowded like an anthill, so that one was in constant danger of jostling against packages or foul refuse, carried on bamboo poles, or even against the broad "Cangue" fixed around some culprit's neck. The "Cangue," a mode of punishment often seen in China, is a heavy wooden collar about three feet square fixed on a criminal's neck, so that he cannot reach a hand to his mouth.

TIENTSIN.

Receiving no encouragement from Sir Robert Hart, the Imperial Commissioner of Chinese Customs, to whom I had forwarded a letter of introduction, to proceed to Pekin, I concluded to go no further than Tientsin, with a view, if practicable, of interviewing the great Viceroy, Li Hung Chang. The voyage from Shanghai was uneventful, but we passed within a moderate distance places which have since arisen into considerable note, including "Wei-hai-wei," the naval port of China, now occupied by the English, Port Arthur and Tah-lien-wan, now in the occupation of the Russians.

Passing the Taku Forts, we entered the muddy and tortuous Peiho River, in whose narrow, undredged channel, and sharp S curves, our steamboat was in constant danger of grounding.

It is, we were informed, the deliberate policy of the Chinese Government, to keep the roads to the capital in a dangerous state of non-repair, and the Peiho river undredged, with a view to impede the advance of any invading army to Pekin.

They have not forgotten the lesson of the Chinese War of forty years ago, when the French and English combined forces, after destroying the Taku Forts, marched on Pekin, and in a disgraceful manner looted the Emperor's Summer Palace. After this, their purposed neglect of the means of access to the capital is intelligible. After proceeding about fifty miles, we stuck fast at last, a few miles below Tientsin, and were obliged to complete the voyage in a "Sampan," rowed by an athletic young boatman. The general physique of the men in North China struck me as being much superior to that of the Southern Chinese. I took special notice of gangs of men unloading rice-junks, who were tripping along with a light, springy step, under bags weighing about two hundredweight each; and a dozen of them would trot up the hill with a heavily loaded cart, in a way that no dray-horse could have done. Indeed, the cart-horse, owing to the cheapness of labour, appeared to be quite "disestablished and disendowed" in Tientsin.

We were under the greatest obligation, during our stay in Tientsin, to the Rev. Jonathan and Mrs. Lees, who were at the head of the London Missionary Society's mission there. Had it not been for their great kindness in inviting us to their home, we could not have remained in Tientsin, as the climate was malarious, and the only hotel was wretchedly damp and uncomfortable. All the missionaries here gave us a warm welcome, and proved helpful to us in many ways. A local banker also arranged for a meeting, to be held in his large and broad verandah, at which the principal English residents were present. During my address, which was afterwards ably commented on in the local press, a Chinese servant noiselessly entered several times, with fresh supplies of refreshing tea, truly grateful in such a sultry clime to a thirsty speaker.

Mr. Bullock, H. B. M. Consul, who was present

at this meeting, when he knew that I wished to see the Viceroy, courteously undertook to arrange an interview for me. Without his help it would have been a much more difficult matter. Mr. Bullock felt an additional interest in my mission, when he understood that I had made the acquaintance of his relative, Mr. W. H. Bullock, the correspondent of the *Daily News*, at Sedan, in 1870. As the nephew of the late General Hall, Mr. W. H. Bullock adopted the name of Hall, on succeeding to his uncle's estate in Cambridgeshire.

The interview with the Viceroy took place on the 10th of July, 1889, and the following report of it which I sent to a friend in England, appeared shortly afterwards in the *Times*.

Interview with Li Hung Chang.

I was anxious to see Li Hung Chang, knowing that next to the Emperor, he was then the greatest personality in China; ex-Guardian of the Emperor; trusted counsellor of the Dowager Empress, whose influence at Court was still all-powerful; senior of the four Grand Secretaries of State; Viceroy of the Province of Chih-li; and President of the War Department. Indeed, he was China's greatest, if not her *only*, statesman.

My main object in going to Tientsin, was to interest this influential ruler in the recent progress in the Western World, of the principle of Arbitration, as a substitute for war. Accompanied by Her Britannic Majesty's Consul, Mr. T. S. Bullock, I

From a Photo by] [G. W. Webster, Chester.

W. E GLADSTONE AND LI HUNG CHANG.

went by appointment to the "Yamen," or official residence of the Viceroy. Etiquette demands somewhat of State, on such visits. Accordingly, mounted in palankins, supported on the shoulders of four coolies, we proceeded briskly for two miles, passing through the native city, with its supposed million of inhabitants, to the gate of the "Yamen." After entering the court-yard, our cards were demanded by an official, and after a few minutes interval, during which I examined at leisure the motley throng of guards and hangers-on, also the grotesque figures—the lions and dragons, with which the enclosure was decorated, being supposed, in accordance with Chinese ideas, to terrify all beholders—we were ushered within the precincts.

Passing through several courts, we stopped at length in an apartment furnished in European style. Here, in a few minutes, a chamberlain entered, and announced the Viceroy—a tall dignified figure in full Chinese costume, wearing a cone-shaped hat, ornamented with a large red silk tassel. He bowed and shook hands; then inviting us into the inner room, seated himself in an arm chair at the head of a table, motioning me to his right, and the Consul to his left hand, the latter being considered the post of honour. His very capable secretary, Lo-Feng-Luh, sat at my right, and proved to be an admirable interpreter.

After cigarettes and long-stemmed water pipes, for tobacco, had been passed round, the Viceroy put to me a series of questions as to the objects of my present travels. In reply, I informed him that, accompanied by my wife, I had travelled through the Australasian Colonies, that I had been accorded interviews by most of the Governors and leading statesmen of those colonies, and that I had addressed many public meetings, with a view of promoting Peace and Arbitration, and that I was now proceeding homewards through China, Japan, and the United States.

I continued, that in the capacity of Secretary of the English Peace Society, I had, in 1887, accompanied a deputation of English Members of Parliament to Washington, to present to President Cleveland a Memorial in favour of a Treaty of Arbitration between our respective countries. It was presumed that the moral effect of such a Treaty, between more than a hundred millions of English-speaking people, could not fail to be very great on the rest of the civilised world. The Viceroy hereupon asked how that deputation was received by the President of the United States. "Very cordially," I replied. I also mentioned that in a private interview that I had had with President Cleveland some weeks previously, he had shown his sympathy with our movement, by attaching his signature to an interesting document which for some years I had been in the practice of showing to influential personages, in my interviews with them.

Producing it on the present occasion, I explained that it was originally given to me as my credentials when commissioned by the "Society of Friends" in England, to act as their representative and the dispenser of their bounty, to the distressed war-victims in France during the war of 1870-1, and that I had subsequently visited Bulgaria in a similar capacity, during the conflict between Turkey and Russia. The Viceroy evinced a marked interest in the signatures on the document, and especially in those of President Cleveland and John Bright.

He then signified his desire to append his own seal and signature. I gladly assented, stating how much I should value such a souvenir of this interesting visit. The Viceroy, however, meant more than this. Turning to his secretary, he desired him expressly to inform me, that his signature might be accepted as a proof of his personal sympathy with the cause which I had come so far as Tientsin to promote.

When his writing materials were brought in, consisting of a camel's hair brush and Indian ink, his Excellency, who has the reputation of being a good caligraphist, traced with his own hand the, to me, cabalistic-looking characters which form his signature, and then attached his seal below. Lo-Feng-Luh informed me that this was his official signature, which the Viceroy only makes use of as Plenipotentiary, in signing treaties and State documents of importance.

In answer to a question from me, the Viceroy said China would be prepared to unite with other Powers in such a League or Treaty of Peace, as had been proposed between England and America. He added, that China had always been pacifically disposed, and that, unless molested by other powers, she would not fight. On my asking whether the views and policy of the young Emperor were equally pacific, he replied that the Emperor's principles were identical with his own.

Further conversation followed, about the proposed High Court of Arbitration; and the Viceroy appeared much impressed by the fact, that in no fewer than eighty cases during the present century, international disputes had been settled by the peaceful means of Arbitration or Mediation. I referred him especially to the well-known *Alabama* case, which had led to such excellent political relations between the United States and Great Britain.

The question of International Arbitration led to the Viceroy asking if I had seen General Grant, of whom he expressed a very high opinion. I said that, although I had not had the pleasure of meeting General Grant, I might mention that he had often expressed his detestation of war, and his desire that Arbitration might become a substitute for it; moreover, that when he was in England, being offered the spectacle of a grand military review, he had declined the honour, saying that he had seen too much of that sort of thing.

General Grant seems to have been equally impressed with the ability, as a statesman, of Li Hung Chang; for on his return to America, after the completion of his tour round the world, he stated that he had seen in the course of his travels the three greatest men then living, viz., Gladstone, Bismarck, and Li Hung Chang.

The Viceroy next inquired if I were going to Washington; and, if so, would I undertake to say something on the unjust laws passed against the Chinese in the United States. I replied that, having no official character, any representations I might make as a private individual would not have much weight; but I should willingly take opportunities in America, as I had already done in Australia, of remonstrating against the injustice done to the Chinese. I added, "China will need long patience. Statesmen cannot all at once settle such questions as they themselves would wish. Intelligent and well-disposed persons acknowledge the Chinese to be industrious, law-abiding, and useful members of the community, and desire to see justice done to them. This is essentially a labour question, jealousy and fear of Chinese labour being at the root of the difficulty. As artisan voters are now a very numerous class, both in the United States and in Australia, the combined pressure which they bring to bear upon politicians, enables them to obtain one-sided legislation, in favour of their own class. Time alone can bring about such a change in public opinion, as may sweep away such unjust laws as those passed against the Chinese."

The Viceroy admitted the difficulties of the question, but appealed to treaty rights, which, he shrewdly observed, "other Powers are not slow in enforcing, when China happens to be in the wrong. If English citizens in China were treated as the Chinese are in America and Australia, should we not very soon see your gunboats in our river?"

Tumblers of champagne being offered us at this stage of the interview, it gave me an opportunity of explaining that my wife and I were members of a Society that abstained from all intoxicating liquors on principle, for the sake of example. Lo-Feng-Luh then asked if I were a "teetotaller." I replied, "yes," and asked him to explain to His Excellency the meaning of "teetotaller." The explanation evidently impressed him, and, looking at me seriously, he rose up deliberately in his chair, made a profound bow, and said with a pleasant smile, "I perceive, Mr. Jones, you are a man of benevolence."

As I declined the champagne, tea in covered cups, was served several times during the interview. On lifting the lid, I observed a straw coloured infusion, with a mere pinch of greenish leaves at the bottom. Tea thus made, though weak, and drunk without milk or sugar, is highly aromatic and refreshing. The Consul remarked to me, after leaving the "Yamen," that I could not buy tea of that special quality, even in Tientsin, at two guineas a pound.

Wishing to approach Li Hung Chang on the opium question, I told him I was intimate with the President of the English Anti-Opium Society, and was much surprised when he promptly asked whether I meant Sir Joseph Pease, with whose name he was evidently familiar. "It would interest the friends of China," I said, "to know how far the Viceroy was satisfied with the existing state of the opium question, or whether there were any changes which he desired in the treaty rights, or in the fiscal arrangements connected with them, as the time for revision of the Treaty was approaching."

The Viceroy replied that he had always been given to understand, that the Indian Government could not afford to lose the revenue from opium, and that therefore the agitation in England against the traffic would prove ineffective. His manner seemed to imply that he had renounced the hope of altering, or amending, the existing state of affairs. I therefore proceeded to remark that many thoughtful persons in England were dissatisfied with the fact of the Indian Government being directly implicated in the manufacture and diffusion of a noxious drug, whose demoralising effects I had frequently witnessed, both in China and Australia; and I should be glad to know how far the Viceroy approved of the efforts that were continually made in England, to induce the Government to wash its hands of the opium traffic altogether.

He replied that if the British Government would indeed wash its hands of this traffic, it would be a great satisfaction to himself; but, he added, "We have already suffered from two wars about opium, and do not wish to incur the risk of a third." At this point, I could not but feel that, for so intelligent a statesman, the amount of interest shown by the Viceroy on a question so vital to the best interests of his country, was rather disappointing. His apparent indifference might arise, in part, from his knowledge of the immense revenue now derived by China from the duties on the Indian drug—a revenue which is largely devoted to the maintenance of the Imperial Navy, of which he was chief administrator. In part also, it might arise, from his feeling the utter hopelessness of further attempts to suppress a practice, which has, alas! become at length deeply rooted in the habits of millions of the Chinese people.

As the Viceroy seemed disinclined to pursue the subject of opium further, he turned the conversation to personal and miscellaneous matters. His thirst for knowledge seemed insatiable, his questions being put with much skill and tact.

A *précis*, it is said, is kept in the "Yamen," of every conversation of importance, properly tabulated and dated for future reference. Repeatedly, while speaking of European armaments, he interjected questions on the military resources and prestige of the various Powers, and on the future prospects of peace or war. Referring to what he termed the constant grasping policy of Russia, which seemed to be his *bête noire*, on the Chinese Mongolian frontier, he asked why I did not go and preach righteousness and justice in Russia. Detecting no trace of a smile at this sarcasm, under his heavy moustache, I replied with becoming gravity,

"Because there is no freedom in Russia, and any such proceeding on my part would probably end in my being thrown into a Russian prison, and perhaps sent to a country (Siberia), which I had no wish to see!" At this the Viceroy laughed heartily, repeating over and over again the Chinese word for *prison*.

He then inquired if I intended to go on to Pekin. I said no, I had given up the idea, as the interview he had so kindly granted me amply repaid me for coming so far north, and satisfied the object I had in view; nevertheless, I added that I regretted, from an antiquarian point of view, leaving China without seeing Pekin and the Great Wall! "Don't go," he said, in a rather contemptuous tone, "there is nothing to see!"

It should be here explained that it is a part of Chinese etiquette, in conversation with foreigners, to depreciate native sights, or objects of interest, as if insignificant, when compared to the sights to be witnessed in the stranger's own land.

Hence Li Hung Chang's derogatory reference to the Great Wall of China must merely be understood from this point of view.

His questions now became amusingly personal. "How old are you, Mr. Jones?" I did not hesitate to tell him my age, but when he followed with the question, "How old is your wife?" I began to think it was time to give the conversation another turn. I suppose that, according to Chinese etiquette, it was my place to have returned the compliment, by asking how old was Madame Li Hung Chang, but I confess that my courage failed me as to putting such a personal question.

Our interview having extended over an hour and a half, the Viceroy desired his Secretary to tell me how glad he was that I had come to see him, and that he sincerely wished me every success in the great object I was seeking to promote. Then, as a mark of special honour, he preceded us as far as the outer door, and again shaking hands with us, bowed us into our palankins. At this, the Consul expressed his surprise to me, saying aside, "He has never done so much as this for me before. It is evidently intended for you; he thinks you to be 'a man of benevolence.'"

It may here be observed that the Mandarin, who interpreted for me so skilfully at this interview—Sir Chih-chen Lo-feng-luh, K.C.V.O.—had been formerly interpreter and Secretary to the Chinese Legation in London, and has since become himself the actual Minister for China to this country, where his well-known ability, his courtesy, and his intimate knowledge of our language and literature, have gained him a distinction above all his predecessors in that office.

CHAPTER XXII.

JAPAN: RAILWAY TRAVELLING IN JAPAN—OSAKA—KIOTO—THE DOSHISHA—"KAGO" TRAVELLING—SUMMER CAMP AMONGST THE HILLS—JAPANESE SIGNATURES—COUNT OKUMA—COUNT ENEMOTTO—JAPANESE "FRIENDS"—SCRIPTURE READING UNION—ENOSHIMA, THE FEAST OF BOATS—RISKY BOAT VOYAGE.—CROSSING THE PACIFIC: THE LONGEST AND CALMEST VOYAGE—THE "GOLDEN GATE"—SAN FRANCISCO.

ON leaving Tientsin it was needful to return to Shanghai, in order to embark on the mail steamer for Japan. The first port of call was Nagasaki, where our steamer anchored in a small harbour enclosed by beautiful hills. We were glad to visit this ancient port, in which for centuries the Dutch alone were allowed, under the strictest regulations, to establish the only European trading factories in Japan, their monopoly being accompanied with conditions of so humiliating a character, that the lucrative nature of the trade alone rendered them tolerable.

We landed at Kobe, after passing through the Inland Sea, so celebrated for the beauty of its shores, though, owing to heavy rain, much of its scenery was lost to us. Here we gladly availed ourselves of the railway recently completed to the capital, Tokio, a distance of about four hundred miles. The whole line, we were informed, had been laid out and constructed by native engineers, the trains also being driven by Japanese engine-drivers. The travelling appeared to be as safe and good as on European railways, though the speed, especially in mountainous districts, was slow. The construction of this railway, in which considerable engineering difficulties have been admirably overcome, does great credit to the skill and energy of the Japanese.

Our fellow railway-travellers were a constant source of interest. As a rule, very few native ladies were seen in the cars. The men for the most part wore European clothing, and were generally polite and sociably disposed towards us strangers, and it seldom occurred that one or more in the company had not enough knowledge of English, French, or German, to render some conversation possible. The line having only recently been opened, the curiosity of the country people appeared to be insatiable. They flocked in crowds to see the trains arrive and depart at the stations. Being detained for about half-an-hour at one road-side station, we got out to walk about the platform. This appeared to give great pleasure to the assembled crowd of men, women and children, who followed us with an amused but respectful deference up and down the platform, the women, who are all little in stature, showing evident surprise at the tall figure of the white lady in European costume.

At the great commercial city of Osaka, said to contain more than 600,000 inhabitants, we rested over Sunday. It happened, however, to be a fête-day, and the fine river was alive with holiday-makers, in brilliant costumes. When darkness set in, the whole scene was splendidly illuminated with fireworks and Japanese lanterns. The crowds were immense, but order and good humour reigned everywhere.

Osaka is one of the most ancient cities in the world, being 2,500 years old. Centuries before the existence of Japan was known in Europe, it was the great financial and commercial centre of the empire. It is now the second city of Japan, and as regards its industries and commerce, is superior even to the capital, Tokio. Its cotton mills are kept running night and day, and thus turn out double the quantity of yarn that English mills produce. Along the wharves of its great river may be seen a seemingly endless array of masts and funnels; but as the largest class of ocean-going steamers draw too much water to enter the river, it is confidently predicted that Kobe will become the chief port for foreign trade.

Before leaving Osaka, we sought out the missionaries, to whom we were recommended, but it being their vacation time, we found the schools closed, and many of the missionaries, in order to escape from the great heat of the city, had resorted to the Encampment and Conference of Missionaries, at a beautiful spot on the hills, which we enjoyed visiting later.

Kioto, the ancient capital, a city, it is said, of 10,000 temples or shrines, possessed abundant attractions, on which I refrain from amplifying. Just beyond our hotel was the noted big bell, cast in 1633, and weighing seventy-four tons. Its tone is marvellously deep and far-reaching, the strokes being given from a wooden beam, swung like a battering-ram against a large boss on the outer side of the bell. Here also is the noted Congregational College, established by American Missionaries, called the "Dosisha," which was also in vacation at the time of our visit. There were said to be 700 young men and 200 young women students in this great educational establishment. Whilst the way was made easy for all to become Christians, no direct attempts, we were informed, were made at proselytising. I have read that since our visit, all the white teachers have been dismissed by the Government, and that the management and teaching are now entirely in Japanese hands; with what results I am unaware. This is in accordance with the deliberate policy of the Government, to substitute as far as practicable, trained natives for European and American employés in all official positions.

Missionaries' Summer Camp.

As we had been invited to visit the Summer Encampment and Conference of Missionaries among the hills, previously mentioned, we gladly fled from the heat of the city, travelling eight or ten miles in "jinrickshas" to the foot of the mountain. Here we hired a couple of "kagos" (pronounced kango), in which, suspended from bamboo poles resting on two men's shoulders, we were each carried up the very steep hill on which the camp was established. Of all the odd contrivances in which we had ever travelled, the "kago" is decidedly the most curious. Some of them are luxuriously fitted up and are stately affairs, but these were simple, home-made cages of green bamboo, and to us long-limbed Europeans, who cannot sit on our haunches like the natives, they were ridiculously inconvenient. They were neither high enough to admit of sitting upright in, nor long enough to contain the legs and feet—these projecting outwards, were constantly butting against the calves of the unfortunate bearer in front, much to our own and to his discomfort. After this we had no desire ever to repeat our "kago" experience, and enjoyed the return journey down-hill on foot.

The day spent in camp with our missionary friends is one to be ever gratefully remembered. Our welcome was of the kindest, and in order that we might take part in the Conference we were made "corresponding members" *pro tem.* The exhilarating atmosphere, at an elevation of 1,700 feet, and the social amenities among a refined and cultured circle of Christian men and women, in the happy enjoyment of their rare holiday, were truly refreshing, and introduced us into a new and delightful aspect of Foreign Mission life. Dr. Gordon, the Principal, together with other members of the "Dosisha," were among those whose acquaintance we were glad to make on this occasion.

TOKIO.

When we first arrived in Tokio, the Cabinet was engrossed with the important work of the revision of the English Treaty, so that I was unable to see any of the Ministers. Ultimately, furnished with a letter from the British Ambassador, I succeeded in getting an appointment with Count Okuma, the Minister for Foreign Affairs. I gave him an outline of our visit to the Australian Colonies; I also referred to the recent visit of the English Deputation to the United States, and its favourable reception by both President and people alike. I ventured to express the hope, that as soon as the proposed Treaty of Arbitration between the entire English-speaking people of the world became an accomplished fact, the two leading Eastern nations, Japan and China, would be willing to join the great international League of Peace.

Count Okuma seemed pleased with the idea, and repeatedly bowed his satisfaction. On describing my interview with the Chinese Viceroy, Li Hung Chang, and showing his signature attached to my document, of which he expressed his approval, he attached his own signature and seal to it. Through his interpreter, the Count said, "The man would be a fool who would involve his country in the losses of war, when there is any possibility of arranging differences by pacific means. It is better even to make concessions than to bring the sufferings and losses of war upon a people. Japan has lived for 250 years without bloodshed, until the great insurrection of about twenty years ago; and her national army is not large. She could get on well without large armies, were it not for the interference of foreign Powers. It is due to these Powers, and not to any aggressive spirit on her part, that she has felt compelled to adopt the conscription, and to organise an army and navy on the modern European systems."

Count Okuma, though quiet and reticent in his manner, struck me as a man of considerable force of character and intellect. On parting, he was extremely affable, saying he would be glad of a visit from my wife and self at his country seat, as soon as he could install himself there; a pleasant wish which, alas, was never realised. Shortly after my visit, a crazy Japanese fanatic assaulted him with an explosive bomb, causing such serious injuries that one of his legs had to be amputated. He survived his injuries, however, and is now able to walk, with the assistance of an artificial leg of American manufacture.

Count Okuma's terrible misfortune put an end to the pleasing anticipation of being his guests, and the opportunity was thus lost to us of being received at a great nobleman's establishment, and of seeing its magnificent surrounding gardens and Japanese landscape.

Count Okuma has since filled the position of Prime Minister of Japan, and it is gratifying to know that his attitude towards England has been specially favourable.

The only other Minister whom I was able to interview was Viscount Enemotto, Vice-Admiral and Minister of Public Instruction. Having been Ambassador to St. Petersburg and Berlin, he was well acquainted with Western customs and ideas, but our intercourse was limited, owing to his very imperfect English. He signed my document with alacrity, and offered to give me introductions to any of the other Ministers whom I might wish to see.

I much regretted having to leave Japan without seeing the Prime Minister, Count Kuroda, to whom I had a special introduction from the British Embassy. The difficulty was, how to communicate with him, as he was travelling from place to place up the country. He sent through his secretary a kind message, that he regarded my object as a most laudable one, and would willingly sign my document as a mark of his approval, if I could send it to him. No opportunity, however, occurred for this before our embarkation for America.

The month spent with much enjoyment in Japan passed rapidly away. It is a land of picturesque hills, and of springs of water, refreshing to every sense, after the dull monotony and sweltering heat of the Chinese coasts. Moreover, we became much interested in its intelligent and amiable people, with some of whom we had personal intercourse at the various missions. Especially interesting to us was the small body who had joined the "Friends'" Mission in Tokio. We were hospitably entertained by their missionaries, Mr. and Mrs. Joseph Cosand, and enjoyed attending their "Monthly Meeting," and witnessing their aptitude in conducting its proceedings.

In their Bible Class, it was interesting to see how ready some of them were in finding the texts, which in the Japanese Bible is more difficult than in our English version. The teacher told us that one young man, who had not been more than a year in the class, was better acquainted with the Scripture than the majority of those of his age whom he had known in America. A Bible Union, for reading portions of Scripture at stated times, which numbered throughout the country about 12,000 members, had recently been established through the exertions of Dr. Whitney and his wife, both members of the Society of Friends.

Notwithstanding his engagements, as the Official Interpreter at that time of the American Legation, Dr. Whitney had found opportunity to establish, and professionally superintend, a medical hospital in the city. Our friend Mr. George Braithwaite, a resident agent for the English Bible Society in Tokio, rendered us much useful service as interpreter, and otherwise. By his help, a large public meeting was organised for me to address on International Arbitration, in the Kosei Kwan Hall. The interpreter, Ishimoto, who had recently acted in that capacity for the late George Müller, the philanthropist, was considered to be the best in Japan. Owing, however, to the "honorifics" in which the language abounds, double the time was occupied in rendering into Japanese what I had uttered in English, so that Mr. Braithwaite was able to take down my whole address in long hand, during its interpretation.

It were futile on my part to attempt to describe the multitude of objects of interest that we saw in Japan. Far more competent pens than mine have already enlarged upon the marvels of the "Land of the rising Sun." I therefore refrain from wearying my readers with lengthy descriptions of temples images, curios, and other well-known objects of interest. Owing to my engagements in the Capital, we did not even attempt the journey of some eighty miles to Nikko, the place of all others remarkable for the beauty and variety of its temples.

Had time permitted, I should have enjoyed seeing, on the road to Nikko, the grand avenue of cryptomerias, *the* tree *par excellence* of Japan, which lines the greater part of the main high road of the Empire,—the famed "Tokaido."

Risky Boat Trip.

With a small party of friends, we paid a visit to the "sacred island" of Enoshima, where we met a number of men and women on pilgrimage to its various shrines and other attractions. It happened to be one of the days of the "Feast of Boats," and the superstitious boatman, fearing the vengeance of the "Spirit of the Boats," refused, at first to row our party across the bay to Kanagawa, where we wished to land, in order to see the great Daibutsu (image of Buddha). At length, our companion, G. Braithwaite, through the mollifying influence of a double or triple fare, succeeded in persuading the boatman to put out to sea with us. The craft proved to be none too large for our party, so that we congratulated ourselves on having successfully resisted the boatman's determination to give a passage to two Japanese women. About half-way across, our two boatmen, who stood up to row, wishing to change ends, thoughtlessly both stepped on the same edge of the boat, bringing it for a moment under water, the consequences of which, had not some of us instantly thrown our weight on the opposite side, might have been most serious to all. A little further on, one of the oars came in two, and the piece floated away. As we were left with only one oar, it was essential to recover the piece, and to repair the broken one; this was effected with some difficulty, and we landed at last at Kanagawa, thankful to escape without further disaster. Our boatmen of course attributed our misfortunes to the vengeance of the "Spirit of the Boats," for our having dared to put to sea during the three days of the "Feast." The Feast of Boats is an annual festival, and is supposed to conciliate the spirits that control the elements. As they are supposed to like fire, a straw boat is towed out to sea, and set on fire to attract the spirits; when these are believed to have entered it, the boat is towed back to shore in a burning condition. During the next three days no boat is allowed to go to sea, on pain of the displeasure of the spirits. At the end of that time, another straw-boat is set alight and sent out to sea, in order that the spirits may disappear with it. Then the boats are under a good omen and may be employed as usual.

The image of Buddha, called the Daibutsu, of Kanagawa, almost fifty feet high, has a very impressive effect on the mind of the spectator, not only from its immense size, but from the remarkable benignity of its aspect. Cast about two hundred years ago, it is a striking tribute to the artistic skill of that day. To convey an idea of its great size, I may mention, that as my wife stood on the platform on which the body of the figure rests in a sitting posture, I observed that the thumb-nail of the image appeared to be somewhat larger than her face.

Among things peculiar to Japan, is the fact that there are no sheep in the islands, and consequently no mutton, unless imported from China. The reason of this is, as we were informed, that the grass of the country, called bamboo-grass, is fatal to sheep. The one specimen sheep, that was formerly kept in the Zoological Gardens at Tokio as a curiosity, had unfortunately died before our arrival. The cicada, somewhat resembling a cricket, which flourishes by the million among the trees everywhere, makes a prodigious noise, so that in passing a plantation we could hardly hear each other talk. One evening, while addressing a meeting, one of these creatures flew into the room through the open shutters, and after buzzing around my head, darted about, squeaking like a mouse, among the congregation, who were seated on the clean, white matting on the floor. The commotion was so great that I had to pause until the disturber of the peace had been captured and carried out, squeaking vehemently. Complying with the etiquette of the country, like everyone else, I left my boots at the door, and preached in my "stocking feet."

To have prolonged our stay in this attractive land would indeed have been pleasant, but the prospect of other engagements in the near future, urged us to hasten our departure for America. Accordingly we took passage from Yokohama, on August 22nd, 1889, in the *City of Rio de Janeiro*, for San Francisco. It was pleasant to find that we could take tickets right through to Liverpool, and at the same time effect a saving of twenty-five per cent. in this ocean and land journey of over 10,000 miles, by paying the fare in Mexican instead of in American dollars. These tickets gave us the option of travelling by any of the five Trunk Railway lines crossing the United States, without further trouble, also the right of passage on any line of steamers between New York and Liverpool.

On our voyage of about 5,000 miles across the Pacific, occupying sixteen days from port to port, we saw not a single sail or passing steamer. The ocean, though very foggy, was true to its name of *Pacific*. The voyage was the longest and the calmest in our circumnavigation of the globe.

Its tedium was much relieved by the pleasant company of two of America's greatest men, in a two-fold sense—Dr. Phillips Brooks of Boston, and Dr. McVicar of Philadelphia. We had previously made their acquaintance at the hotel at Kioto, where their stature looked absolutely gigantic in comparison with the little Japanese waiters. Like ourselves, they had been enjoying a holiday in Japan. The interesting conversations on deck which we enjoyed during the whole passage, with these able and courteous fellow voyagers, are a pleasing reminiscence.

When we touched the 180th degree of longitude, we had, what occurs on every voyage towards the East, the, to us, novel experience of an extra day in the week, our captain humorously offering to accommodate us with a Thursday forty-eight hours long, or with two Thursdays of twenty-four hours each! By means of this extra day, our reckoning was kept right, so that on landing our dates corresponded with those kept on shore.

Passing through the famed "Golden Gate," we entered the fine harbour of San Francisco, and, after landing, our first care was to notify friends at home of our safe arrival. This was done in a telegraphic dispatch of one word, "Flourishing!"

CHAPTER XXIII.

AMERICA — SAN FRANCISCO — SAN JOSÉ; RICH FRUIT COUNTRY — GREAT "LICK" TELESCOPE — MARIPOSA GROVE—YOSEMITE VALLEY—SALT LAKE CITY—MORMON TABERNACLE—GRAND CAÑONS—KANSAS YEARLY MEETING—EFFECTS OF PROHIBITION LAWS—OKLAHOMA NEW TERRITORY—NIAGARA—HOME AT LAST.

I DO not propose to encumber this book with details of the numerous assemblies which I addressed in 1889, during our three months tarriance in the United States. The work was, in character and effect, similar to that in which I had been engaged during my visit to the States in the previous year. As a number of local Peace Societies had in the meantime been formed throughout the country, by the Peace Department of the Women's Christian Temperance Union, which was founded at the Convention at Nashville in 1887, it was thought desirable that I should visit as many as possible of these Associations. In the main, however, my labours were confined to the principal cities, and to some of the Universities, Colleges, and Schools. The number of young people whom I had the privilege of addressing, on the subject of Peace and Arbitration, from the colleges in California in the west, to those of Providence

R.I., in the east, amounted, in all, to between three and four thousand persons. No work in which I have, in my lifetime, been engaged, has so thoroughly enlisted my sympathies as these efforts to influence the young of both sexes, in favour of methods of adjusting international differences which appeal to reason, justice, and conscience, rather than to passion, violence, and bloodshed. Considering that these young persons would each become, in degree, centres of influence hereafter, in their respective spheres, as citizens of a great country, I felt that my efforts for this class, in particular, warranted hopeful feelings, in regard to the potential results.

CALIFORNIA.

We made no long stay in the busy, bustling city of San Francisco. Some of its "lions," however—notably the "sea lions" in the bay—claimed our attention. The clumsy gambols of the latter huge, uncouth animals on their rock island, a short distance from shore, attract many visitors, for whose delectation a large telescope is provided, near the adjacent hotel, through which, at a small charge, the huge, amphibious creatures may be watched at leisure—their curious hollow-sounding "bark" reminding one of a pack of hounds in full cry.

China-town, with its dense population, and, in general, the fine streets and noble public buildings of this Western Capital, are too well-known to need any description here.

It was with a feeling of relief that we exchanged the bustle of San Francisco for the comparative quiet of San José, fifty miles further south by rail. Here we found rest and refreshment among hospitable friends, there being two "Friends' Meetings" in the city.

California is the country of fruits, *par excellence*, and in San José, for example, one could buy excellent Muscat grapes for five cents (2½d.) per pound. At the fruit farm of a "Friend" in the neighbourhood, although the season for apricots and peaches was over, we saw the process of preparing plums, rivalling in quality the finest dried prunes of France. They are first dried in the sun, exposed on large wooden trays, then dipped in a certain preparation in order to preserve them from mildew. Thus prepared, Californian plums find a ready market in both hemispheres. Dried apples, peaches, and apricots are also largely exported.

THE "LICK" OBSERVATORY.

One of our "Friends" of San José kindly drove us in his carriage to Mount Hamilton, for the purpose of visiting the world-famed "Lick" Observatory. Mount Hamilton is twenty-six miles by road south-east of San José; the last six or seven miles include the circuitous way up to the summit, which is 4,250 feet above the sea, and is distant only thirteen miles in an "air line" from San José.

The Observatory was constructed and finished from monies donated by the late James Lick, a successful merchant, a part of whose deed of trust reads as follows:

"To expend the sum of seven hundred thousand dollars (£140,000) for the purpose of purchasing land, and constructing and putting up on such land a powerful telescope, superior to and more powerful than any telescope ever yet made . . . also a suitable Observatory connected therewith."

The remains of the donor himself were interred under the foundation stone of the great telescope, and a tablet is placed thereon, with an inscription to his memory.

The committee who had the matter in charge, after extensive inquiries, concluded to erect a refracting telescope, having an object glass not less than thirty-six inches in diameter, with a tube about sixty feet in length. The floor on which the telescope stands is seventy feet in diameter, and is raised by four hydraulic rams. It is so exquisitely balanced that my wife being invited to raise it, together with the large heavy telescope and its adjuncts, found but little difficulty in doing so by simply turning a wheel.

Furnished with a letter from the Chairman of the Trustees, which we presented to the person who admitted us, we were informed that Professor Holden, the Director, to whom the letter was addressed, was absent, but he, the speaker, opened the letter himself, and said it would be "all right." This action made me scrutinize him more closely, and I soon found that the man whom I had taken for the hall porter, being dressed in rough corduroys, was none other than the great astronomer, Professor Burnham, himself. We were courteously received and entertained on the premises for the night, thus preventing the necessity of our returning after dark to the hotel at the foot of the hill, a distance of seven miles.

After supper we adjourned to the observatory, where Professor Burnham explained to us the mechanism of the great telescope, and then directed it to the most interesting objects then to be seen in the heavens. Among these were four of the moons of Jupiter, which were very clearly defined. Saturn, with his rings, was unfortunately below the horizon, and the moon was not visible. Professor Burnham now turned the telescope towards some of the double stars. Here we were more successful, and saw several of these wonderful combinations. But I was much struck with the fact that some which the Professor stated were ternary or quaternary groups, to my powers of sight were only double stars. I remarked to him, that he must naturally have stronger sight than other people, his hawk-like eye seeming to confirm the fact. "That is not so," he replied, "it is all a matter of training. Suppose you were a botanist, you would discover plants more quickly than anyone unpractised in field botany; or, you may be an artist, and you will see in the landscape, pictures invisible to another, unless pointed out to him. It is just so with the astronomer, his eye is trained to narrowly scan the heavens, hence he discovers combinations that are invisible to an untrained eye."

Professor Burnham's antecedent history was remarkable. Engaged in a subsidiary official position in Chicago, he had erected a good six-inch refracting telescope in his own back-yard, by means of which he had discovered and fixed the position of upwards of two hundred compound stars, hitherto unknown to astronomers. The published catalogue of these stars created a profound sensation among astronomers, and Mr. Burnham's name became famous in all the observatories of Europe. His fame having travelled back to Chicago, his fellow-citizens said in astonishment, "Can this possibly mean our own Burnham?" His merits, as an astronomer, were now recognised by the United States Government, and he was placed upon the staff at the "Lick" Observatory. At the time of our visit, he had extended his catalogue of compound stars, discovered mainly by means of the great telescope, from two hundred up to twelve hundred!

In the early morning we took a stroll on the Observatory Hill, to view the extensive panorama spread out before us. We found the summit dry and warm, bathed in sunshine. So free from moisture is the atmosphere, that we were told that a polished steel plate left out all night, would show no sign of rust in the morning. Not so, however, was the case in the valley below. For a distance of fifty miles, as far as San Francisco, it was filled with an extremely dense white fog, pierced at varying distances, by rugged peaks or rocks, standing boldly out, like islands in the ocean. The effect was heightened by the extensive Bush fires which were then raging on the distant hills of San Matteo.

Before leaving the Observatory, we were shown over the establishment, and had the various transit and other astronomical instruments explained to us by Professor Schweniger and others. We also examined a number of interesting photographs of the moon and other celestial objects, which had recently been taken.

We returned from this remarkably instructive visit to Mount Hamilton with feelings of gratitude for the great courtesy which had been extended to us by the whole of the Observatory staff.

After returning to San José, we proceeded (as everyone who visits California is advised to do) to visit the Mariposa Grove of trees, twenty-eight to thirty-three feet in diameter, and the Yosemite Valley, but I spare my readers the descriptions of these well-known places. The passage of a coach, however, through a burning forest is not an every-day experience. It fell to our lot on our way to Yosemite to feel the fierce heat of such a forest fire upon our faces, and witness the frantic fear of the horses, which were with difficulty induced to pass by it.

Both the valley itself and the grove of great

Sequoia trees exceeded our expectations, except that, owing to a drought of five months, there was a woeful lack of water. Indeed, in the great Yosemite fall of 2,500 feet, noted as being the highest in the world, not a drop of water was to be seen, except a tiny stream in the third or lowest fall.

The time had now come for our departure eastward for our engagements in Kansas. The railway journey over the Rocky Mountains, especially over the Marshall Pass, nearly 11,000 feet high, afforded magnificent views of this lofty range, which constitutes the backbone of America. Much of the grand scenery, however, was lost to view as the train passed through gloomy snow-sheds erected to protect the line from avalanches in winter.

Salt Lake City.

Wishing to take a few hours rest from continuous travelling, we stayed one day in Salt Lake City, which gave us an opportunity of examining the Mormon Tabernacle, so remarkable for its acoustic properties, which we put to the test, so that whether in the gallery or under it, or in the centre of the room, one could hear a whisper, or a pin drop, on the platform. The building, which is said to hold 11,000 people, makes no pretension to architectural beauty; it is indeed distinctly ugly, the roof resembling an enormous oval dish cover. There is evidently something, however, in the internal arrangements of this great structure, from which our British architects might derive a lesson: how to improve upon the acoustic properties of many of our public buildings.

The electric street railway cars which run to all parts of Salt Lake City, with overhead wires, travelled at a speed which might be considered dangerous in our crowded thoroughfares, but were said to be well under control.

The shores of the great Salt Lake, along which we skirted, are very flat, presenting no features of interest. So strongly impregnated is the water of the lake, that it is said to yield twenty-two per cent. of salt, being about the same proportion as is contained in the brine which is ordinarily pumped up from the salt deposits of Cheshire. Heaps of salt were visible near the lake, the water having been evaporated by the sun.

We continued our journey over the waterless alkali plains, where, amid sage-brush and "jack-rabbits," no human beings were to be seen, except the patient Chinamen, who act as the lines-men, and cabin-keepers, in this dreary region, in which men of no other nationality can be induced to live. The railway took us through the Black Cañon of the Gunnison, with its lofty cliffs towering on either side. It was near here that, a few weeks previously, the main line train had been attacked and "held up" by robbers, when the passengers had their valuables taken from them, but no lives were lost. This circumstance did not diminish the eager interest with which we watched the narrow gorge in the brilliant moonlight.

This cañon, however, will not compare in grandeur with the Royal Gorge of the Arkansas, which is more than eight miles in length. When we arrived there, we entered the roofless observation car, at the end of the train, and thus obtained an uninterrupted view of the lofty pinnacles, the highest towering to 3,000 feet or upwards in height. The gorge is so narrow in places that the railway has been suspended above the river from iron girders, fixed into the solid rock. The passage of this grand cañon was a novel and striking experience.

KANSAS.

We arrived in the city of Lawrence in time for the commencement of the Kansas Yearly Meeting of "Friends." The large array of "buggies" and wagons drawn up in the yard attached to the large Meeting-house, was an indication of the energy and perseverance with which many of these Kansas farmers had travelled from homes, distant from one to two hundred miles, to attend their Yearly Meeting. Some of them had spent eight days upon the journey, bringing their food with them and sleeping in their wagons at night. The earnestness of spirit with which they attended the various services was quaintly expressed by one who said he had found it "to be a bigger thing to attend Kansas Yearly Meeting than ever he thought!" This earnestness pervaded the assembly, and seemed to be the key-note of the whole of the sittings. This will be, in part, explained when we consider how isolated are the homes of many of these "Friends," and how rare their opportunities of uniting with others in public worship.

Among those who appeared much to enjoy the services were several Indian converts, from the Reservations under the care of "Friends." There is something in the spiritual form of worship of "Friends" which seems specially adapted to the Indian nature, trained, as they are, from their childhood to believe that they are children of the "Great Spirit." A remarkable instance of this we noticed in the striking address, in his own tongue, of an old Seneca chief, named John Winney, which was well interpreted by his Indian wife, a member of the Wyoming tribe, and who, having been educated in the "Friends'" Schools, was now acting as Clerk to the Indian Monthly Meeting of Friends.

Here we had also the pleasure of meeting with Jeremiah Hubbard, whose success in civilizing young Indians was honourably mentioned to me by the Methodist Bishop of Nashville, Tennessee.

We made a point of inquiring how far the Prohibition Laws in Kansas were carried out, and were informed by Dr. Coffin, that they were kept even better than the laws against stealing and other crimes. This was corroborated by a policeman, who told us that their gaols and lunatic asylums were empty, and that the duties of the police consisted largely in watching the chemists' shops, in which alcohol was sold as a "drug." No drunken or ragged adults, or children, were seen anywhere by us during our stay in the State of Kansas.

A short time before we arrived at Lawrence, the new territory of Oklahoma was opened for settlement. It had previously been a portion of the Indian Reserve Lands, which, for some reason, the United States Government now offered to the public. On a certain advertised day the United States Marshal appeared on the ground, in order to proclaim the opening of the land to the public. A large number of speculators and settlers having assembled, precisely at noon, when the Marshal declared the lands to be open, they made a simultaneous rush to their pre-emptied claims. The result of these proceedings was, that upon land which in the forenoon had not an inhabitant upon it, there was erected, before evening, a city of booths and tents, containing about four thousand inhabitants. With the usual American promptitude, a Mayor of the City was forthwith elected by popular vote, in the person of John D. Miles, a well-known Kansas "Friend."

We heard a good story of General Grant's energetic administration, in connection with these Indian Reservations. One of the superintendents, (who happened to be a "Friend") being greatly troubled by the incursions of white men, trading "fire-water" and firearms among the Indians, and settling upon their lands, causing him much difficulty in the management of these people, called together the Indians under his charge and urged them to keep the peace, until he went to lay their case before their "great Father" at Washington, and, in an interview with General Grant, explained the matter fully to him. Grant, who was a man of few words, promptly told him to go directly back and use his influence to keep the Indians from retaliating upon the whites: "and I," added he, "will answer for order." Before the Superintendent could reach his home, a detachment of cavalry had entered the Reservation, and entirely cleared it of every white man.

Eastward and Home.

Proceeding, *via* Chicago, to Richmond, Indiana, where we stayed a few days, we were interested in seeing the domestic use which is made of the natural gas, both in cooking, and in heating the apartments. This gas issues, at a high pressure, out of the ground, at various points over a wide district.

At Earlham College, Richmond, in which some hundreds of young men and young women of the Society of Friends are educated, I had much pleasure in responding to their invitation to deliver lectures on various topics.

Both at Earlham and subsequently at Penn College, Oskaloosa, after a course of lectures on Peace and Arbitration, I was amused to find that nothing would satisfy these keen young students, but that I should enlighten them also upon the

Irish "Home Rule" question, respecting which, however, I was careful to say I was not an authority.

As my wife had never seen Niagara, we planned our eastward route so as to include it in our journey. The great Falls have been so often described, that one need only say they have left an impression never to be obliterated while memory lasts. It was the last day of the season for entering the cavern behind the Falls, known as the "Cave of the Winds," and my wife courageously ventured in. For this purpose, visitors are carefully apparelled in a flannel suit, covered with oilskin. Proceeding then, in charge of a guide, they descend a long flight of steps, and cross a wooden bridge, exposed to the spray falling like a shower bath from the American Falls. Entering the cave behind these Falls, the deafening noise, the fierce cross-currents of wind, the bewildering blinding spray, cold as snow, dashing against their faces, are almost enough to deprive them of consciousness. With the help, however, of the strong hands of the trustworthy guides, they emerge, breathless and dripping, on to the wooden stairs, delighted no doubt to get safely back to *terra firma*. Decidedly, the experience is one not to be repeated, leastwise in the chilly weather of the last day of the season.

The remainder of my time in America was devoted to addressing meetings in Baltimore, Philadelphia, New York, Boston, Providence,

R.I., and other places, in the course of which we met with friends, who, not only helped and encouraged us in our work, but also did all in their power to render our stay interesting and agreeable. Space, however, forbids my recording particulars of these numerous visits.

Our homeward voyage, from New York to Liverpool, was comfortably accomplished in the ss. *Teutonic*. No incident worthy of note occurred, except that owing to dense fogs, we got out of our course and sailed about sixty miles to the south of Ireland; thus, failing to call at Queenstown, our vessel was not signalled to Liverpool until we passed Holyhead some hours later.

Our voyages and travels having occupied over fifteen months, and the circuit of the globe being completed, we landed, thankful to arrive in safety, in our native land, which, after all the attractiveness of foreign climes has been summed up, was, in our sincerest convictions, THE COUNTRY OF ALL OTHERS TO LIVE IN.

CHAPTER XXIV.

FIFTY YEARS' RETROSPECT—WONDERS OF ART AND SCIENCE—THE LEGACIES OF SEVEN GREAT WARS—RESCRIPT OF THE CZAR ON ARMAMENTS—CONCLUDING NOTES.

THE period of my life has extended over portions of three reigns, those of George IV, William IV, and Queen Victoria. During the latter half of the Nineteenth Century the development which has taken place in every department of the Arts and Sciences, especially in their application to every-day life, has been one of unparalleled progress and completeness. Railways have been introduced and brought to their present perfection, ocean steamers, wholly unknown in my youth, are now found in every sea, electricity, formerly the mere toy of science, has been wonderfully utilized and adapted for many commercial and domestic purposes, whilst the telegraph and the telephone, marvellous as their growth has been, seem to be as yet but in their infancy.

Equally conspicuous is the progress that has been made as regards some of the amenities and moral aspects of social life and customs. Prize fighting, patronised in former days by the highest in the land, has, with bull-baiting, cock-fighting, and other kindred brutalities, almost disappeared ; and duelling among gentlemen, being no longer enforced by the absurd and unfair "laws of honour," has ceased in England.

Surely facts like these are suggestive of yet greater advances to be realised in the march of civilisation in the near future. Is it too much to infer that the life-time of another generation, may see the duel between nations, the barbarism of war, no longer enforced by so-called "National honour," nor tolerated by the enlightened Christian conscience of civilized and intelligent people? May it not even be thought possible, that the clergy will cease to regard it as a Christian duty to invoke the blessings of Heaven upon warships and regimental colours, destined for purposes which manifestly contravene the commands and the example of the Great Teacher, the Prince of Peace?

Glancing back over the past half century, among the strongest impressions left on the mind are the well-remembered grief and sorrow that were felt by thoughtful minds throughout this country when the forty years' Peace of Europe, undisturbed since Waterloo, was rudely broken by the disastrous Crimean War. The reign of Peace being thus violently terminated, there followed, in deplorable succession, the Franco-Austrian War in Italy, the American Civil War, the Austro-Prussian, the Franco-German and the Russo-Turkish Wars, and, we may now add, the recent Spanish-American War—seven great and sanguinary conflicts, by which Christendom has been scourged and desolated.

Whilst these wars have left behind them, among the nations of Europe, a terrible legacy of international jealousies, and of oppressive militarism, there has been, on the other hand, a substantial and cheering progress in the adoption of the principle and practice of adjusting quarrels by pacific means. During the same period, fully a hundred cases of disputes between nations have been successfully settled by Arbitration, or Mediation. Were the proposed Treaty of Arbitration between the two great English-speaking nations, England and America, to become an accomplished fact, as seems now probable, it would, in the words of John Bright, be a "grand step forward in the world's march," and doubtless the example would not be lost upon other Christian peoples who, in this day, are longing to be rid of their military burdens.

In this connection, a brief reference may here be permitted to the Rescript issued by the Czar of Russia, August, 1898, in the interests of a "real and durable peace," suggesting to the Governments of Europe, that the moment was favourable for seeking to put an end to the progressive development of the present armaments, which are "transforming the armed peace of our days into a crushing burden, which the people have more and more difficulty in bearing."

It would be contrary to all experience, if this proposal of a European Conference, in order to seriously discuss the desirableness of gradual Disarmament, were not strenuously opposed by the large and influential class, who are more or less interested in the maintenance of the military system. But by the over-taxed and conscripted victims of militarism, as well as by every lover of Peace, this "Olive Branch from the Neva" was hailed as a boon fraught with untold blessings.

Assuredly no more weighty proposal bearing upon the happiness and prosperity of the toilers of the world has been uttered in my lifetime. The fact of the *word having been spoken* cannot fail of being productive of solid and lasting benefit to the human race, as was evident from the outburst of enthusiastic approval with which the appearance of the Rescript was hailed throughout Europe.

This noble effort of the youthful Czar, in the cause of humanity, has transferred, as with a stroke of a pen, the great topic of Disarmament, from the hands of those who have hitherto been regarded as visionary enthusiasts, to the consideration of the Councils of Europe.

The fact with which responsible European Statesmen have to deal is, that a question of momentous importance to the well-being of their several countries has been placed before them by one who, as the master of armed battalions, speaks with authority. Thus, whether the proposed Conference result in its main object of preventing the further increase of armaments, or not, solid and lasting advantages are certain to accrue from this noble personal effort on the part of the Czar of Russia, in the interests of Disarmament and durable Peace.

It is, moreover, in the educative effect which such an appeal is bound to have on the minds and consciences of the nations that in the future its greatest influence may consist.

That it has been put into the heart of this youthful Ruler to utter this great word in the cause of humanity, is indeed cause for thanksgiving and praise to Him "who ever ruleth in the Kingdoms of men."

In concluding this book, I lay down my pen with feelings of thankfulness that in this special field of service I have been permitted to be a humble follower, at however great a distance, of noble workers like John Bright, Henry Pease, Henry Richard, the Bishop of Durham (Dr. Westcott), Hodgson Pratt, Frederic Passey, Dr. Channing, and many others. There is, however, no ground in this for self-gratulation. However earnest may have been my willing service, in this and in other directions, I am deeply conscious, that in regard to my final acceptance with God, I have nothing to build on, save only the Divine goodness and mercy which have followed me all the days of my life, leading me to faith and simple trust in the Lord Jesus Christ.

> "I know not what the future hath
> Of marvel or surprise,
> Assured alone that life and death
> His mercy underlies."
>
> —*Whittier*.

INDEX.

Lightning Source UK Ltd.
Milton Keynes UK
UKHW022141100521
383500UK00003B/180